LITTLE SHIP OF FOOLS

<< CHARLES WILKINS >>

LITTLE

SHIP

(OF)

FOOLS

16 ROWERS, 1 improbable BOAT,

7 tumultuous WEEKS on the ATLANTIC

GREYSTONE BOOKS
Vancouver/Berkeley

Greystone Books
343 Railway Street, Suite 201
Vancouver BC V6A 1A4
www.greystonebooks.com

Cataloguing data available from Library and Archives Canada
ISBN 978-1-55365-878-8 (pbk.)
ISBN 978-1-55365-879-5 (ebook)

Editing by Lucy Kenward
Copyediting by Peter Norman
Cover design by Peter Cocking and Jessica Sullivan
Interior design by Jessica Sullivan
Cover photographs (top) courtesy of Charles Wilkins
and (bottom) iStockphoto.com
Interior photographs courtesy of Charles Wilkins
Map by Eric Leinberger
Printed and bound in Canada by Friesens
Distributed in the U.S. by Publishers Group West

We gratefully acknowledge the financial support of the Canada Council for the Arts, the British Columbia Arts Council, the Province of British Columbia through the Book Publishing Tax Credit, and the Government of Canada through the Canada Book Fund for our publishing activities.

Greystone Books is committed to reducing the consumption of old-growth forests in the books it publishes. This book is one step toward that goal.

To be complete
one must hold the whole sun
wholly
in the marrow of the bone

One must celebrate
how to be one
with everyone
yet forever alone

DOROTHY LIVESAY

It began on a boat, like *The Tempest,*
like *Moby Dick,* a finite enclosure of floating
space, a model of the world in little.

JEANETTE WINTERSON

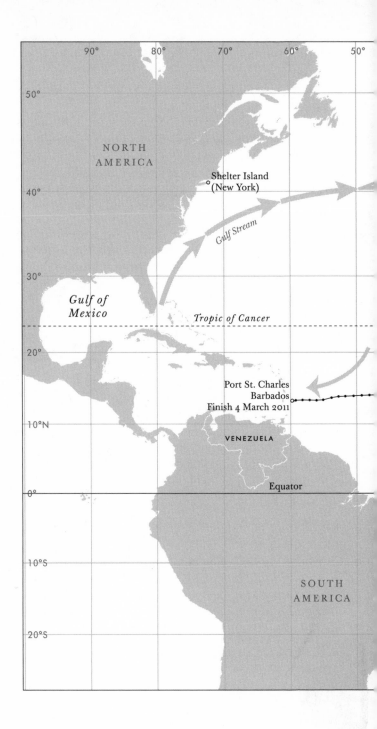

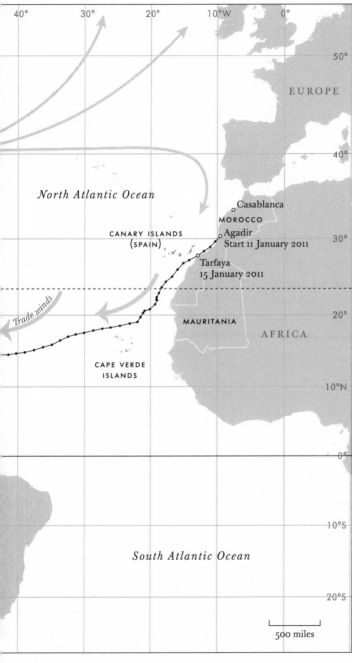

40° | 30° | 20° | 10°W | 0°
50°

EUROPE

40°

North Atlantic Ocean

Casablanca
MOROCCO
CANARY ISLANDS   Agadir
(SPAIN)   Start 11 January 2011   30°

Tarfaya
15 January 2011

MAURITANIA

Trade winds   20°

AFRICA

CAPE VERDE
ISLANDS   10°N

0°

10°S

South Atlantic Ocean

20°S

500 miles

Big Blue's Transatlantic Crossing

PROLOGUE

WEEKS LATER WHEN I spoke to my buddy Steve Roedde, who had been a mainstay of the voyage, he was still rattled, still aggrieved about it all. He said among other things that he had been unable to free himself of the specter of what might have been: better discipline, better cargo control, a lighter boat, a better chosen departure date, more confident and forthright leadership—in all a more Homeric journey and, as imagined in the palmy days of the project, perhaps a world record.

What he got—what we all got—was something botched and bastardized, something at times almost biblical in its run of torments and dark forces. We got failure, we got fuckup, we got farce. And I, more than some, was a contributor to that failure and farce.

And yet I don't regret a minute of it, for the simple reason that what we got besides—what we got because—was something weirdly and wildly beautiful; for some of us something magnificent; for a few even romantic, and in the ensnarement of romance I include myself. For amidst the strain and privation and exhaustion, I grew to love that botched journey; to love the boat, to love the people, the little ship of fools, as I came to think of them, a crew fancifully and farcically, and always it seemed fatefully, intertwined.

What Steve got finally that none of the rest of us got was himself, a man bent to an all-but-impossible standard—to ambition, to truth, to exactitude; to discipline and excellence.

And he got Margaret—incorrigible, shape-shifting Margaret, a woman who if she had paid her dues and done her time and been a half turn more circumspect might have been his ally instead of his nemesis.

And he got Angela—sweet, wounded Angela, whom he liked well as a human being but whose disinclinations as a commander he couldn't abide.

And he got me—brought me to the expedition, as he did so many others; encouraged me; mentored me; laughed with me on the long night watches; poured out his history hour after hour (his boyhood, his insecurities, his marriage).

Over the long weeks of the voyage, he showed me not just his commitment and sensitivities but his hypocrisies and shortcomings. He showed me his rage.

And I showed him mine.

And how different they turned out to be. And how integral to the pages that follow.

Whereas Steve championed ideals—ascendancy, superiority, a will to win—I was juiced by what was; by the boat and sea and by the other wastrels aboard.

All of which is at the heart of the story I am about to tell. To which honest end, I wish to say that I no longer think of our epic travels as a journey in the strictest sense of the word. I recall them rather as a kind of fable, a nuthouse opera, written not by cynics or pessimists (who to my mind miss the point) but by dreamers, by stargazers, by minstrels. I recall the fable's jittery, soulful currents, its nightmares and eloquence, the worst and best of it captured indelibly for me by an incident that occurred on January 29, 2011, amidst seas so high that for hours they had been threatening to knock us off our rowing seats. Just after 2 a.m., word came up from the captain's quarters—a fusty little spook hole in the cabin of our experimental rowboat—that we were through for the night and should quit rowing and try to get some rest. For a few seconds, having shipped my oar, I slumped forward in my seat and stared blindly into the rowing trench beneath me. We were just nineteen days out of our starting port of Agadir, Morocco, and already I was down twenty pounds and was losing strength. And didn't know what to do about it. I hadn't brought enough food. Or the right food. I had come aboard as a kind of test of what was possible for a guy my age—a test that at the moment I was failing with flying colors.

Meanwhile, the fog was so dense, the night so black, that even with the deck lights on we could barely see our own feet. Nevertheless, within minutes we had unpacked the sea anchor, a colossal underwater parachute, and had pitched it over the bow on 200 yards of line. Even on a night so unruly, the anchor could pretty much neutralize the drifting of the boat.

By the luck of the draw that night, I was among the first four chosen for watch duty and was given the initial shift alone. And so I took my place on the bridge while a dozen others slept in the cabin and my watchmates took to the holds.

For the next few minutes, I did what I always did during cold nights on watch: enacted a tiny private indulgence, let us say a comfort, by wrapping my hands around the flimsy metal stanchion that supported the running light atop the cabin. And there I stood, as tranquil as Aquinas at prayer. While the light's plastic housing shed no warmth, the chromed metal post that held it aloft transmitted a matchstick's worth of heat from the electrical activity inside. But compared to the weather, it was as soothing as a woodstove in the Arctic, perhaps the only item warmer than the human body within a hundred miles of the boat.

As I absorbed the benefits of this pitiful dollhouse furnace, a wave exploded over the bridge, putting me ankledeep in brine. As the flood dropped, a small dark shadow fluttered in behind me, pushed by the wind, and a little black bird, a storm petrel, thwapped off the cabin door and was suddenly at my feet on the bridge, apparently as surprised as I by the turn of events. For nearly three weeks I had watched with great respect as these delicate bat-like irregulars bopped along the wave tops, pulling up tiny surface fish with their dangling and witchy feet. What I did not know at the time (it would have increased my respect significantly) is that these four-ounce strafe-artists never alight, either on water or land, except for two or three weeks a year during which they fly to distant islands to breed. Immediately, my little visitor was aswim on the painted plywood, thrashing its limp legs, while its weight rested on its spread wings and belly. Initially, I believed it must be injured—or perhaps just exhausted. I knew the feeling.

It was not until I had watched the thing struggle for a few seconds, unsure of what to do to help, that the truth dawned on me: the bird's longish legs and claws were so well adapted to snatching up tiny fish that they had become entirely too spindly for walking. Pained by its thrashing, I reached down and picked it up, quickly discovering the other thing aboard that was warmer than the human body, and considerably softer. I closed my hand over it, holding its wings gently in place until its eyelids fluttered and closed and it went calm. Intimacy was nothing new aboard, but the daily intimacy of naked bodies and raw emotions at close quarters seemed suddenly impertinent compared to the more primitive annunciation of the little winged creature whose heart and nerves, and whose uncertain fate, had quickly become one with my own.

Ten minutes later, I would hold the bird high, would open my hands and expel it into the night, unsure whether I was saving or dooming it. And would rejoice with it, in miniature, as it caught an updraft and was gone.

But for now it sat, poignantly and crushably vulnerable, in the hands of a stranger, on a turbulent night in the middle of the Atlantic Ocean, every instinct undoubtedly telling it that the jig was up, that this is how it ends.

For our purposes, of course, it is not how it ends but how it begins. Always: A dark and stormy night. An ocean. A boat. A cast of strangers. A blackbird.

A story. A storyteller.

Listen up.

I{T WAS TO BE} an expedition like no other—a run across the Atlantic from Morocco to Barbados aboard an experimental rowboat the likes of which no one had ever seen. Powered by a crew of sixteen, backed by the west-bound trade winds, the radically designed catamaran, dubbed *Big Blue,* would be capable, it was hoped, of making the 3,200-mile crossing in record time—max thirty-three days. The boat's crew, the largest assembled on the Atlantic since the days of the Norse longboats, included several veterans of U.S. college rowing, a number of marathoners and triathletes, and a woman who had rowed both the Atlantic and Indian Oceans. There would be no support vessel, no stored water, no sails or motor. No certification or assurances.

The venture, to be sure, was no laughing matter.

Well, unless you consider that one of the crew was a scrawny and bespectacled sexagenarian, the pinnacle of whose sporting career had been a couple of seasons of high school basketball and a season of hockey with the Forward Pharisees of the old Toronto Church League. This notable human blight on an otherwise durable roster had, until recently, never swung an oar in earnest or even sat on a proper rowing seat—indeed, did not know the names of even the commonest parts on a competitive rowing vessel. It is worthy of Mrs. Malaprop that on training maneuvers, when a reference was made to "the riggers" (the mechanisms that hold the oars in place), the duffer in question assumed it was the *rigors of the anticipated crossing* that were under discussion.

I am speaking of course of myself, Monsieur la Mer, Charles Wilkins, dad of three, fervent narrator, aging expeditionist; and I must reluctantly report that when I stepped on deck wearing my glasses during the earliest hours of the voyage I was told by one of our toughest rowers, Ryan Worth of the University of Tennessee, that I looked as if I were on my way to the library.

I suffered but did not protest the appraisal, and a mere eight hours later, as I came off the 2 a.m. watch, had a chance to reassess it with a vengeance. For at that point I would willingly have traded the last shreds of my dignity to have indeed been on my way to the library—to have been pretty much anywhere on earth other than where I was.

If I could claim one rueful victory as I settled to my bunk, it was that I no longer *looked* like a guy approaching a library. For one thing, every item of clothing on my carcass—ball cap, socks, sneakers, plus several layers of "warmth" beneath my rain gear—was oozing sea water. My newly cropped hair was the itchy amassment of brine and microorganisms that it would remain for days, and my hands and toes (the latter from being wedged into my salt-soaked shoes) were a bleached mess of tortured skin and broken blisters.

I was cold, I was exhausted, I was starved. Dinner, many hours earlier, had been a bowl of partially rehydrated macaroni and cheese followed by a cup of greenish pond muck (the latter cleverly presented as Wilderness Kitchen no-cook key lime pie). And yet I had no inclination to fiddle open the "all-organic GREAT TASTING one hundred percent natural" protein bar that was left from the day's snack pack. Even had I been ravenous for this questionable pretense to food, its unwrapping would have required a modicum of coordination from hands that had been reduced to crooks and were temporarily useless for small-motor chores.

What's more, I had been beaten up—slapped around by waves that sometime before midnight had started coming hard out of the northeast onto our port flank. Many of them had broken over the gunnels into our laps, onto our chests, into our faces. At one point, when for the briefest of moments my focus had lapsed (my brain having detoured into fantasies of my former life as a human being), a wave had snatched my oar, driving the handle into my chest, pinning me with savage efficiency against the bulkhead that defined the prow end of the rowing trench. My right ear had taken so much salt water that it had effectively gone deaf.

As if it all weren't enough, for perhaps twenty minutes toward the end of the watch I had experienced a running hallucination—a sense that a monstrous rusting scow, the ss *Apocalypse,* perhaps the moldering container vessel we had seen at dusk, had reefed out and sunk and was somehow lying just beneath us, or was about to surface in the mists off our bow.

I had been told that at times like this I would be unable to remember my own address, or my mother's name, or where I had gone to school. Or who loved me.

I could remember it all just fine.

Unfortunately, I no longer cared.

Meanwhile, if I was lucky, I had ninety minutes to sleep before being jarred awake for my next two-hour stint on the oars. That was the deal—two hours on, two hours off, for whatever number of days it took to get from Africa to North America. When you weren't in your bunk, somebody else was: in my case a mindfully ambitious emergency room physician named Sylvain Croteau from Gatineau, Quebec. Such were the good doc's focus and self-possession that a week earlier, in Agadir, when he got news that his dad had died, he had, rather than wilting or packing up, taken an hour in the boatyard where we were getting *Big Blue* ready, reflected on the life of his estranged *papa*, and gone industriously back to work.

As for the rest of the crew, I can say now that if we had known what lay ahead, some of us mightn't have been there. In the desultory losses and recrimination that would ensue a couple of weeks hence, one or two considered putting ashore at the Cape Verde Islands. I believed at the time, and said so, that if anyone wanted to go, he or she should get in a lifeboat and do it. And good riddance.

Which isn't to say I did not have traitorous thoughts of my own, among them a scorching heresy that, had I divulged it at the time, would have had me vilified, if not shunned, by some aboard: Namely, that my one-time interest in establishing a world record (the very reason for the voyage) had largely been displaced by a fascination with the journey itself—what it would require of me, what I could give to it and what it might give back. At the same time, there is a competitive and cement-headed part of me that would have reveled, have danced naked on the roof, to set a world record. One of my sustaining fantasies during the endless weeks of training was a mental projection of the last hours into Barbados, the old guys saving the day, persisting through the night, winning the battle against the clock—the lot of it an echo of my own internecine war, the one in which, as Mr. Donne put it, we are all finally trumpeted from the field.

As for what the journey would require, on that first night out of Agadir it was demanding everything I could offer in the way of wits and sanity. I had determined days ago that if I was to fulfil my duties to the boat during those early hours aboard, my biggest responsibility would be to myself—specifically to establish sleeping and eating patterns. Suffice it to say, my survival plan had already gone to hell, replaced by lesser, stupider efficiencies. I imagined, for example, that to save time as I came off the 2 a.m. watch that night, I would attempt simply to sleep in my wet clothes.

First, though, I had something to attend to in the darkness of the cabin—and must at this point grant a moment's shore leave to anyone of delicate nature. For even so early in my story, I must thrust into the limelight a part of my anatomy typically off limits to nonprofessionals or to those whose house key does not match my own. By which I am referring to my ass. To what was left of my ass.

My problem astern, I am embarrassed to report, had begun earlier that evening, barely out of Agadir, when, in a moment of distraction and weariness, I had dropped my precious gel seat cushion overboard into the sea. It was an item that had taken me weeks of sampling and experimentation to decide upon and buy, and as I stood on the bridge watching it disappear into the depths, a little part of my optimism for the trip disappeared with it.

Now, in the darkness, tummy-down in the bunk, I raised my hips a few inches and, using my thumbs as grappling hooks, eased my Class-3 high-tech rain pants onto my thighs. By this time I had endured three watches in succession with no seat pad, or with replacement pads so woeful (a pair of gloves, a folded sweatshirt) that none at all might have been an improvement. With the help of my stubbly chin, I pried open a tin of Penaten Medicated

Cream and, working blind, pressed great sticky gobs of the sweet-smelling emollient onto the weeping sores, one of them as big as a Ritz cracker, that had been grated into my backside by the rowing seat.

If I had any reason to feel positive as I lay in my soaked garments—or at least to feel less negative—it was that I was considerably better off than a couple of my cabinmates. One of them, Dylan White, a dazzling young musician and biologist from Toronto, who occupied the bunk opposite mine, had developed muscle spasms in his thighs and abdomen and for several hours had lost the ability to urinate. This one-time football player, little more than a third my age, had told me earlier in the evening that after three frightful watches he was no longer sure he was cut out to row the Atlantic.

Above him, on the upper bunk, lay Tom Butscher from Toronto Island, a former Canadian speed skating champ, a guy who at sixty-seven hoped to become the oldest man to row the Atlantic. Meanwhile, he had contracted severe gastrointestinal poisoning in Agadir, an illness that had wrecked him to a point where his normally elfin face had entirely gone missing beneath a mask of sagging wax. Unable to row, he could for now do little more than lurch back and forth between his bunk and the alfresco toilet within sniffing distance of the port stroke seat—or lie gazing at the cabin ceiling hoping that somehow his affliction would go away. Which, with the help of medication, it eventually did.

Had it not gone away, Tom would, like any other crew member postmortem, have been accorded what a prospectus for the trip had called "immediate burial at sea"— preferable one assumes to less timely options, such as, say, stowage in the food locker in a hundred degrees of heat, or being trussed up in a sleeping bag in a shared bunk and thus transported through the tropics (I had a morbid cartoon fantasy of being bound up in a blanket and thrown overboard, and somehow picking up the trade winds and beating the boat to Barbados).

"How ya doin'?" I asked Tom quietly in the dark, when I had reinstalled my soaked and now frigid pants.

"There's blood," he whispered.

"Ya gonna make it?"

After a lengthy pause, he said, "I dunno—at least it's calming down out there."

Ten seconds later, as if cued to his utterance, a fifteen-foot wave exploded over the bridge, astern, and sloshed through the cabin door, which we had not yet learned to keep closed.

When the shrieking had died down and those closest to the door had rescued their skivvies from the cabin floor, Dylan looked across at me and said, "I dunno either." And in self-mocking insolence (the last luxury available to us under the circumstances), we began to laugh.

I F FURTHER EVIDENCE is necessary of either the mirth or sobriety of this fanciful and fateful expedition, consider that by the time we cast off I, like the rest of the crew, had invested US$10,000 in the boat and several thousand more in travel and training (this at a time when an American greenback still bought half a tennis ball and the treasury in Washington had not commenced perforating its currency and dispensing it on a roll). What's more, having begged my way aboard as a chronicler of the follies to come, I had spent nearly a year and a half in arduous training in order to be ready. This grossly protracted fitness spree left me so exhausted at times that toward the end of it I began seriously to wonder if I had the jam to do what dozens of far stronger athletes had failed to do in the past. Of the 700-odd fools who had attempted to row the Atlantic during the past hundred years, a mere 400 had made it—compared, for example, to the roughly 5,000 who have reached the summit of Everest.

That said, there is a part of me (the mating of Puritan and cockroach) that thrived on the training and exhaustion, that looked forward to the salt drenchings and sun, to the scouring of the hands against the oars. "Everest Shmeverest," I told a mountain climber at one point, jestingly contemptuous of those who needed Sherpas and oxygen and Depends to fulfil their questionable goals where I needed only blind determination and stupidity—well, and a crew of much stronger rowers than I... oh, and a mini-Everest of 222s, the wobbly pharmaceutical crutch on which I have stumbled along for a dozen years, six a day, taken as a stop-gap against arthritis and muscle pain and migraines.

Fortunately I did not need privacy. For when we weren't rowing or soaked, or under other pestilential influences, we lived like gophers, far more scuzzily than you might imagine, in a cabin about the size of a Volkswagen van. It was a cell that, for reasons easily imagined, I came to think of as the Gas Chamber—or, in airier moments, the House that Dave Built: eight bunks, upper and lower, each about the dimensions of a pygmy's coffin, on opposite sides of a narrow central passageway, and a Lilliputian fore-galley which on the third day at sea was colonized by the boat's captain, Angela Madsen, and converted into a berth. In that tiny enclosure, our oft-inscrutable commander had almost enough space to lay out a sleeping bag, but not enough to roll over in the night or even to stand up without sticking her head and upper body out the ventilation hatch on the inclined front wall.

By Dave I mean David Davlianidze, the unflappable Georgian expat—hawk-nosed, brilliant, soft-spoken—in whose boat shop on Shelter Island, NY, our eccentric craft had taken shape. In the days after Georgia gained its independence from the Soviet Union in 1992 and was plunged into civil war, this gentle, free-spirited economist and entrepreneur carried a Smith & Wesson .38 revolver and ran with other gun-toting "paramilitarists" in order to guard the money he was making by importing cigarettes from Austria and selling them out of what he refers to as his "boutique" in the Georgian capital of Tbilisi. His introduction to the Land of Hope and Glory, which we shall visit in due time, was as outrageous and picaresque as that of a character in the boldest and most subversive fiction. He had for months been an outlaw. But for most of us he was all hero—a guy you could trust with your life, as we did literally from the moment we signed on.

The question no one dared ask during the days leading up to our departure was whether our trust was justified. Would the spidery and eccentric vessel Dave had built hold up on the Atlantic? Would the beams connecting the hulls do their job? Would the boat surf, as any rowboat riding the trade winds has to do?

At least one person, a naval architect in Agadir, had been decidedly non-committal in assessing *Big Blue*'s seaworthiness. When asked, as he was several times, he would roll his eyes, shake his presumably knowledgeable head, and allow that he would certainly not want to be aboard.

In effect, we were test pilots for a boat that might at best become a model for the future of the sport—or at very least an honorable experiment. At worst, *Big Blue* would end her days as a scattering of expensive flotsam amidst an array of kit bags and life preservers on the lonely and heaving surface of the Atlantic.

MY FIRST AWARENESS of this fanciful experimental rowboat had come sixteen months earlier, during late August of 2009. On a visit to Thessalon, Ontario, to lead a weekend of writing seminars, I had an opportunity to catch up with my old friends Steve Roedde and Janet McLeod, whom I had met nearly a decade earlier while I was on a sixty-three-day solo hike from Thunder Bay, Ontario, to New York City. At the time, they had hosted a dinner for me at their home on St. Joseph Island, in Lake Huron, east of Sault Ste. Marie. Like any number of generous and adventurous irregulars whom I met en route, they eventually became characters in the book I wrote about the walk, and we kept in touch. By August 2009, however, we had not seen one another for several years. So we enjoyed a welcome reunion, over dinner with others, and eventually got to questions about what everybody had been up to in recent months.

"Wellllllll...," said Janet, when it was her and Steve's turn, dragging out the syllable as if hesitating to announce, say, that they had turned to gambling and lost everything, or had bought a herd of rhinos and it wasn't working out.

"I'll let Steve fill you in on the details," she said after a few seconds, "but he and Nigel are in training to row across the Atlantic Ocean."

Nigel is their twenty-three-year-old son, and as Steve took up the tale, I heard, as if through radio static, the phrases "crew of fourteen"... "world-record attempt"... "four months from now"... "tropical Atlantic." By the time he had uttered half a dozen sentences it no longer seemed as if anyone was actually speaking to me, answering my questions, attempting to impart information. It was rather as if a kind of force field had descended, reducing me first to defenselessness, to purest susceptibility, then to a single evolving compulsion. During the minutes that followed, every other thought in my head was displaced, if not eradicated, by an outlandish inner hankering to be part of the remarkable expedition Steve was describing. I love boats, particularly those without motors; love outdoor adventure. I had in fact been stirred in recent months toward what I felt might be a last grand attempt to do something extraordinary in the realm of travel, something that would push me hard up against my limits, perhaps even my mortality. What that might be, I didn't know, and could never have named it as specifically as it had just been named for me. Beyond my private ambitions, the writer in me was fascinated by the idea of being out on the ocean, at sea level, in a rowboat of all things, and of having to be fit enough to power such a vessel across an ocean.

When later I cornered Steve about the possibility of my being included, he allowed that there happened to be an opening on the crew and a *very* remote chance I might be taken on, although probably not—the cherished record was more likely to be broken with young titans at the oars than with skinny old writers.

Nevertheless, I got the name and phone number of the boat's builder and captain, Roy Finlay, and a few nights later found myself on the phone with him explaining in immodest bursts what a sterling chap I was, exemplary in the clutch, durable, disciplined—how I had once walked 1,400 miles from my home in Thunder Bay to New York City, overcoming poor training, infirmity, injury, blizzards, heat waves; I had written a book about it! I would send him one! He could read for himself about the extraordinary creature I am!

For reasons too trifling to mention, I hesitated to note that I am an arthritic and near-sighted rack of bones, who had done nothing aerobically challenging for three or four years and, at the time, would have been hard-pressed to row across the St. Lawrence River, let alone the Atlantic Ocean.

SIXTY MAY WELL be the new fifty, as the culture-clappers would have us believe. At the same time, I am deeply aware that if there is an axiom for self-deceit among guys my age it is that somehow we can forestall the diminishments of time—or even reverse them—and rise to physical demands that would have defeated us at thirty or forty.

This is perhaps why, when the captain called eight or ten days later and announced to me that I would be allowed to come along as a writer, provided I could row, I hung up the phone not, as one might think, gripped by elation or a sense of triumph but in a welter of ambivalence—excited, yes, but appalled too over what I had gotten myself into. For the first time it occurred to me that at my age I couldn't possibly get fit enough to row day and night on the high seas—to keep up with a dozen or more tough athletes, most of whom were less than half my age and either elite rowers or front-line endurance competitors in other sports.

His belief, the captain told me, was that I would have a stabilizing influence on temperamental young crew members (a first, let it be said, in that for years I have more often been cited as a *de*stabilizing influence on the orderly progress of the universe).

If my skepticism needed burnishing, it got it a few days later, when, en route from my cottage in Muskoka to my home in Thunder Bay, I stopped overnight at Steve and Janet's on St. Joseph Island. Steve had a rowing machine in his basement and was going to show me a few things about technique.

"Promise me no tests at this stage," I told him, to which he responded that I should "just get on for a while—see what it feels like. No numbers."

The Concept2 rower is a long, Inquisitional-looking contraption with a flywheel, pull chain, and sliding seat—and a computer. And as soon as I saw it, I realized in dismay that anything I did on it in terms of speed, power, or distance would be recorded, almost certainly exposing me as a fraud, perhaps even a fraud with a defective heart (to go with what was rapidly being exposed as my defective brain).

To this day, it is a reminder to me of how badly I wanted to do this that as I got onto the rower I found myself thinking *and not particularly caring* that if I was going to show Steve and the others I had the mettle to go out on the Atlantic with them, I would need to push myself to where I would unquestionably be risking a heart attack (heart attacks being what happen to out-of-shape sixty-two-year-olds who push their tickers up to 85 percent of capacity and attempt to hold them there for... well, the time it takes to row across the Atlantic Ocean). My best chance of surviving the next hour, I suspected, lay not in the resilience of my arteries but in the fact that Steve and Janet were both practicing emergency room physicians.

And so I rowed. And my heart pounded. And my lungs wheezed. And my heart pounded harder.

When it was over, I am relieved to report, I had not only survived but had put up numbers that moved Steve to enthuse that I was "*probably* going to be okay" and that he would hasten to let the others know that I would at least be able to lift my own oar onto the boat.

Later, in Steve's absence, Janet told me how utterly relieved she had been to see me row, surely feeling that had I wobbled or begun to complain after a few minutes, the voyage, not to mention the lives of her son and husband, would have been that much further compromised and at risk.

And so began my training—the run-up to an adventure for which I still believed I had just three months to prepare. Throughout September I spent four or five hours a day at the Canada Games Complex in Thunder Bay, jogging on the track, lifting weights, pumping the rowing machines... and further pumping them... and pumping them some more. Part of my challenge was that the rest of the crew, already far stronger than I, had been training for nearly half a year. The previous February, a kind of cattle call had gone out over an array of rowing and sporting websites. The message was that Captain Roy Finlay, boat designer extraordinaire, was looking for hard-nosed rowers with an epic sense of adventure to take an experimental rowboat across the Atlantic during late 2009, and to take it across in world-record time. Steve and Nigel had been among the dozen hardy souls— from Canada, from the U.S., from Europe—who gathered at Shelter Island, showed Roy what they could do, and departed, dreams burnished, passports as good as stamped. The early instalments of their $10,000 participation fees would begin building the boat, which at that point was itself little more than a dream.

By September, the hulls had been built and the construction schedule was on catch-up—could the boat possibly be ready for mid-November, when it would have to be shipped to Morocco?

My own game of catch-up was every bit as frantic as Roy's. While my official goading to be up to speed by the end of October came from headquarters, my real regimen came from Steve Roedde, who emailed me twice a day with endless encouragement and challenges—for this afternoon's workout, for tomorrow's simulated row, for the weekend's marathon. What rattled me particularly as Week 1 slid past was my utter incapability merely to stay perched on the rowing machine. I would very shortly be expected to sit for two hours straight, six times a day, quite literally working my ass off, when for now I could barely go twenty minutes without having to get off and grimace and massage, as if I'd been flogged at the mast or thrown down the stairs. When I complained, Steve informed me that my problem was nothing more than the muscles being crushed by the pressure of the seat—"pulped," I believe was his word. As for mental conditioning, I was led to think of it as something real ocean rowers, leather-butts, didn't worry about because once you got out there it was pretty much a crapshoot of stresses and unpredictability and we were all more or less nuts anyway.

Gradually, I increased my "sit time" to half an hour, then forty minutes, but never really did get much beyond the latter. Even on the boat, I'd get up and stretch and adjust my cushion, or take a leak, or take off my T-shirt, or reapply my sunscreen—whatever little chore provided a modicum of cover for the fact that I simply could not sit there pulping my bony posterior for much more than half an hour at a time.

The second and third weeks of my training called for three- and four-hour rowing sessions at a level of strength and cardiovascular fitness that my second week told me I would not be achieving any time soon.

In response to these exaggerated demands, I was going through Gatorade by the gallon and eating whole chickens, whole lake trout, whole apple pies. At one point in October, I boiled up a five-pound bag of potatoes, *tout complet,* and ate them with a pound of butter and another of old cheddar within perhaps eight hours.

Meanwhile, I agonized over what I perceived to be my painfully sluggish progress, more fretful than ever that I would not be ready and would end up disgracing myself. My greatest fear was not that I would drown or be ship-wrecked or die of a heart attack aboard; it was that I would simply not be equal to the task, would end up huddled and whimpering in a corner of the cabin while the others debated whether to euthanize me humanely or just throw me to the sharks.

At the same time, there was something crazily exhilarating for me in the fact that, at the ripening age of sixty-two (when, as Shakespeare put it, I might better be pulling up "the lean and slipper'd pantaloon"), I had committed myself to an adventure that I would not even have contemplated at times in my life when I would more likely have had the physical capabilities to survive what I planned to do.

In a magazine story on my training, I wrote with utmost sincerity that at twenty I would not have had the inner strength for such an endeavor, at thirty the imagination, at forty the time. At fifty I would have lacked the all-important awareness that I gained as I approached sixty: that mortality is just another setting on life's cruise control, neither to be feared nor particularly avoided, and that the true gist of the ripening season is one's compulsion just to go, to ask what would happen if rather than simply enduring risk and uncertainty as we add years, we decided instead to embrace risk, juice up on it, reclaim our bodies, re-establish ground—in short to reinvent ourselves, or at very least to discover what an adventure might turn up about the human comedy and how best we might play out our roles in it as we age.

WHEN WORD CAME from Roy Finlay in mid-October that the boat was not ready and that, given the shipping time to Morocco, we could not mobilize until February, I was surely the only crew member who felt even a remote sense of relief, in that I now had time to get properly into shape, as well as to sort my finances, get my will updated,

and so on. Some of my fellow crew members were outraged. A few had taken specific time off work in order
to participate, or had other obligations in February and
couldn't make the adjustment.

No one responded more adamantly than Steve. He
and Janet have a maple syrup operation on the island,
and he had to be there tapping trees and boiling sap
during late February and March. I had access to some
of Steve and Roy's correspondence at the time. I am not
free to quote from it, but will submit that Steve went at
the captain with an all-but-animal rage over his perceived
delinquency in not providing fair warning as to what was
going on with the boat. It was Steve's contention that
Roy must have known weeks earlier not only what shape
Big Blue was in but what sort of effort would be required
to get her to Morocco.

By the time the ensuing quarrel derailed, Steve had
pronounced Roy a liar and closet fraud, and Roy had
declared Steve an insubordinate meddler (in words
slightly more colorful) who could not accept authority
and who would not now, *ever,* be part of the crew that
would eventually row *Big Blue* to her rightful moorage in
the record books.

When I spoke to Steve shortly after the announcement,
he told me he was "devastated" that his eight months of
training and anticipation—in effect the reshaping of his
life to the exotic prospect that lay ahead—had come to
nothing. Even if he could patch things up with Roy, there
was the more concrete obstacle of the sugar bush.

We had barely absorbed this new and shattering reality, when an announcement came that it was now all off
for a year. The proposed February departure could not be
accomplished either, after which, for nine months, there
would be too great a likelihood of tropical storms and

hurricanes. For crew members such as Steve, this opened new possibilities—if and only if he could work things out with Roy. A new concern, however, was whether he could withstand another year of the sort of training that, at this point, had taken a toll not just on him but on his marriage.

For others who had stayed with the voyage, it was the last hatchet blow, and within days the crew was down to seven or eight committed rowers. One of them, fortunately, was Nigel Roedde, Steve's son, who was determined to see the voyage through, thus significantly increasing the chances that Steve would find his way back aboard.

As rowers abandoned ship, my own sense of commitment deepened. By this time, I had borrowed a rowing machine and was often on it for three hours a day. At the height of Roy's flare-up with Steve, I emailed them both, confirming my participation, hoping it would not be read as a betrayal of my friendship with Steve. Which clearly it was not. When I visited Steve and Janet at Christmas, Steve and I "raced" on a pair of machines in their rec room, after which he informed me that I was now functioning at "the fitness level of the average twenty-five-year-old" (he did not mention which species, although I assumed he was talking about human beings and on that basis permitted myself a moment or two of satisfaction over the progress I had at times doubted I was making).

If I had a training predicament it was this: that, while I was supposed to be putting on weight, the better to survive the physiological dunning of the Atlantic, I was actually losing it, couldn't gain an ounce no matter how many gallons of oatmeal and pounds of spaghetti and handfuls of cashews I consumed. My intention was to get up to 180 pounds from my customary 160, but I knew from experience that I would have to put the weight on gradually—couldn't hope to add that much muscle and lard during the last couple of months.

The other hitch in my training was my tendency to go too hard and thereby to risk injury, this against the advice of every knowledgeable athlete and trainer I encountered. My friend Peter White, a Thunder Bay lawyer and former competitive rower, would remind me every time I saw him that it was crucially preferable to under-train than to over-train, and that I should simply not allow myself to fall into the "harder, faster, longer" syndrome. Nevertheless, in February, while attempting to set a personal best for power and "speed" on the machine, I messed up a disc in my back—felt it pop—and for nearly three weeks could barely walk, let alone row. At the height of my discomfort, it took me ten minutes to get out of bed, another ten to get my pants on, another ten to get downstairs to the kitchen. Shortly after it happened, I attended a dinner party and spent the entire evening pitched forward at a forty-five-degree angle from the waist, as inflexible as a 5-lie hockey stick, explaining to stupefied friends that I would soon be reclaiming my youth by powering my way across the Atlantic. A week after that, still folded like a jackknife but gussied up now in an Italian tux, I lurched around a "grand" charity ball, a literary affair, at the Royal York Hotel in Toronto, explaining to writers who thought they'd seen it all that in tossing off the shackles of the years I would, among other things, be testing the resiliency of the human carcass.

Meanwhile, I learned what I could about the route, the weather patterns, the prospects. I also devoured anything I could find about modern ocean rowing—not as it is practiced by fishermen or lifeguards in wooden dories or double-enders off the coasts of, say, Newfoundland or

Australia, but by the hardy extremists ("the global-village idiots," as I have heard them called) who for nearly fifty years have made a kind of game of racing one another, or the clock, across the oceans of the world.

No one would have predicted much of a future for such a game when it debuted during the summer of 1966 (indeed, in considering its history, few free of dementia would predict much of a future for it now). On May 21 of that year, while others of their generation were rolling weed or stringing flowers in their hair in Kensington Gardens or MacArthur Park, a young British pair named David Johnstone and John Hoare, motivated by heaven knows what, left Virginia Beach, Virginia, aboard a craft named *Puffin,* rowed for 105 days in the direction of home, and on September 3 (as their recovered log revealed) disappeared forever from the face of the planet. A second British team, John Ridgway and Chay Blyth, set out from Cape Cod, Massachusetts, two weeks later than the doomed pair, and upon their arrival in Ireland on exactly the day their cohorts are thought to have gone to the bottom, became the first of the new-age rowers to cross the Atlantic.

In 1972, after three false starts, another pair of Brits, John Fairfax and Sylvia Cook, aboard *Britannia II*, became the earliest to cross the Pacific (she the first woman to cross any ocean), rowing from San Francisco to Hayman Island, Australia. They did so in a sprightly 361 days, including food and water stops on a variety of shores and islands.

Of the thirty rowing crews that attempted ocean crossings between 1966 and 1982—attempts now referred to as "historic" ocean rows—just fifteen were successful, while three were lost entirely. The most compelling of the disappearances was that of an Englishman named Kenneth

Kerr, who departed St. John's, Newfoundland, in May of 1979, rowed for fifty-eight days on the North Atlantic, gave up, and was rescued by a passing cargo ship. He set out again several months later, this time from Corner Brook, Newfoundland, rowed for 108 days, and is believed to have been wrecked and drowned, possibly within miles of his destination on the English coast.

What distinguished those first thirty attempts from rows that have occurred since was that they were undertaken without life rafts, satellite phones, or desalination equipment—or any navigational conveniences such as an autopilot or a GPS (which had of course not yet been invented). A broken rudder or oarlock meant the end not just of the voyage but quite possibly of those aboard.

Peter Bird of the U.K. had already rowed both the Atlantic and Pacific when, in August 1982, he introduced modern desalination and communications equipment to the sport during his 294-day odyssey from San Francisco to the Great Barrier Reef in Australia. Between June 1992 and June 1996, Bird would make five more attempts to row the Pacific, all of them unsuccessful, invariably from the east coast of Russia with the hope of reaching the west coast of the USA. The fourth attempt lasted 304 days before he gave it up. On his fifth attempt, he rowed a couple of thousand miles east from Vladivostok, made his last contact with land on Day 69 of his voyage, and was never heard from again.

A pair of Soviet rowers, Alexander and Eugene Smurgis, embarked from Tiksi, Russia, on the Arctic coast, during the summer of 1993, and reached London, England, in 131 days. Less than three months later, Eugene, alone on a relatively straightforward run across the Atlantic, disappeared somewhere above the Mid-Atlantic Ridge and, like Peter Bird, was not seen again.

During the decade to come, Smurgis's route, an approximation of our own, emerged as the standard transatlantic crossing, beginning either on the northwest coast of Africa or in the Canary Islands and moving westward for some 3,000 miles, aided by the trade winds, to the outer islands of the Caribbean. The less common and tougher Atlantic route, eastward from North America to Europe, is aided by the current of the Gulf Stream, which arcs north and east up the U.S. seaboard, past Newfoundland, and eventually across to Ireland.

While fewer than thirty rowboats successfully crossed any of the world's oceans during the first thirty years of the sport, the next fifteen years—from 1997 to the present—witnessed so many attempts that successful crossings now number somewhere over 400. This is a result largely of the introduction of a transatlantic rowing race, the Atlantic Challenge, in 1997. In October of that year, thirty boats, all pairs, left the Canary Islands. Twenty-four of them eventually reached Port St. Charles, Barbados. In 2003, the race became the Woodvale Atlantic Rowing Race, a contest that every second year sends as many as forty boats out from Tenerife in the Canaries. The sport is regulated and archived by an English organization called the Ocean Rowing Society, which logs the details of all crossings, sets the rules, and keeps the record books. Those rules stipulate among other things that boats must be self-sustaining from start to finish, must touch neither land nor any other vessels en route, and must run entirely without motors or sails.

Big Blue, I had realized by now, would be running not just without a motor or sail but without a toilet—the absence of which was apparently to be addressed by a handle astern, to which one could cling while dangling one's posterior above the ocean. During my training,

I read numerous accounts of excursions such as ours, at least one of which mentioned the unsettling sight of sharks, big ones, that occasionally surfaced as someone was doing his or her business over the rail. Beyond the risks of being lost at sea and the (admittedly slim) threat of having one's hindquarters removed by a man-eating fish, the hazards of ocean rowing, as I was able to assess them, ran to sunstroke, dehydration, exhaustion, malnutrition, extreme weight loss, supertankers in the shipping lanes, salt sores, mid-Atlantic delirium, breakdown of navigation and desalination equipment, antipathies among crew members, and bad weather.

There were also, I came to understand, great pleasures to be anticipated on such crossings: parades of porpoises, pods of whales, glorious night skies, intense camaraderie, the satisfactions of high-level fitness. One crew member from a previous crossing described his boat surfing for miles at a stretch—"as thrilling as a rollercoaster"—on twenty-five-foot waves sent up by the trade winds, which would be of primary importance to us as we made our way across. Or so we believed.

A **S THE WINTER** deepened, Roy's communication with the crew became increasingly fitful. There were stretches when we didn't hear from him for weeks. He had taken time away to build another rowing boat, a smaller craft, for a team of British rowers—three of whom, ironically, had in recent months departed our own dwindling crew.

Roy's own abrupt departure from the expedition in the late spring of 2010 might have been predicted. By that time, he had apparently fallen out with David, and the project was sinking into debt. The boat was far from ready for the ocean. No one knew quite what to do or think about Roy's going. On the downside, we had lost our captain, a mercurial mastermind who had brought multi-hulled boats to ocean rowing and in so doing had revolutionized the sport. What we had gained, meanwhile, was the freedom to reshape the adventure, free of the singular fixations of an increasingly unpredictable leader.

Until now, the greatest mystery for the crew had been the nature of David and Roy's connection, and of David's connection to the boat. In the early days, David had been pitched to the crew as an engineer who would be aboard but not rowing, presumably as Roy's assistant. Steve believed David was the money man, and that Shelter Island Boats was Roy's operation. But with Roy's departure, it quickly became clear that David, a man with the subtlest of egos, owned not just the boatyard but the boat and that he knew a good deal more than we had imagined about boatbuilding. Indeed, with a gaggle of his Long Island pals, two of whom were fellow Georgians, he was prepared now to take over the project. His motivation compared to Roy's (whose was creative and competitive, as well as financial) was largely a matter of integrity. He and Roy had accepted money from those who had signed on, and David was not about to stiff them if he could help it.

Almost immediately, Steve, who with Roy's departure was back in the fold, broadened his influence on the voyage. My own hope was that he would assume the captaincy, which would have been his for the taking. But he didn't want it. He was an experienced Great Lakes sailor but did not feel confident in his navigational skills on the Atlantic. I think he believed too that the captain of an ocean rowboat should have made the crossing at least once as a crewman. However, he did set about bringing new people to the expedition, as did Nigel—an effort that would eventually put seven Canadians, a modest plurality, aboard an essentially American boat.

For the moment there were twelve of us. David wanted sixteen. Steve's foremost acquisition, as it turned out, was not a Canadian but a Californian whose route to *Big Blue* was more circuitous, unlikely, and coincidence-ridden than the plotting of a Victorian novel. It began perhaps three months after Roy's resignation, when a Thunder

Bay skier and endurance cyclist named Frank Pollari, a friend of mine who is legally blind, had an inkling he might like to join our little band. He began to train. However, before he committed to the voyage he wanted to test himself on the ocean, in particular to see if an old vulnerability to seasickness still existed. Through Google, he located a veteran female rower in Long Beach, went out to see her, went rowing, and spent much of his time aboard with his head over the rail, puking into the California surf. And came home. And more or less forgot about ocean rowing.

Until a day in late September, when he received an email from Steve, who knew of Frank through me and wanted to know more about this mysterious, good-natured woman who had taken Frank rowing on the Pacific. Steve could not help but notice on her blog that she had rowed both the Indian and Atlantic Oceans, and had returned recently from a triumphal row around Great Britain.

The question was: Would she row for us? Might she accept the vacant captaincy? There is in the sport a prestige in being at the helm, where she had not been on any previous row. Plus, it was assumed that the boat's experimental design and the desire for a world record would interest her. Steve petitioned her in an email—and received an answer the next day. And sent word to the rest of us that she was at least open to the idea.

We held our breath as she flew cross-country to New York to meet David and to check out the boat. And celebrated quietly as news came down, beneath the radar, that she had liked what she'd seen.

So it was a week or so later that the soft-spoken grandma from Xenia, Ohio, via Long Beach, was introduced to the crew, via email, as our new commander,

Cap'n Angela—excited, as she put it, to be part of "this historic ocean row."

MEANWHILE, in Thunder Bay, not everyone was as magnanimous about my decision to row the Atlantic as I might have liked. "Are you doing this because you want to die?" I was asked at one point by a smart-aleck acquaintance—to which I responded, in finest mock Confucianism, that I was doing it "because I *didn't* want to die."

"But what is the *meaning* of it?" I was asked by a nettlesome neighbor.

"Discovery," I thought to tell her, adding that I assumed I would be better able to report on such abstractions when I returned.

"And if you don't return?" she said slyly.

For now, I told her, I had discovered meaning in my training, which, happily, in mid-June, moved outdoors onto water—at Clear Lake, in the Muskoka region of central Ontario, where the family keeps a summer cottage. What a relief it was to be splashing, to be *moving,* to see shoreline passing, after ten months indoors on the old black C2 torture machine. My outdoor rowboat, it needs be said, was not one of those spiffy needle-nosed skiffs that you see rowers using in the Olympics but an old Norwegian sailing vessel—a Gresvig 5—given to me by my parents on my twelfth birthday. With a tuck here, a tap there, I converted it into a rowboat that worked the muscles of the upper body and abdomen to the point where several times that summer I was approached by people speculating on how youthfully and seductively "ripped" I must be somewhere beneath my T-shirt. And of course I was. Profoundly. However, as you might imagine with a guy of my age and inclinations, mine was more a metaphysical ripping, an inner muscularity, than one merely of the flesh.[1]

And the ripping did not stop at my pecs, nor in the well-lit recesses of the *chi*. A further feature of this dutiful if moldering craft was that its old centerboard slot, which transected the seat directly beneath my hard-working glutes, regularly ripped holes right through my pants and on into what was left of the underlying muscle. To someone of lesser ambition this might have presented as a drawback. However, because of it I was infinitely better prepared for the salt and "rub" sores that accrue to all transatlantic rowers.

In contrast to the skepticism of my detractors, I enjoyed the acknowledgment and encouragement of, among others, bank executives, artists, politicians, lawyers, professors. Some said they'd love to be going with me. There were times when I wished they *were* going with me. Or going instead of me. For despite my anticipation and training, I harbored little in the way of certainty about the upcoming months. Which was preferable, I believed, to being too certain. Ricky Wallenda once told me that a wire walker is more likely to fall if he succeeds in overcoming his fears. So he nurses those fears as he weathers the improbability of his choices.

Likewise, I nourished my own modest fears and uncertainties, in the hope not just of weathering but of welcoming the consequences of this thing I had chosen to

---

1 Meanwhile, anyone who'd like to see what a skinny old guy looks like, and talks about, while preparing to row the Atlantic should get on the web and locate a short film, made in March 2010 by the Canadian director Kelly Saxberg, about my training and seafaring ambitions. Entitled *Life Is but a Dream*, the nifty little movie was chosen from some 200 mini-docs from around the world to be shown at the big international documentary festival, Hot Docs, in Toronto in May of that year.

do. And therein I located both the thematic and narrative arcs of the next few months of my life—arcs animated increasingly by my improbable makeover as a high-stakes rower, an extreme athlete, or, more pertinently, an extreme convert to the uncertain art of keeping the adventure alive.

WHILE THE CREW trained, David and his Shelter Island kinsmen were at work on the boat—strengthening it, rebuilding parts of it, generally gussying it up and fitting it for the ravages of the sea. David believed that Roy, whose idea was to keep the boat's weight down at any cost, had somewhat under-engineered the vessel, perhaps leaving it vulnerable to the tough going ahead. Roy's earliest plan had not even included a cabin; crew members were to have slept in compartments in the hulls or on an open platform between them. In defense of Roy's standards, it should be said that in 2006 he had built an ocean rowboat named *Orca,* a gorgeous tri-hull (two of the hulls were in effect sealed hollow outriggers) in which he and three others raced across the Atlantic against a boat named *La Mondiale,* piloted by the famed Scottish ocean rower Leven Brown. Coincidentally, it was *La Mondiale*'s crossing time of thirty-three days (*Orca* crossed in thirty-four) that established the world record we were about to go chasing.

But *Big Blue* was more vulnerable than *Orca.* As a catamaran, she would be subject to enormous structural pressures in that her hulls would be torqued hard and constantly in opposite directions by the waves. The cabin would be pounded from below. Her advantage was that her twin hulls would allow eight rowers to work at once, more than had ever rowed together on an Atlantic crossing.

From afar, Roy protested the contamination of his design, while David made it clear that it was his boat now and that the safety of the crew would not be compromised beyond the fateful compromises that were already intrinsic to such a voyage.

Impressed by *Big Blue*'s design—by "David's vision," as she put it—Angela nonetheless initiated two small changes: the addition of a toilet and of a small gas burner for heating water. Where there was a grandma on the raging main, there would also be a cup of tea.

SIX WEEKS LATER, in mid-November, fourteen of us flew or drove to New York City and rode in crowded vehicles out the Long Island Expressway, past Amityville and Fire Island and the Hamptons. Eventually, at Greenport, we caught the night ferry to Shelter Island, where, during a three-day trial, our experience of the Atlantic began.

At this point, I had not actually seen the already storied rowboat that had occupied my thoughts and dreams day after day for so many months. And I had developed a deep hankering to do so. And was not disappointed. As we spilled out of the van that had transported us from JFK, the boat sat dramatically before us in the lights of the boatyard, spidery and futuristic in its new coat of paint. For half an hour or more, we circled it in a kind of trance, patting and rubbing at it, tummying up to it, peering into its recesses, fiddling with its hatches and seats, unable to get the smiles off our faces. The $10,000 I had put in, which at the time had struck me as a chunk, seemed suddenly small, while the boat, or at least its aura, expanded like Topsy in our midst.

Structurally, *Big Blue* is a study in simplicity: two narrow hulls, each nearly forty feet long, joined by aluminum beams so they sit twenty feet apart. Each hull has four rowing positions, while the joining beams support a tidy little spaceship of a cabin.

"It looks big, but it'll be very small on the ocean," growled a low voice behind me. I turned and a man a few years older than myself was looking at me with drooping but animated eyes. He said, "You must be Charlie; I'm Tom Butscher." He was one of Steve's would-be recruits, as yet undecided, who had traveled by train from his home on Toronto Island in order to mingle with the crew, take a trial row, and make up his mind. (The following morning he said to me quietly, "Ya know, I don't think I'll bother making up my mind—too much pressure. I'll just go." And he committed to the journey then and there.)

In all, meeting the crew was like encountering the characters out of a novel I'd been reading for weeks: Ernst from Vienna; Sunshine Liz from the north side of the island; Aleksa the firefighter from Deer Park; Rowboat Ryan from Chattanooga; Louise from bluegrass country; Sylvain from Gatineau; Paul from Shelter Island.

Paul was not a rower but had our respect and attention because he had worked on the boat, as had the pair of Georgian expats, relentless smokers, who shook hands dutifully and went back to building the rudders.

And of course David—*David*—that most honorable of guys, who had picked up the pieces in Roy's absence and had made a boat that with any luck would bear us all off to sea.

Of the lot, it was Angela who seemed most like a character who had somehow found her way into the wrong novel. More subdued, sweeter tempered, driftier than any of us had imagined, she was, at six-foot-two, an impressive assemblage of tree trunks and upholstery and scar tissue. Thirty years ago, as she had explained to us on the way up from JFK, several of her vertebrae had been smashed while she was playing basketball for the U.S. Marines. It was her first game; she was to have been a star. A dozen years later, the military's best orthopedic surgeons had botched the operation that was intended to fix her up. "No hope, no recourse," she shrugged—adding that, these days, with the exception of short hauls, where her leg braces were all the support she needed, she traveled in a wheelchair. "Or on a surfboard," she brightened. Or on her beloved rowboat back home in Long Beach.

On the morning after our arrival, David hitched his wide burgundy half-ton to *Big Blue*'s trailer, and, following a police escort, pulled her ceremoniously from the boatyard. In our scarves and squall jackets, we fell in behind, pilgrims to Canterbury, chattering and laughing as we walked a mile or more of treed residential roadway to the launching ramp.

There, over a period of several hours, in the cold November afternoon, we attached the rudders and rowing riggers, ate lunch, kibitzed and fussed until, finally, at perhaps 5 p.m. we slid the boat ever so gently off its trailer into the shallows of the Atlantic Ocean. And watched in fascination as it floated free, seeming barely to create a ripple.

Off we rowed into a grayish and misty twilight—up the east side of Shelter Island, not far from East Hampton and Montauk, where my only previous look at the local waters had come from the Steven Spielberg movie *Jaws*.

For sixteen hours straight we worked exactly as we would at sea: two watches of rowers in two-hour shifts, alternating port and starboard hulls, in order to balance the strain on the shoulders, neck, and torso. During the year or more I had been involved in the expedition, I had been asked perhaps a dozen times: Why two hours—why not three, to allow a decent sleep? And the simple answer is that three hours (great for sleep) is too long a period for rowing. At least over a period of days—or in our case weeks. According to Angela, no crew that has tried has ever been able to stand such a schedule for more than a few watches.

My plan all along had been to position myself with the second watch. That way I could simply observe for the first two hours, after which I intended to row in the bow, so that nobody would actually see me or be aware of my ineptitude. However, as we pulled away from the dock I unwisely positioned myself on the bridge beside the commander, who quickly realized there was an empty seat on the starboard hull. She invited me quite jauntily to take it.

What was I to say after fifteen months of training—no thanks?

Within seconds I was in the seat, feet in the stirrups, pulling furiously on my big sweep oar. As fate would have it, I was seated behind Ryan Worth, a former collegiate rowing star and now a coach at the University of Tennessee. I am not exaggerating to confess that during the first twenty minutes aboard I clattered my oar off Ryan's perhaps twenty-five times, each time offering up a plaintive little "sorry, Ryan"... "oh, sorry, Ryan"... "woops, sorry, Ryan," etc.

It perhaps goes without saying that banging your oar off the oar of the rower in front of you is an unacceptable blunder, a no-no of the first order, among practitioners of this ancient team sport. Thus it was that about twenty minutes in, Ryan shipped his oar (which is to say drew it aboard without releasing it from its rigger), turned to me and said in a most patient and amicable voice. "Okay, I see where we're at, Charlie. And what I normally take about three months to teach my freshman rowers I'm going to teach you in thirty seconds"—in other words, listen and listen good! And he proceeded to give me three or four fundamental instructions—about leg extension, about shoulder positioning, about pace and control and breathing—all of which I began immediately to incorporate into what I might presume to call my technique.

The next day, I got further instruction from Liz Koenig, a former varsity rower from the University of Rhode Island, also a coach, and within twenty-four hours was, if not exactly rowing like a pro, or even a "real" rower, rowing with sufficient awareness and capability that I was able to present a plausible impersonation of a guy on an ocean rowing team.

On Saturday night, we gathered at the Shelter Island Community Hall, a rustic old place without heat, where we met several dozen residents of the island, many of whom had seen the boat taking shape and had been invited to come out and meet the crew. One by one, we stood to introduce ourselves and to say something about our reasons for being here. Sylvain spoke about the need to challenge himself and to excel—said that by pushing the physical body he hoped to expand the spirit. Steve said he wasn't sure what exactly had motivated him, except perhaps a desire to drive himself to the limit, in effect to see what was out there.

Aleksa spoke of a love of whales, Ryan of the pleasures of risk, Zach of a fascination with the unexperienced world. Tom said he had met the crew, had fallen in love with them, and wanted to consummate the romance. At sixty-seven, he also wanted to become the oldest person to row an ocean. Liz, meanwhile, said that as a twelve-year-old rower she had looked at the map and wondered if it would be possible to row the Atlantic—and was about to find out.

Louise had set out to row the Atlantic several years back, with another woman, and had had to stop just two days out of the Canaries because of her partner's acute intestinal poisoning. "I love the sea; I love adventure," she said with characteristic aplomb. "This time I'm going to make it."

David said his motivation was to get us home safely and in one piece. It was no small order. Indeed, a question I'd been asked several times in recent weeks was what sort of safety equipment we would have aboard. "None," I liked telling people, adding that we'd at least have a set of oars in case the engine broke down. We would also have life jackets and safety lines and survival suits, plus a pair of inflatable life rafts.

And we would have EPIRBs (Emergency Position Indicating Radio Beacons). Until recently, I had never heard of such devices, which when activated send a distress signal to computers ashore, showing their location on a life raft or capsized boat, or with a swimmer. As I understood it, at least a couple of our crew would be bringing EPIRBs of their own, while the boat too would have a pair.

Privately, my concerns were less about the *un*certainties of our travels than about the fateful certainties: exhaustion, salt sores, inadequate nutrition, plus what was invariably referred to as "extreme weight loss." I also admit quietly to a lifelong neurosis about storms on water, which I had so far managed to suppress (or perhaps to face, as Mr. Jung might have seen it); and to an all-but-daily paranoia over whether or not my many months of training would hold up once I got out there on the main.

If there was a hitch in the weekend, it was (seen in retrospect) that our new captain was perhaps a *trifle* remote, reluctant to take the initiative and gather us in a group so that we could raise questions and discuss issues or information pertaining to the weeks ahead. But having little perspective and not wanting to seem impatient or overanxious, we let it go, allowing that Angela probably had too much on her mind for now, and that the time for more detailed discussion would come.

More importantly, we left Shelter Island with the deeply heartening memory of how *Big Blue* had coursed along the island's east side after being launched, sitting as high and light as a water spider, touching speeds of nearly four and a half knots.[2] And how the following day on the north side of the island, with a little current beneath her, she had clocked out at nearly seven knots, a speed we imagined she would touch again easily with the trade winds behind us and the equatorial current underneath.

Back home, satisfied that the adventure was a go, we bought our air tickets for Morocco and began buying food and kit. At Shelter Island, David and his lieutenants put the finishing touches on the boat. During the first week of December, having done what they could for now, they took *Big Blue* apart, packed her into shipping containers, and hauled her to the docks in New Jersey, from where she would begin her voyage to North Africa.

---

2 A knot is one nautical mile per hour or 1.1 miles per hour.

4

O**N DECEMBER 23,** I bid a quiet farewell to my children in Thunder Bay. Eden, who was fifteen and in Grade 10, had in recent months grown somewhat cavalier about any show of affection toward me and was brisk, even jokey, in her goodbyes. Georgia, my seventeen-year-old, had woven me a little gold bracelet, about the thickness of butcher cord, which she fastened to my wrist with instructions that if I kept it on she would always be with me and that I would have safe travels and a safe return. (In the weeks to come, as it wore thin, I would reinforce it with everything from electrical wire to fishing line to duct tape, increasingly paranoid that it would fall off and I would lose my angelic protection.) While I am anything but an ideal father, I am tearfully close to my children, and when I had exchanged hugs with the girls, Matt, my oldest, then twenty-two, asked me quietly if I was sure I was doing the right thing.

"No, I'm not," I felt obliged to tell him, "but I'm going anyway," to which he offered a rather pensive smile, not so much at me as at the floor.

"Well, good luck, Dad," he said after a few seconds, "I understand." And they hugged me and were gone out the door, clearly under the impression that they were unlikely to see me again.

The next day, Christmas Eve, I flew to Toronto and spent Christmas with my friend Trish, with whom I had had a close, sometimes fiery four-year companionship.

Five days after that, on the morning of December 29, Trish dropped me at Billy Bishop Airport on Toronto Island, where I rendezvoused with Steve and Nigel for our flight on to Montreal. For Trish and me, it was a landmark parting, uncharacteristically affectionate and gentle—in all a heartening sendoff. The previous afternoon, I had sat at her dining room table in east Toronto and penned a farewell to those who had sustained and befriended me during the long months of my training:

December 28, 2010

Hello again to all of you who, in your variety of ways, have so faithfully supported my Atlantic adventure! And goodbye, too—or let us say, farewell, as I count down the hours to my departure for Casablanca tomorrow, then on to Agadir the following day. With luck, *Big Blue* (which as I write is rocking her way across the Atlantic aboard a thousand-foot container vessel) will reach Agadir about the time we do.

We expect to have her reassembled, provisioned, and ready for the crossing by January 8 or 9, although the actual date of departure will depend on the weather.

Our route will take us about 400 miles south along the African coast from Agadir to the little fishing port of Tarfaya, in what was once the state of Western Sahara, now part of Morocco. After a stop there, we will continue southwest in an attempt to pick up the westbound trade winds and equatorial current, which, if our hopes are fulfilled, will carry us out to sea. I find it fitting that we should be starting this undeniably remote adventure on the coast of Africa, which to me has always seemed the "remotest" and most mysterious of populated continents.

Most of my food is already with the boat in the shipping containers, on its way to Morocco. It includes a lot of freeze-dried stuff: Thai noodles, stroganoff, macaroni and cheese, rice and beans, bacon and eggs, potatoes with ground chicken, plus dozens of half-ounce packets of powdered Gatorade, four boxes of protein bars (twenty-four to a box), and twenty vacuum-packed cheese and bacon sandwiches. These last delicacies are of a sort reputed to have been sent into space with the astronauts and have a "best-before" date that I will not have to worry about in this lifetime.

My kit, as prescribed by Angela, is a strange little doll's closet of trinkets, electrical gadgets, and toiletries: headlamp, flashlight, pens, folding scissors, razors, a waterproof digital camera, waterproof containers of one sort or another, a sleeping bag, an odd little blue velour "traveling" pillow, a Moleskine notebook, reading glasses (two pairs), sunglasses (two pairs), a couple of plastic "sporks," a water bottle, an insulated mug, a food bowl, sunscreen, various heady-smelling ointments (including diaper rash cream), sea soap, a "miracle" towel, mechanic's gloves, half a dozen asthma inhalers, and clothes for a variety of conditions that will include daytime temperatures as high as 100 degrees Fahrenheit in the deep tropics and night lows of, say, 50 F, and, of course, rain and wind.

Most importantly, I have a seat cushion made of a thick honeycombed gel which took me weeks to decide

upon and buy and which I have been using to magnificent effect on the rowing machine for the past ten days.

If you to go to bigbluerow.com or to rocexpedition.
com, you will find photos of the boat and of our training, will get at least sporadic updates from the journey
and will be able to follow our progress on a map of the
Atlantic, where we will appear as a tiny dot. We will also
appear as a tiny dot in real space and time on the actual
Atlantic—but let us not get poetic. If all goes well, the
dot will reach Barbados sometime around mid-February.

As you know, we will be chasing not just a world
record but a fine six-person rowboat, a tri-hull named
Hallin Marine (formerly *Triton*), which will be leaving the
Canary Islands a week or more prior to our own departure and may well establish a new record before we get to
Barbados. So in effect we will be chasing *Hallin*'s record,
not the existing thirty-three days. A more conventional
single-hulled rowboat named *Sara G* will also be setting
out from the African coast at about the time we do. So
we are braced for rivalry against muscular British rowers
who I am led to believe carry far higher pedigrees than
do we. Indeed, our respective crews remind me of those
dog teams that compete in the Alaskan Iditarod or Yukon
Quest dogsled races across a thousand miles of subarctic
wilderness. Some of the teams are highly pedigreed pure-
breds, or carefully bred crosses, while others (the canine
version of the *Big Blue* crew) are made up of strays from
the pound and are apparently the more resilient for it.

All of this "racing," I might add, is unofficial—a projection entirely of our being out there at the same time as
the other boats and with the same ambition. Yet another
vessel, *Britannia II,* will be leaving Africa or the Canaries
with, I believe, a crew of eight just after our departure,
except with no stated ambition to set a record. For all

of this, it is unlikely that we will either see or hear from any of these boats, before, during, or after our respective crossings, unless of course we should happen to meet on the sea floor or fetch up within a couple of hours of one another on the coast of Mauritania or Gran Canaria.

The final two members of our crew of sixteen were added this week. Unfortunately, we lost a rower, Anne Maurissen from Belgium, who signed on a few days after our training session but fell on the ice on Christmas Eve, in Brussels, and fractured her wrist. I never met her, but in her emails sensed a kindred spirit, so I will miss what she undoubtedly would have brought to the crew.

Our latest additions are a twenty-four-year-old British medical student named Liam Flynn, who rows recreationally on the English south coast, and a thirty-one-year-old Tasmanian woman, Margaret Bowling, who is reputed to be an organizational whiz and will apparently be assisting Angela with the command.

While I have been attempting to play down any symphonic goodbyes, I want to say that I have appreciated the good wishes that so many of you have sent my way. As of the moment I have received well over a hundred messages, some of which I can barely read for the depth of their grace and goodwill.

I am heading out optimistically and with great respect for my fellow crew members, for our builder, David, and for our captain, Angela. And of course for the ocean. As the writer Simon Winchester said of the Atlantic, "It is a gray and heaving sea, not infrequently storm-bound, ponderous with swells, a sea that in the mind's eye is thick with trawlers lurching, bows up, then crashing down through great white curtains of spume, tankers wallowing across the swells, its weather so often on the verge of gales, and all the while its waters moving with an air of settled purpose, simultaneously displaying incalculable power and inspiring by this display perpetual admiration, respect, caution, and fear."

We will be counting on the trade winds to move us along—and on all the energy we can muster for our rowing.

And so I go—deeply appreciative of your support and of your good wishes for the trip.

I look forward to reporting to you all upon my return. Happy New Year! Farewell for now.

Sincerely and affectionately,
Charlie

AT TRUDEAU AIRPORT in Montreal the next afternoon, as I lay on a padded bench attempting to get a little rest, I mentioned to Steve that I had a swelling and an ache in one of my ankles. I believed I had picked up a minor injury in training that had been accentuated by long hikes around downtown Toronto as I tried to find anything I was missing in clothing and kit items. Ever the pragmatist, Steve informed me that if it was blood-clotting—"thrombosis," I believe he called it—it would either shake loose unannounced and kill me instantly (in which case I had nothing to worry about) or would dissolve without shaking loose (in which case I would live on and had nothing to worry about).

At perhaps 5 p.m. (having found something to worry about) I went on an extended tour of the airport in search of Tom, who had taken the train from Toronto rather than flying with the rest of the Canadians, and with ninety minutes to go till boarding for Casablanca was nowhere to be found. I called his wife, Luisa, who said he had left on a later train than he had intended and should now be in Montreal.

A kind of gallows watch ensued, during which one or two of us would saunter down the long row of international gates, hoping to catch a glimpse of Tom's distinctive bald head or hear the equally distinctive kazoo of his voice. My concern was that as we got to within forty-five minutes of takeoff, he would, for security reasons, not be allowed on the plane.

The flight was eventually called, and the six of us lingered in the departure lounge until I, for one, couldn't stand it anymore and said to Dylan White, "We'll see him in Agadir." And I got up, showed my passport at the gate, and walked into the tunnel that led to the big Royal Air Maroc jet. But I felt wretched knowing that Tom, who did not like money transactions or even using a credit card (he had gotten Steve to buy his plane ticket), would probably get hit for four or five hundred dollars in rescheduling fees, as well as having to find a place to stay for the night and to negotiate Casablanca and Agadir on his own. If there was even the faintest comfort in any of it, it was that he speaks fluent French, so would be okay both in Montreal and on arrival in North Africa.

As the line at the aircraft door shortened to six or seven people (there were already several hundred aboard), only Steve hung back at the top of the tunnel, hoping against the hopelessness of the situation that Tom might still show up. As far as we knew, he had never checked in for the flight.

If I were to tell you that as we howled down the runway for takeoff, an elfin sixty-seven-year-old apostate waving his arms and wearing a little red gob hat came sprinting along beside the plane, leapt onto a wing, made his way forward along the fuselage to the door and thence inside with a grin, you might question my reliability as a storyteller. But in my memory of the evening, that, within a hair's breadth of the truth, is what happened. Had Tom been thirty seconds later than he was, there would at lift-off have been six distressed, not seven relieved, Canucks in the front right quarter of perhaps the dingiest jetliner, with the cruddiest bathrooms and toilets, that I, or perhaps any of us, had ever been on.

Typically, as in days to come, Tom was the first one asleep, passed out like a lizard in a patch of sunlight, while the rest of us fidgeted and shivered and wrenched our thin blankets around us, attempting to dispossess ourselves of the stresses of the past few hours, not to mention the past few months. We had worked hard, very hard, for a reward that lay bristling before us and, for each of us, would redefine what working hard could mean.

Finally, in the darkness over the eastern Atlantic, a grumpy stewardess with breasts like warheads and the eyes of an executioner served something approximating breakfast and, in a great arcing swoosh, we rode the rising sun into Casablanca, where the airport at 6 a.m. was populated by a dozen healthy-looking cats and a scattering of unhealthy-looking human beings.

We flew on to Agadir, across the Atlas Mountains, aboard a rickety twin-engine de Havilland, the proverbial flying coffin, which might have been disconcerting had we been awake enough to notice. And drove on into the city—twenty miles in a big Mercedes cab: past date palms and argan orchards and palmettos; and bursts of bougainvillea on the cinder-block shacks; and little roadside stalls selling French pastries and used car bumpers and chips of burnt meat on a stick; all of it spread out against the unending brownish rock that, whether in mountains or coastal plains or city outcrops—or reduced to sand by the wind—is the fundamental landscape of North Africa.

FOR THE NEXT twelve days, the men of the crew lived in a windowless backstreet apartment that had been rented for us by David. This morose concrete grotto was crammed with lurid Moorish furniture: ensembles of leopard skin and red vinyl and purple plush, with big velveteen cushions, and tassels on everything, and poorly dyed carpets. All the trappings of whoredom, right down to the red lightbulb in the front hall. So much attention to tactility but with no actual comforts—not even proper light, or hot water, or even a table to eat off. And of course no art or books. The bathroom, whose encrusted shitter was surely a castoff of Royal Air Maroc, both looked and smelled like a leprosarium. I admired Steve's response when, together, we laid eyes on the bowl: the double take, the queasy smile, the glance my way as if to say *It's you or me, brother,* and the immediate commitment (his) to scouring the thing out.

The kitchen wasn't much better, and since there was no means of dealing with the trash produced by a perpetually famished rowing crew with little inclination to clean up, it simply accumulated: first in garbage bags, six, seven, eight of them, crowding the kitchen floor, and then in an impassable knee-high heap of loose egg cartons, cereal boxes, orange peels, soup cans, cookie packages; plus the endless plastic bottles and tubs in which Moroccan dairy products are sold and go moldy and die.

The highlight of my days on Rue Salaam (Peace Street)—a lovely address, I thought, for a place that even our gentle-tongued crewmate Sylvain referred to as "a bit crappy"—came on a morning when I had risen in the predawn so as to be early to the boat, and Steve, as a reward for my diligence, placed a saucepan of heated water in the bathroom that I could mix with cold tap water in a grubby plastic bucket that subbed as the apartment's shower.

Ten of us lived ass-over-chinstrap in this weird little den—all the men but David, who was installed in the Ibis Hotel, a nice-ish two-star a fifteen-minute walk away, with his dark-eyed fiancée, Lali, who was visiting from Tbilisi. Because she spoke only Georgian, Lali could do little more than smile at the rest of us, and languish, and look longingly at David. They were tender and smoochy with one another and spoke softly, probably about taxi fares or laundry, and yet it always sounded intimate and mysterious. At the boatyard, she would stand motionless and decisive-looking beside *Big Blue* with her hand on the gunnels for a few seconds, then would pirouette suddenly and take a step or two and put her hand on the rudder and stand there for a minute—then would stand on the ladder that led up to the bridge, while David, a few feet away, sweated and hung upside down, fussing with the wiring, or whatever, in some impossible-to-reach place inside one of the holds.

I had an urge to talk to Lali, to be friends with her; she was so alone. Plus, I knew she had lots to say, having survived a ruinous civil war in Georgia, as had David, after the break-up of the Soviet Union. But to carry on even a few minutes of conversation would have required focused translation by David, who spoke a poetically quirky English, cut with the inevitable shorthand of television and the web. But he didn't have time, what with getting the boat ready twelve hours a day. So our discourse was limited to a daily morning greeting—"Hi Lali!"—to which she would respond brightly, "Hi Chordly!"

The women meanwhile lived in a tidy resort apartment five miles from the men, near the waterfront and the port entrance. The place had a contemporary kitchen, a television, two cushy bathrooms with hot showers, plenty of dishes and towels and bedding. About the only thing it had in common with our place was that its furniture appeared to have been swiped out of the same hellacious cathouse. The place had originally been rented by Angela and her partner, Deb Moeller from Bakersfield, California, a woman who put heart and soul into looking after not just Angela—whom she called "Madsen" and treated with tender exasperation—but half of the administrative chores around the expedition: communications, website, media relations, plus any sort of messaging and boat contact that was required from land once we set off. From the time I met them at Shelter Island, it was hard to imagine that Angela could have carried on as she did without Deb, who was her "girl," so to speak, her adjutant, as well as her manager, advisor, and agent; and driver and photographer; and social coordinator and lover—all of it puttied up and patted into place with painstaking care and affection. If you wanted the lowdown on Angela, you went to Deb; if you asked Angela directly, she'd say, "You'd better ask Deb."

Above all, Deb protected Angela. On the way into New York City in the van after the training weekend, she had confided to me her rather poignant (and ultimately accurate) fear that people would "take advantage of Madsen" because she was so essentially gentle and unassertive. It was an image that did not seem to jibe with that of a woman who, before her spinal injury, had been in the police corps of that toughest of military branches, the U.S. Marines. The truth was, she had joined the Marines with the hope of becoming a mechanic like her brothers and dad before her, and it was only because of her size (not to mention her reluctance to refuse) that the towering recruit had been pushed into police work. She told me one night over dinner in Agadir about being summoned repeatedly and unhappily to deal with domestic violence at the residences of Marines who had returned from conflicts in, I believe, Southeast Asia. "All these guys," she said, "had taken 'desensitization' training so they wouldn't be affected by orders, say, to go into villages and slaughter women and children, which was bad enough. But when they got home, nobody 're-sensitized' them, so they were equally insensitive to their own wives and children."

Originally the whole crew was to have lived in the men's flop pad. But when Liz Koenig and Aleksa Klimas-Mikalauskas arrived a day or two past New Year's, after detouring to Marrakesh, it was all quite natural that they settle in with Angela and Deb. For one thing, the four of them were well acquainted after an agonizing seventy-two-hour snow delay at JFK in New York, over Christmas. Plus, they had all endured horrific problems with Royal Air Maroc, which had lost not only Liz and Aleksa's luggage (it eventually arrived) but Angela's custom-built ultra-light wheelchair, which the airline replaced with a flimsy little rickshaw of a thing that would occasionally drop a part or two on the sidewalk—not at all the sort of appliance to carry a 250-pound woman with very specific ergonomic requirements.

The boatyard where we worked was within the high guarded walls of the officially designated "Port of Agadir"—a square mile or so of docks and warehouses and boat-building facilities spread out along the seashore at the city's north end. Immediately to the east rose a desert-dry mountain whose top formed the old-city kasbah, the only remaining feature of ancient Agadir, which had been destroyed by an earthquake in 1960. The city had been rebuilt and was now uniformly modern, including the *souk*, a vast walled city-within-a-city, where vendors sold everything from handmade leather goods and furniture to fabrics, shoes, handicrafts, fresh fruit, spices, appliances, electronic goods—anything you might want, up to and including the illicit hashish for which Morocco, perhaps the most liberal of Muslim countries, is renowned. Donkeys waited outside by their owners' carts, amidst street garbage and squawking chickens and the occasional dead rat or dog.

Each day began for us with a long, sometimes harrowing ride from the apartment to the boatyard in one of the hundreds of tiny orange fender-bashed taxis that pinballed around the city, honking, squealing, blasting Arabic hit-parade music, throwing soot or brake parts or tire-tread. At the port gates, we showed our passes—ragged bits of tissue paper bearing a line or two of smudged Arabic—and careered on through to the Chantier Naval Hesaro. There, in the sunshine, we went at sweaty chores on a half acre of dusty concrete, amidst partially built fishing trawlers, or yachts being refurbished, one of which, a doozy built in 1948, belonged to a member of the rock band Pink Floyd and was in for a million-dollar refit that we were told had been ongoing for years.

From New Year's Day forth, David applied himself relentlessly to getting the boat wired and rigged and (more or less) safe for the sea. He had not just the crew's help, but the contracted assistance of a young aide-de-camp named Hassan, whose knowledge of Agadir was encyclopedic, as well as one of the yard's most capable *artigianos,* an endearing and hard-working machinist named variably "Yaya" or "Shacky," depending on who you asked. He also had the help of a yard journeyman and, later, an electrician name Essaidi, a devout Muslim with whom I occasionally attempted to converse. Unfortunately, he was a thinking man (problematic in any culture), and his ambitions to discuss political and social philosophy with me—and on one occasion the thoughts of his fellow North African, Albert Camus—went as pearls to swine in the context of my pathetically verbless and largely brainless French.

One of the most important and time-consuming jobs was getting new hardwood handles into the dozen oars (including four spares) to which we would be entrusting our progress in the days to come. The new ones were a pearly white ash, as hard as gun metal yet less apt to cause blisters than are the state-of-the-art neoprene-wrapped handles on many sculling oars and virtually all rowing machines these days. It took four of our young crew members the better part of a week to break the old handles out of their graphite sleeves, a sliver at a time, and get the new, longer handles epoxied into place. More grueling yet was the effort of getting the "trampolines" constructed and attached—taut nylon "decks" on both sides of the boat, linking the hulls to the centrally positioned cabin, giving us a crucial six-foot-wide walking and living platform to both port and starboard.

Before we left Canada, Steve and I had agreed that we would work on the tramps together. However, in the end,

it was Sylvain and Tom who were Steve's ranking assis-
tants, while I tootled around poking at oar handles and
doing fussy work—and of course note-taking, preparing
to write, which as the novelist Don Bailey once pointed
out is largely a process of gazing out the window or down
the beach, or peeking over the fence. At times, craving a
little detachment, I simply slipped out the boatyard gate
and enjoyed brief walks around the port. Anywhere there
was a bit of spare ground, boatbuilders with mallets and
four-inch-wide chisels banged away, hand-hewing bulgy
little cypress-wood dories, or sixty-foot trawlers, gorgeous things that echoed the centuries and would, on
completion, become part of the Moroccan sardine fleet,
the biggest in the world.

The truth was that after the intense training of the
fall and early winter—not to mention the travel, the jet
lag, the abrupt change of diet and sleep—there were
hours during that first week in Agadir when I didn't feel
like doing much of anything. My mood had not been
improved by four days of stomach flu and now a mouth-
ful of cankers, for me a sign that something is amiss that
will only be righted by a little down time. One day Liz
Koenig and I chanced a keelhauling by sneaking out of
the yard for an hour to look for souvenirs that we could
send home—I to my children, she to her parents and
friends. And I was glad we did; it gave us a chance to get
to know each other and exchange a story or two, which
to my perhaps deluded mind was as important as busting
ass all the time. But you couldn't be gone long or you'd
get a frosting when you got back—mostly (and justifi-
ably) from Steve, who was working like a mule and had
thereby established himself as the company yard master
and conscience.

At the age of twenty-three, Liz was nonetheless among
our most experienced and talented rowers, having taken

up the sport when she entered St. Anthony's High School on Long Island. She was eventually scouted by a number of universities, offered several scholarships, and ended up at the University of Rhode Island. There, during a four-year Division I career (2005–2008), she trained eight hours a day, six days a week, sufficient to put her on the podium a dozen or more times with different crews of eight at some of the sport's premier regattas. "My one huge regret," she said as we walked, "was that I never got to row in an NCAA final. It's just *so tough* in that conference, with Harvard, Yale, Princeton, Boston—all these rowing powerhouses. We came *so close so many times,* and just never quite got there."

Liz has a glamorous side. Yet like Angela (and the rest of us), she has her insecurities. That day on the promenade, she said to me quietly, "Charlie, there was something I wanted to mention to you."

After a few seconds of silence, I asked, "What is it, Liz?"

"I'm not quite sure how to put it," she said staring out to sea, "except that I've been feeling a little... you know... *bulky.*"

I assured her she didn't *look* bulky.

"No, but I *feel* it," she protested. "I packed on an extra twenty pounds for the crossing, and most of it went... you know... exactly where I didn't want it to go." She smiled self-consciously. "I was just gonna say that if you're going to put photos in your book, I'm wondering if you'd allow me to see what you're going to put in that might have me in it?"

I assured her she could approve any photos that were used (the irony being that one of the two or three she eventually liked was a glorious shot of her taken from behind as she sat topless on the prow of the port hull, in a high wind, her hair flying, her arms thrown to the sun—a shot featuring the very portion of her anatomy that she had apparently been so reluctant to expose).

While they are not the least bit alike, I tended to think of Liz and Aleksa as a pair, a sort of matched Island set—in part because they are the same age and because Aleksa too attended St. Anthony's High School, although she did not start rowing until she enrolled at Stony Brook University on Long Island. She eventually rowed for Dowling College, where she now coaches and from which she holds a post-grad degree in early childhood development. It is an unlikely complement to her full-time job as an emergency first-responder in North Babylon and her part-time career as a volunteer firefighter in Deer Park. Both are jobs in which she sees and must take in stride what she called "some of the most shocking violence" known to humanity. Meanwhile, there is a small-town innocence to Aleksa, epitomized in part by her admission that if she had to get off Long Island, driving on her own, she would be "totally unable" to find her way through the merciless bottleneck of freeways, underpasses, and bridges that connects the island to New York City and to the rest of the world beyond.

As with Liz, there were aspects of Aleksa's person that she wanted neither exposed nor discussed in a book—she made it clear that any violations on my part would be treated with murderous severity. She was in other areas a kind of free-flowing WikiLeaks on everything from her occasionally heavy partying to her seditious pleasure in social media to the endearing intricacies of her life as the daughter of Lithuanian immigrants. The family had escaped the old country when it was under the most dispiriting influences of the Soviet regime and, during thirty years on Long Island, had enacted a transcendent commitment to the preservation of Lithuanian culture, much of which had been kicked to the dogs under Muscovite imperialism. Aleksa spent her childhood and teenage summers at what she called "Lithuanian camp" in the mountains of upstate New York, putting on the costumes and learning the language, dances, music, and stories of her ancestry. Her affectionate, sometimes poignant descriptions of it all reminded me of Ray Bradbury's novel *Fahrenheit 451,* in which those who love literature (most books having been burned) hide in the woods, passing memorized novels and poems on to their children.

ALONGSIDE WORK on the boat, Angela engineered a Herculean six-day bee of food sorting and packing, during which there were at times several thousand food items laid out on the concrete in sorted lots, as well as hundreds of Ziploc bags and hundreds more garbage bags, not to mention a dozen ten-pound logs of mauve-colored cling wrap.

The arrangement was this: we had all brought our own food, or had at least ordered it from the expedition supply houses, and had had it sent to Shelter Island, where it had been packed with the boat and shipped to Morocco. Most of us had brought additional food in our luggage and had picked up items from the market and stores in Agadir. The Great Sort divided it into days and, further, into lunches, dinners, and snacks. The plan was that Angela would supply some level of breakfast each day but that otherwise we would take turns cooking in pairs for the crew (which for the most part meant nothing more than heating water and adding it to envelopes of dehydrated rations).

All of this started well. However, on the fourth day rats got into the storage quarters where we kept the food at night. They ate and crapped selectively, mostly in Angela's boxes, requiring her to pitch hundreds of dollars' worth of meals. From that point forward the whole extravagant exercise began to seem somewhat oppressive. The harder truth was that, whereas some crew members had attempted to minimize their nutritional requirements in order to keep the weight of the boat down, others had brought what seemed a vast surfeit of entrees and desserts and snacks—and sub-snacks and pick-me-ups and treats.

Part of the disparity was that Angela had convinced some crew members they would need 10,000 calories a day—four meals, plus snacks. Roy had told us months back that no one needed or would eat more than 5,000 calories, that we simply wouldn't feel like it, given the exertion and heat and exhaustion. He believed that when your daily ration of 5,000 calories was used up, your stored fat, if you had any, would see you through (and that when it was gone, you died).

At times I wondered what the Phoenicians or Vikings or, centuries later, the Spanish, French, and Dutch had eaten on their sea voyages. Certainly not foil packs of Bubba's Kountry Kitchen Dehydrated Crab Gumbo (MSG-free). Or U.S. *Challenger* freeze-dried ice cream bars. The English, according to our British crew member Liam Flynn, ate hardtack and dried lard—and "probably lots of other really dodgy and awful stuff."

Steve, more than I, was appalled as all of this provender, pack after pack of it—in garbage bags, in duffel bags, in dry bags, dozens upon dozens of them—was shoe-horned into the holds and hulls and onto the galley shelves of a vessel that was already weighed down with perhaps a ton and a half of hardware and appurtenances that were not aboard when we feathered so delicately down the channel off Shelter Island.

Since then, David had added four monstrously weighty solar panels that lay atop the cabin; and a pair of wind generators whose whirligigs, half as big as airplane propellers, sat twelve feet above the bridge on steel stanchions; and a thick and complex wiring harness that carried power to heavy storage batteries in one of the holds and from there to the GPS and autopilot systems, and to deck lights and running lights, and to a pair of bulky desalinators in the front holds, as well as to a half-a-dozen wall sockets where camera batteries and iPods and the boat's two SAT phones could be recharged. He had added cooking equipment and first-aid supplies and tools; and a spare rudder; and four spare oars; and a porcelain toilet; and sump pumps; and extra bracing; and a pair of inflatable life rafts; and survival suits.

And now of course food. And more food. And bedding. And clothing. And two more people than we had had aboard at Shelter Island.

IF STEVE WAS aghast over the weight of food, he was dismayed tenfold by the arrival on January 6th, just five days before departure, of Margaret Bowling, the young Tasmanian woman who had rowed the Atlantic a couple of years earlier and to whom Angela had given first mate's status specifically for the experience she would bring in the areas of navigation, weather awareness, charting, and so on. She would also, it was assumed, bring moral support to Angela in her attempts to direct a crew not one of whose members had rowed an ocean or rowed even a hundred miles out on one.

Unfortunately, Margaret did not have commensurate experience in handling human beings—at least those of the sort that had signed on with *Big Blue*. While I had my differences with her, especially over her damnable habit of telling people what to do when no telling was necessary, I eventually came to an understanding of sorts with her and found her variously exasperating, vulnerable, somewhat lonely, and perhaps a trifle nuts, although no more so than a few others aboard the boat, including myself.

If I remember correctly, it took about ten minutes on the morning of Margaret's first working day at the boatyard for her to run afoul of Steve, from whom she demanded a "complete list" of all the medications on board.

"There's really no need for that," Steve told her. "Sylvain and I know what's on board, and either he or I will be prescribing, so we'll just leave it as is. Plus, I'm *very* busy right now, as you can see."

"Well, I'd like that list," she insisted. "I'd like it by sometime tomorrow."

Others balked at Margaret's adamant vetting of our kit based on stringent new limits for weight and bulk—this after we had accumulated such kit according to different, although still quite disciplined, standards. My own response, largely unspoken, was that it was a little late to begin compensating for our massive burden of food and hardware with an enforced jettisoning of light little kit items such as T-shirts and flip-flops and other bits of clothing and footwear.

Margaret's vetting of Tom's rather arcane paraphernalia came down to an absurd head-butting that might well have been lifted from the scripts of Harold Pinter:

MARGARET: But, Tom, don't you see it's not fair to the rest of the crew for you to take extra weight?

TOM: Yes, I'm sure that's true, Margaret, and I sympathize with them; I'm all for fairness—but I'm not leaving my favorite blue jeans behind to save the weight of a few ounces of denim.

MARGARET: But, Tom, we *all* have to make sacrifices!

TOM: Yes, I know that's true, Margaret, and I'm very happy to make sacrifices—name one, I'll make it. Meanwhile, I am not leaving my jeans behind.

MARGARET: Tom, do you know what sacrifices the others are making?

TOM: No, they haven't told me. But I'm sure it's all very difficult for them and I'd like to know so I have a better idea what I'm up against in not leaving my blue jeans behind.

A week later, at sea, Steve was infuriated to discover that Margaret had allowed at least one of the young women on the crew to bring aboard substantial bottles of hair care products, while some of the men had been cited over significantly lighter, smaller items.

In some cases, Margaret was indisputably right in her decisions, insisting for example that Ernst Fiby, he of the Viennese wit and shaved head, leave behind a pair of clunky, high rubber Wellingtons—for the sheer space they would command, as well as the weight. She was outraged to realize later that he had snuck them aboard, although he did finally toss them in the sea, where they may yet be doing thousand-mile circles in the currents of the mid-Atlantic.

EVERY EVENING at about seven o'clock, we'd slump out of the boatyard in the winter darkness, one of us pushing Angela in her wheelchair, up the mile-long hill outside the port walls to where the city proper began and we could organize our taxi-sharing for the long ride back across Agadir to the apartment. And from there on to a restaurant for a blessed hour of nourishment and relaxation. Restaurants are an adventure in Agadir, and our search for a decent tagine or couscous led us variably to little family bistros such as Daffy's on the back side of the city's tourist area and into the visceral horrors of the restaurant at the Riad Hotel, where, had the tagine I ordered been 50 percent better, I'd have suspected it of coming out of a can. At the same place, Tom's much-anticipated sixteen-ounce "Entrecote USA"—"premier slice beefsteak, fired out on our uniquely charcoaling grille"— turned out to be a slab of unidentifiable zoological matter so thoroughly ridden with fat, bone, and gristle as to be entirely inedible (it would have been funny had some poor goat or donkey not died in the service of this reprehensible restaurant).

However, for the most part we ate in a breezy little outdoor barbecue in a non-tourist neighborhood near our apartment. We referred to this decidedly unregulated kitchen as "the meat place" because it served meat, bread, and pop only, the meat purchased by the customer on skewers at the fly-ridden butcher shop next door and carried a few feet to the restaurant, where it was thrown on the grill.

One night as Steve and I and a few others sat there in the company of sparrows and cats and one or two rib-thin mutts, a guy in his early twenties came along banging his palm on the metal table tops, demanding money. I reached into my pocket, realizing when I pulled my hand out that my only cash was a pair of 200-dirham notes, worth about forty bucks each, and some Canadian coins worth perhaps a dollar. So I gave him the coins and felt anguished five minutes later when he came raging up to the table and threw the money clattering down in front of me, accompanied by a blast of indecipherable scorn.

It had been stupid of me, no doubt—lazy both culturally and morally, in that I knew the coins were of limited or no value to him. But it served as a chastening, as one's experiences on the road, particularly the embarrassments, tend to do. Happily, a couple of nights later I saw the same guy at the same place, and was able to give him a twenty-dirham note that he pushed into his pocket without a peep as he brushed past me.

THAT THESE PRECIOUS, nervous days in Agadir were winding down was impressed upon me on the 8th of January, when David did not show up at the boatyard until nearly noon—and eventually did so in tourist clothes, subdued, having taken Lali to the airport and seen her off to Tbilisi.

Late that afternoon, with our chores done, our spirits high (and about to get higher), Steve and I left the boatyard half an hour early to get our hair chopped short at Coiffure Paris, a tidy little barbering salon that we had passed numerous times within a few blocks of the apartment.

There was only one chair, and as Steve sat down, the barber, an amiable Arab of perhaps thirty-five, asked in rough, gentle English if we'd like a shot of "Moroccan whisky." We would, and immediately he dispatched his young friend, who returned minutes later with a pair of juice tumblers full of a steamy amber-colored fluid.

It was not until I had drained this earthy potion and Steve and I were exchanging seats so that my own shearing could begin that Steve, wearing a broadening and relaxed grin—indeed, showing a state of relaxation that I had not seen in him since our arrival—wondered aloud if I realized we had been drinking marijuana tea, quite strong marijuana tea as it turned out. As a matter of fact I had not (there was a hint of peppermint to it, perhaps masking the main ingredient). But given the new tingling in my extremities and the fact that the modest barbershop, with its antique television and shelf of bright pomades, had just now begun to seem like the funniest entertainment on earth, I did not question the news.

Having been at first somewhat nervous about the threat of hepatitis, which can be contracted through a barber's nick, I was soon sensitized to the point where I was enjoying with a kind of dreaminess the buzzing of the clippers over my skull, then the sound of the straight razor rasping down the skin of my neck and behind my ears, emitting what for me at that point was a quite euphonious *pop* with the snapping of each individual hair.

But the sense of well-being was short-lived. As we emerged from the barbershop into the crowded and noisy street, a kind of cloud descended around me, a sense of vulnerability, and I was reminded with considerable force that I was at that moment sixty-three years gone, an old man, without language, in the backstreets of a Muslim city, stoned on an illegal drug, as defenseless as a baby— beyond which, of course, I was facing a challenge in the weeks to come that would either kill me ingloriously or fortify me for life's home stretch.

At the meat place, we ingested skewer after skewer of chicken and pepper sausage and steak. And floated home. To the whorehouse. Where that night I had a staggering dream, a kind of *fin du monde,* in which a bloody and beheaded man appeared at the door of the apartment asking for me, attempting to push his way in, determined that he should find me. As Nigel and the others forced him from the room, he hollered over their shoulders that he knew I was in there, knew my name, knew everything about me, said he would track me down, would not rest until he had found me. And then he was gone, and in the hallucinogenic logic of the dream world, I was left pondering who he was, whether he would be able to pursue me with no head, and perhaps most significantly in this twisted Jungian conundrum, why he had been wearing my shoes.

THE BIG MORNING arrived, and in a pilgrimage more spirited than our parade to the launch ramp at Shelter Island, we grouped up around the boat as a smallish tractor hauled it at an emperor's pace out the boatyard's wide front gates. Each of us had a job, mine being to carry a sheet of bendy galvanized steel that could be thrown down over a rough patch in the road to allow any of the four dollies beneath the hulls to pass smoothly overtop.

As we heaved through the potholed streets, the tires on the casters, frightful little things on stamped rims and hubs, began to disintegrate. Meanwhile, a crowd of chatty and inquisitive rubberneckers fell in around us— kids with soccer balls, men in work clothes or business suits, women in Muslim head coverings, yapping dogs, gulls, gannets, the lot of them making a carnival of it, the centerpiece of which, our space-age rowboat, was a clearly irresistible piper to those who were seeing her for the first time. Left and right we went, this way and that, eventually down to the port's monstrous boat ramp. There, the broad concrete aprons were a dry-dock for trawlers and dories and tugboats, dozens of them, beyond which, in the inky waters off the docks, floated an armada of sardine trawlers and rusting freighters, some of which gave the impression of having been there for decades. It was all quite a contrast to *Big Blue,* which by the time she sledded into the shallows, to a modest cheer, had made dump waste of her dolly wheels, an appropriate symbol, I thought, of her being free at last of the land.

Not quite free, as it turned out.

For as six or eight of our crew leapt aboard to row the boat over to the marina, it was clear that a bit too much of the land had been launched with her. The hulls were sitting perhaps six inches deeper in the water than at Shelter Island, a signal that the boat was now several tons heavier than it had been. To my eye, she seemed to wallow slightly as the rowers pulled away from the ramp.

Fortunately, we had a 250-mile shake-down run ahead of us on the way down the coast to Tarfaya, where we would stop briefly before heading properly to sea. If necessary, we could offload weight. We would also be consuming fifty pounds of food a day—and shedding body weight, a process at which I, to quote the television program, would eventually be the biggest loser.

My chief concern of the moment was that the interior of my mouth was still a nasty little nettle patch of cankers—a dozen or more of them, including one beneath my lower lip that was pretty much as big as a dime.

I have Margaret to thank for my timely recovery. As the lot of us fussed around the marina on the morning of Sunday, January 10, addressing last-minute adjustments to the boat, stowing kit, gathering fresh fruit and snacks for the run down to Tarfaya, she said to me, "Charlie, I have a job for you."

My truest ambition for the next few hours had been to curl up in my bunk aboard the boat and there to log three or four hours of much-needed sleep. I had slept very little the night before and had been up early that morning to help empty and clean the apartment. I raised my eyebrows, feigning receptivity to whatever was coming, and she said quite gaily, "I want you to take a taxi to Marjane and get us eight or ten more packages of prepared cereal for the boat."

Marjane is a cavernous supermarket at the far end of the city, near the men's apartment, where I had already been that morning on behalf of the boat and to which I had no intention of returning—especially in one of Agadir's sooty little orange taxis. Not that I didn't enjoy Marjane. I did. It was an entertainment unto itself: aisles heaped with groceries and Moroccan clothing, kids in little *djellabas*, women gliding mysteriously past the bully beef display in their floor-length wraps and head scarves. Scruffy little sparrows that had undoubtedly lived their entire lives in the store darted around, chirping and shitting among the bulk nuts and fruit.

I agreed reluctantly to go, and was on my way down the promenade to catch a cab when I ran into our crewmate Louise Graff, who asked me with her customary affability if there was anything I needed at Marjane; she and her friends Noreen and Julie, who had their own apartment nearby, were on their way there now to get sandwich foods and oranges for the boat.

I had liked Louise immediately when we met at JFK on the way up to Shelter Island. From the start, we conversed easily and could always find something to laugh about. On the first night of training, after a couple of exhausting watches, she had endeared herself to me by reaching across from her bunk and holding my mittened hand for a minute, a gesture of graciously affectionate solidarity, which, for me, cemented our friendship. It would come as a laugher of a surprise to me when a few days hence, at sea, Louise revealed to me that Noreen, whom I had taken for a mere pal, was actually her husband, her lover, when all along I had joked with and related to her—indeed to both of them—as if they were single gals for whom I should best be on my toes as a (just slightly diminished) representative of the testicle-bearing class.

Within twenty minutes I was sacked out on the couch at their apartment, where I slept soundly for four hours and awoke as they came yoo-hooing up to the door to get me. The plan, if you had not guessed, was that I would parade over to the women's apartment with them, hauling the cereal I had so responsibly acquired at the supermarket.

As we arrived, Margaret emerged from one of the bedrooms, looked at me quizzically and said, "That was *quite* a shopping trip, Charlie!"

Unsure whether she was on to me, but not about to concede, I said, "It was!" and neither of us said another word.

In the meantime, I felt infinitely better for the sleep. By evening my cankers and digestion had improved to the point where I was able to eat a walloping chicken tagine and drink a pint of beer at one of the restaurants along the seawall—a restaurant, as it turned out, that would come perilously close to killing poor Tom.

WE SLEPT the night on the boat, and awoke in a cool pre-dawn mist with no wind to speak of. At about 6:30, in the darkness, Steve and I walked to a restaurant along the seashore for a bite of breakfast and a last cup of decent French coffee. By the time we returned, Ryan had popped a bottle of champagne, and the countdown had begun. Behind us to the east a band of cloud-rippled azure was broadening above the mountains. A brigade of noisy gannets was aloft in the motionless air.

There were no heroics or theatrics as we pulled away from the dock at 8 a.m. sharp. Angela gave the "easy out," eight blue blades made their first tentative strokes, and we cruised out into the harbor. And from there around the breakwater. David's Moroccan adjutant, Hassan, and a few faithfuls from the boatyard had gathered to see us off. As had Deb, Noreen, and Julie. There were a few tears, probably of relief that we were finally leaving. Meanwhile, our Canadian friends, Damien Gilbert and Kelly Saxberg, climbed into an outboard Zodiac and banged out past us on the swells, shooting footage for the film they were making of the expedition.

A couple of days earlier Ernst and I had gone with Kelly and Damien up to the kasbah on the mountain behind the city to get some footage. From the thousand-foot elevation, the Atlantic had looked unspeakably vast. By comparison our little boat—our Tinkertoy experiment, *just* visible in the harbor below—had looked ridiculously small and fragile.

"Vare za motore on zis sing?" I had been asked the previous day by a German tourist who had wandered down the pier from Central Casting.

I tightened my bicep and patted it, and he said in dismay, "Vee are pawddling zis sing?"

"Rowing," I said, at which point his chin began to tremble, and he howled, *"Izz too zmall! Vee are dying in zis sing maybe!"*

And yet as we rowed away that morning, put our backs at last to work, the boat seemed bigger, solider, heavier again. It was no cinch to move. At the same time, paradoxically, it seemed smaller than ever, compared not just to the ocean with its wide and glassy undulations but to the mountains behind the city, the rocky jawline of the continent, running as far to the south as we could see and then disappearing into the desert dust and mists. Of the four rowers on my side of the catamaran, Liam rowed lead, in the stroke seat, closest to the rear hold, while Ernst rowed second and Steve third. I sat in the bow, the back and least consequential seat, where if you blew a stroke or fell out of sync it made little difference to the other rowers.

All day, we seemed barely to move relative to the great solid wall of northwest Africa. Then at dusk the lights came on, a million of them running for miles south of Agadir, a kind of earthbound Milky Way that threw a mile-high glow and blotted out the light of the stars.

While I will not relive the ignominy, I had by this time lost my seat cushion, and because of it was in a colliery of despondency. I have wondered since what enabled me to get past the loss of something so indispensably crucial to my survival on the voyage and have come to believe that some deeply intuitive, deeply innocent part of me was able to interpret this private calamity—"repurpose" it, shall we say—as a kind of spiritual means assessment, some cosmically applied test of my durability and will. At the time I was desperate enough and detached enough from normality to accept almost any lifeline that appeared.

Even *with* the cushion, my rear carriage had quickly become bruised and strained. I had toughened it on the rowing machine over the months, but with the pounding of the waves and the constant drenching in salt water, it was absorbing several times the punishment it was accustomed to.

Lifeline or not, at about 8:15, as I sat on my damp bunk, I was possessed suddenly by a sense of hopelessness. What on *earth*, I thought, had I gotten myself into? *I can't do it,* I thought, unaware in my evolving isolation and uncertainty that others were undoubtedly feeling much the same way. Across the aisle, above me, Tom was moaning with dysentery, while beside me Dylan was all but paralyzed with cramps. Out on deck, Nigel, who alone had fallen seasick, was retching up what little he had been able to consume in the way of solid food.

Ninety minutes earlier, as I rowed, I had coughed up a kind of hairball, an alarming thing that I had half expected to get up and walk down the trench and out the scupper. I had figured all along that if I had a ghost's chance of keeping myself together it would be fueled by minimally a hundred minutes of sleep between the night watches, plus regular napping during daylight. But it wasn't happening—indeed would never happen in the weeks we were aboard. The tension of cramped and twitching muscles, the exhaustion, the trauma of the boat being smacked around simply did not lend themselves to transport into the dreamtime. At the end of each watch, I would lie in my bunk buzzed and twitchy and wide awake, and though I had promised myself that I would hold off writing even a note, a jot, until I had properly established sleep, in sleep's absence I had (you guessed it) time.

To write. So had embarked like a mad scrivener in getting it all down: my lacerated hindquarters, the incessant cramping, the pallor on Louise's face as she came off the afternoon watch, the sight of fishing trawlers and container ships and of ships' lights now that it was dark—all of it witnessed in some curious transposition, as in a dream or a movie, or through somebody else's eyes.

Back at the docks, Sylvain had given us "patches" for seasickness that we stuck behind our ears. And they apparently worked; I had no inclination to vomit. At the same time, I had the feeling that somebody had pushed a tennis ball well down into my esophagus, or at other times had dropped in a lit match. There was talk of "acid reflux," which until then I had associated largely with Pepto-Bismol ads or with life under the Golden Arches. However, another twenty-four hours would pass before I'd realize when my patch fell off that it was the medication, not the sea or the effort, that was making me sick.

In the meantime, the lovely little down sleeping bag I had borrowed from my daughter Eden had gotten drenched by a wave that had breached the cabin door at some point during the afternoon. Immediately, I had hung it outdoors in the sun, where it seemed to be drying nicely. However, at dusk, as I rowed, Angela, thinking to get the bedding out of the weather before nightfall, asked if I wanted her to take it in. "Yes! Thank you!" I called above the wind. "Put it on my bunk if you will." I did not realize till the watch ended and I entered the cabin that she had simply tossed it in the door, onto the floor, where it had been doused by another wave and people had walked on it, their feet kneading the sea water into every feather and inch of fabric.

If there was a grace note amidst the turmoil it was that just before sunset we caught a glimpse of our first dolphin, which had stirred me—and then a whale, a fin whale of all things, the fastest and one of the biggest of the cetaceans. And, sadly, one of the most endangered. Just 100,000 of these magnificent beasts remain, a number barely above the survival line for breeding, while the Icelanders and Japanese continue to hunt them into extinction.

Now, on the 10-to-midnight, Steve was pushing a no-nonsense agenda, as if our relatively slow pace was the fault of the rowing, of the commitment, a storyline into which I was already reading pretenders such as myself. To protect what remained of my rear end, I had fashioned a seat pad of an old sweatshirt that, lumpy side down, afforded roughly the cushioning that might have been provided by a sheet or two of folded newspaper. The result was that when I came off watch, my hindquarters had gone numb—were in effect anesthetized from the small of my back to the middle of my thighs.

I told Dylan I believed my ass was in shock, to which he responded weakly that at least it was still healthy enough to *go* into shock. I couldn't see him in the darkness. However, at sunset, the rings around his eyes had been the color of old asphalt and as big around as hockey pucks.

"I dunno if I can do this," he said after a silence. "I can't eat, I can't sit, I can't sleep."

The only thing I could think to say to him by way of encouragement was that it would take time to adjust.

"If I can do it, you can," I said.

By this point, I had more or less decided that if I could do it anybody could.

B<small>Y DAWN OF</small> the second day out of Agadir, the mountains were smaller, reduced not from the top, as mountains are reduced by the ages, but from below, by the curvature of the earth, as the sea dissolved their foundation.

Throughout the pre-dawn watch, I tried desperately to find some inner equilibrium. At perhaps 9 a.m. it occurred to me with a scintilla of optimism that rather than wallowing on, suffering with makeshift or with other people's seat cushions, I must make a new one, a decent pad being vital not just to my functionality but to my sanity. And must do so immediately. To that end, I scoured the holds and came up with a couple of book-sized slabs of cheap foam, one thin and dense, the other thick and porous. I believe they were leftovers from Angela's determined attempts to make her bunk more comfortable, but I did not ask and no one told me not to use them. I bound them together with duct tape and celebrated on the 10-to-noon as the new appurtenance, while far from ideal, assured me more or less that it was now only the rest of my body and soul that would have to be rescued out of hell.

Throughout that second afternoon, the breakers came hard onto our starboard hull, with the result that by sundown even Steve, whose Crohn's disease had been acting up, admitted that it was all he could do to get through a shift. "What time is it?" we'd plead from the rowing seats as each watch deepened, attempting to sound casual, as our thighs cramped and twitched. However, anyone who had a timepiece and was in a position to respond knew it wasn't the time of day we wanted but the *time remaining* in the watch. A response of anything less than twenty minutes seemed to come directly from the angels, whereas a report of, say, half an hour carried an implied knife in the gut, a despondency that sometimes I could manage only by starting literally to count seconds, to count to sixty and start over, thus reassuring myself that minutes *were* passing, that we *would* get through, that at some measurable point before we perished we would rise from the rowing trench, stagger inside, and collapse into our dear mommies' arms.

Night-time was the worst. Imagine someone heaving a five-gallon pail of cold sea water into your face in the dark, four or five times an hour, without your knowing when or from where the next violent soaking might arrive. No matter how carefully I fastened my jacket around my throat, the water forced its way in, or up from underneath, ran gradually down my back and abdomen and eventually into the ass of my pants. There, it puddled on the seat until either it drained or I shipped my oar and stood up and let it run down my legs into my shoes. The whole awful progression, Steve and I agreed, resembled some perverse strategy of the CIA—something marginally less than pure torture but, like torture, bound to weaken and demoralize and desensitize, to leave the nerves not so much raw as plain gone, with no memory of, or discernment for, what was normal or sane or livable.

When ten minutes remained, whoever had a watch would deliver the sweetest news any of us was likely to hear in this life or the next: that there were *ten minutes to go,* a cry offered partly for our watch's benefit, partly as an alarm for those who now had to wrench themselves from their bunks.

Five minutes later, as we rowed down the minutes on deck, Sylvain, who was always first out of the cabin, would appear on the bridge, serious and groggy but a step ahead of the werewolf, and would stagger down the tramp to relieve whoever was rowing in the third seat. A few minutes later Margaret and Ryan and David would appear, generally with the werewolf still on their backs.

IT WAS NOT until dawn of the third day that the sun rose directly out of the sea, and we were at last out of sight of the land. By that time Tom was all but a corpse from his intestinal infection. Steve and Sylvain had him cranked up on antibiotics, but so far the medication had not reduced his symptoms. Meanwhile, Angela, in her wisdom, had decided he should be rowing, or trying to, declaring more or less openly that there was no place aboard for anyone who couldn't pull an oar. And so the following day, our fourth out of Agadir, Tom rowed, if weakly, with Steve sitting behind him for moral support, while Dylan, whose health had improved, moved into Steve's seat in front of me. *Big Blue* was a society, I hardly need add, in which irony went largely unacknowledged— as, for example, when Angela herself fell out of the rotation a few days later and stayed out for weeks because of her sore back, taking not a sidling glance back at her declaration regarding Tom.

Steve suspected she was "setting Tom up," wearing him down with the rowing, so that he would be more likely to withdraw from the expedition when we reached Tarfaya a day hence. To be fair, she may merely have been testing his resolve. Even so, it would seem highly *un*fair to have "tested" him while he was still suffering what appeared to be a potentially deathly illness.

In a surprise turn of events, it was Angela herself who came closest to withdrawing from the expedition—this on the morning of day five, in Tarfaya, on the edge of the Sahara, where we suffered our first, and one of our foremost, crises of personnel.

Our approach to Tarfaya had in a sense begun the previous afternoon, when after a day of relative calm we were picked up and driven south by a hard and exhilarating northeast wind. Whereas the previous day the boat's speed had peaked somewhere under three knots, we were quite suddenly plunging along at four-and-a-half knots, a speed that had it continued would have put us in Barbados in record time.

One of the more debilitating influences on our approach to Tarfaya was that in the rush of the past few weeks, or out of simple neglect or budget consciousness, no one had bothered to acquire detailed charts of the Moroccan coast. So we had no clue what to expect in the way of shoals or sudden depth changes as, in the early morning, we bore down hard on the little sardine port. So fragile was our control in the high seas that a mile or so out we stopped rowing altogether and simply drifted, knowing that at the point we passed the end of the town's breakwater, which extended out into the sea, hooking sharply to the south, we would have to make a hairpin turn east into port. All we could hope was that the wind and waves would not carry us past the harbor mouth onto the surrounding rocks, against which our boat would almost certainly have been demolished.

If our confidence was further diminished as David scanned the shoreline through binoculars, it was because the captain was at that moment fast asleep, seemingly comatose, in the bunk she shared with David inside the door. She had retired to bed before dawn, complaining of what she called "sinusitis," apparently having taken a painkiller or sleeping pill or perhaps some powerful sinus medication. A couple of us tapped her on the shoulder, or called her by name at close range. However, if the calamitous bouncing of the boat and the yattering of excited voices within inches of her bunk had not been enough to waken her over a period of an hour, it seemed unlikely that any amount of polite prodding would do the job. Nobody knew what to think—she was the captain! We were in a potentially fatal situation.

As we swept across the harbor mouth at a bad angle heading for the rocks, David, who had assumed command, gave the order, and our eight rowers dug in hard at perhaps thirty strokes a minute, across the wind, and in no time had pulled the boat within the lee of the breakwater. But there wasn't a moment to relax. For by now a deflected wind had picked us up and was pushing us at speed across our limited refuge, amidst dozens of dories and larger cabin vessels. I give credit to Margaret for her pluck in leaping into the water in an attempt to set the anchor, which would not catch in the sand. As she climbed back aboard, she slipped on the steelwork of the bridge and injured her foot, and was clearly in severe pain.

After several attempts to anchor the boat, or moor it against the harbor's stone wall—and with advice flying in six directions—David decided to let it drift toward the docks and then to run, prow first, onto a small adjacent

beach on the harbor's south side. There, the impact of the
bow sprits on the sand made a heavy, grinding thud.

Off we jumped, happy to be briefly on land, a little
wobbly on our legs after four days aboard.

However, we had not been there an hour when we
were suddenly in boat trouble again as the tide began
to recede. Ryan noticed it first and hollered a warning,
but by that time the boat's stern, which had been floating free, had dropped to the point where the rudders,
the lower thirteen or fourteen inches of them, had been
driven hard into the sandy sea bottom. For an hour or
more we shoveled and levered and heaved, standing up
to our waists in water, attempting to free *Big Blue* from
her unexpected incarceration. If the rudders broke we
were finished; we had no way of repairing them in Tarfaya. The greater fear was that with the boat so heavy and
resting on its rudder mounts, the transoms themselves—
the back walls of the hulls—would be unable to take the
weight and would crack.

Eventually, David gave the order just to leave it; he
had faith that both the rudder posts and transoms would
hold until the tide came back in and sucked the boat out
of the mud.

Meanwhile, Angela had popped from the grave like
the Elect on the Day of Reckoning. She lowered herself
with some difficulty from the boat, whose decks were
sitting five feet above the beach, called Steve aside and,
based on her intuitions of four days, informed him in so
many words that there was not *quite* enough room for
both of them aboard. She believed his tendency to shape
command, coupled with the obvious inclination of several crew members to look to him for leadership, would
compromise her own authority, and she was thereby prepared to abandon the voyage.

Angela was not always flawless in her assessments, but she was bang on here. Steve can indeed be a menace to authority, especially when he perceives such authority to be anything less than fully proficient or committed or confident. He is also a man of hair-trigger sensitivity, and quickly now concluded that it was he, not Angela, who should jump ship and be gone.

There was one problem. Steve's son Nigel was aboard, as were five others, including myself, whose presence on the boat was Steve's doing and who would have been extremely unhappy to see him go. Likewise, he didn't feel he could abandon us.

So an agreement was reached. Privately. Both he and Angela would stay and would do so in mutual respect (and throughout the trip would suffer about equally for the decision).

Perhaps an hour later, one of our younger crew members asked me in genuine perplexity why, if Angela was "so concerned about the possibility that her authority was being compromised," she wouldn't have gotten out of bed that morning and taken the helm and shown everybody who was boss. It was a question that was on most of our minds, a tough one to answer. A senior crew member postulated that, under the circumstances, a more experienced crew might have demanded at that point that she resign—as we might have demanded it ourselves if we'd had someone to "do the demanding" and had been sufficiently confident in our navigational capabilities to carry on in her absence. It is also possible that she had simply been knocked right out by some combination of microbes and medication, and had been unable to answer the bell.

For now, Steve quietly informed those close to him that he would be laying back, and that any matters requiring his perspective—at least matters concerning the functioning of the vessel—should be addressed to Sylvain. Who would of course pass such concerns along to Steve (who would present them to his alter ego, Cap'n Kafka).

TARFAYA, it must be said, is one of the windiest, dustiest, most godforsaken places on earth—a town barely hydrated by the Atlantic and simultaneously sucked dry by the ceaseless winds and dust off the Sahara Desert. It is also the place where the legendary aviator and writer Antoine de Saint-Exupéry kept a station for the French airmail service Aéropostale during the 1920s. As such, it figures indirectly in his novella *The Little Prince,* written in New York in 1942 as he reflected on his time in North Africa and on his near-fatal crash in the Sahara during the 1930s.

As a crew, we were in momentous need of the Little Prince's wisdom as the lot of us settled onto the sand for a crucial midday conclave, our first of the voyage—in fact, our first since we launched the boat at Shelter Island.

The sun and wind were by this time so fierce that at one point, overwhelmed by the heat and dust, I jumped up and ran to an upturned fishing dory near the seawall and hid under it for a minute while I regained my cool.

The first item on the agenda was Tom, who was still, as he put it, "shitting blood" and whose whole being had been reduced to a kind of rumpled effigy of himself. His voice had fallen husky and faint.

Having learned by now that there was a bus out of Tarfaya that could take him up to Agadir or Casablanca, from where he could catch a flight home, Angela asked him rather brusquely, "So, what are you going to do, Tom?"

He thought for a moment and said, "What are my options if I stay aboard?" He clearly meant options for medical care or emergency transportation if his health did not improve.

"Well, there's always burial at sea," said Angela, to which Tom howled, "I'm not interested in burial at sea! I don't consider dying an option! I have responsibilities to my family!"

"Well then you should probably stay here," she said, to which he responded that he would think about things through the afternoon and would give her his answer by four o'clock.

The next item of business, our grossly overweight boat, prompted a reluctant commitment to jettisoning food and kit items that might be considered unnecessary. (Not that we didn't believe a lighter boat would make easier rowing—it was just that, well, *surely* it wasn't *my* or *my* modest belongings or provisioning that was slowing things down.) In the end, the most compelling part of the ensuing offload was not the actual weight reduction, minimal at perhaps 300 pounds, but the poignant sight of the impoverished man who, at the request of our French spokesman, Sylvain, had been chosen by the port authority to receive our bizarre largesse and who came trundling along the beach with his sweet-faced daughter, pushing a rickety wheelbarrow, followed by a guilty-looking little dog. When they reached the pile of stuff, they stood frowning at it (including the dog), intrinsically humiliated by the obscene imbalance of riches that had created it. Slowly they began loading it in: dehydrated dinners, bags of protein powder, nutritional supplements, Gatorade, granola, nuts, raisins, dried fruit, candy—plus odds and ends of clothing and footwear and assorted junk; and for some reason three air mattresses, one of which Sylvain and I could have used a few days hence when the one on our bed sprang a leak that we were unable to fix.

When the wheelbarrow was stacked two feet above its lip, the girl stood up on its wheel bracings and held the load in place while her dad tucked in every last pathetic item, including a few chunks of Styrofoam and some lumped cling wrap that we'd neglected to toss in the garbage. Then he hefted it all with his skinny brown arms and wobbled back up the beach, and I thanked God that he had not demeaned himself by expressing gratitude to us for the awful pile of rubbish that was our gift to him and to his town.

Before the meeting broke up, Angela, who was now as bright as a whitecap, asked if anyone had anything to add. Liam immediately piped up that one person on our watch had been late getting out of the cabin. *Aw, come on,* I thought, *surely, he's not . . .* at which point I heard him say my name, and then heard my own reedy voice, like some school kid's, as I have heard it all my life, muffled by the blood-rush in my ears or in this case the roar of the sea, attempting to convince yet another self-appointed ethics inspector—*just this one more time, please*—that they should overlook my screw-ups while I try to *improve* things, while I try to *correct* things, the sales pitch of the moment being that I believed I *was* improving my tardiness and had actually been doing a pretty *good* job of getting out on watch on time.

Later I said to Liam, "Why wouldn't you just speak to me privately about that?"

"I thought you needed the reprimand," he chirruped, to which I had no civilized response except to nod in disbelief and to offer my appreciation for his concern over my needs.

Meanwhile Ernst, in an attempt to stanch Tom's diarrhea, had offered him some sort of super-Imodium, one tablet of which, he told Tom, would dry him up for two days. Two, he said, and Tom would not "shit till Barbados." Three, it seemed, and he would "never shit again." Tom, bless his heart, took three. And by four o'clock felt well enough to tell Angela that he was back aboard and ready to row.

Steve and Sylvain were not impressed with Dr. Fiby's Desert Sands prescription service—understandably, since it would no longer be clear to them whether Tom was actually free of his bug or merely plugged up. The important thing to Tom was that he *felt* better after three days of pretty much grave-ready infirmity and torment.

As if anything could get wackier, during the early afternoon a young male journalist came bounding down the breakwall onto the beach, having driven across the desert from a nearby town to get the scoop on the zany American rowboat that had pulled ashore at Tarfaya. He told Liz that, through the military, the Moroccan royal family had become aware that we were moving down the coast and that an order had gone out to mariners and the media that if there was any contact with us they were to treat us with respect and generosity, presumably a kind of sop to U.S.-Moroccan diplomacy. The twist was that we had landed illegally in Tarfaya, having officially signed the boat out of Morocco five days earlier through the Customs and Immigration office in Agadir. As such, we were prohibited from re-entering the country, even landing on its shores, without renewing our papers and passport visas. All of which was clearly immaterial to the little immigration office in Tarfaya, which, beyond an obvious sense of wonderment at our outlandish craft, treated our visit with unregulated autonomy. Had it been otherwise, ironically, the royal hospitality might well have had to be extended to us through the bars of the local jail.

THE PLAN WAS to leave Tarfaya at 10 p.m.—high tide. We needed the depth of water not just to float the boat and lift the rudders but to keep us off the coastal shoals

formed by the fine sand that swirls endlessly off the
Sahara and settles anywhere up to half a mile offshore.
Or settles on the town.

Late in the afternoon, feeling mopey and isolated, I
walked up behind the port buildings toward the village
mosque, where waist-high dunes, as fine as gunpowder,
wound sinuously across the road or lay settled against
the stone wall that separated the road from the beach, in
some places burying it like snowbanks after a blizzard.
A scrawny Arab, perhaps fifty years old, came shuffling
along wearing filthy seersucker Capri pants and a T-shirt
emblazoned with the words "Bombay Sapphire Gin." His
teeth looked like poorly driven tent stakes, and when
he smiled and nodded I asked in my poor French how
the town got rid of the sand so that it didn't eventually
just cover everything up. He seemed pleased to be asked
a question to which he knew the answer and, through a
series of charade-like gestures and growled phrases, gave
me to understand that there were *vingt hommes* and *beau-
coup de pelles,* and perhaps a loader of some sort, and that
these *vingt hommes* worked full-time shoveling the sand
into *deux camions,* which delivered it back to the desert, from where it began blowing again into Tarfaya. It
reminded me of writing, although I didn't bother saying so—time was short and my French poor, and I knew
that somewhere back on the beach there were masters to
appease and world records to consider, and I thought I'd
best get going. But I regretted, under the pressure of the
afternoon, that I did not feel comfortable going farther
into town to seek out the Exupéry museum, or the monument to the great French writer, which I have seen a number of times in photos. (I might add, incidentally, that *The
Little Prince* is the best-selling novel ever, at more than 200
million copies, in dozens of languages, and yet has the

happy quality of seeming entirely non-commercial, a new and provocative experience for everyone who reads it.)

As I returned to the boat, it occurred to me in a modest satori why the port police had been able at a moment's notice to produce a shiny new shovel to aid us in our battle with the rudders. Clearly, people here kept a sand shovel at the ready on the stoop or in the vestibule, the way Canadians keep a snow shovel by the front door in winter.

For now, if we needed a reminder of the potential hazards offshore, we had only to glance a few hundred yards beyond the beach to where the wreck of the immense car ferry *Assalama* sat rusting against a sandbar on which it went hard aground in the spring of 2008. As with all shipwrecks, above or below water, there was a creepiness to it, a nightmare factor, that hinted at one's own potential for a bad end at sea. I had declined to take a photo of it that morning, spooked by an irrational fear that having its image onboard, even in digital form, might somehow affect my dreams or bring malevolence to the cabin.

During the mid-afternoon, when we notified the port authority of our departure plan, they warned us that we would be risking our lives to leave the harbor and to attempt to navigate the coastal shoals in darkness—and strongly urged us to wait until sunrise. Warnings, of course, don't apply to amateurs with dreams of world records or to rowers with such obvious navigational confidence that they have rejected the use of coastal charts in favor of *guessing* where catastrophe might lie. In the end, the ferocious north wind that had driven us into port that morning, and continued apace, proved irresistible to the boat's brain-trust and trumped any concern we or the port authorities might have had for our safety. The decision to launch was reinforced by news that the wind was likely to blow at its current strength for just twenty-four more hours.

Thus it was that at about 7:30 p.m., in fading light, we eased *Big Blue* off the beach, gave the rudders a cursory examination ("They'll be fine," I heard someone say), and stroked confidently out of the harbor, into the night.

I CAN ADMIT now as I could not then that the choice to launch in darkness caused me fleeting but sincere doubts about the judgment of those in charge of our crazy little two-hulled ship—not to mention about the future of the expedition. It was one thing to wreck on sandbars a few hundred yards offshore, near a harbor full of fishing dories, quite another to suffer bad navigational or deployment choices in the middle of the Atlantic in sixty-knot crosswinds. In the days to come, such doubts became a sporadic theme in late-night conversations between Steve and myself, culminating a week or so hence when I informed him reluctantly that my suspicions about Angela and Margaret's state of mind had led me to a secret search of their possessions to see what I could find out about their identities.

"Annnd?" he said expectantly, to which I responded that the news was not good—indeed, that I had found in Angela's document folder a yellowed newspaper clipping from the *Des Moines Expositor* detailing her and Margaret's escape from the Iowa State Hospital for the Criminally Insane. According to the story, they had formed a rowing team, mixed quads, had made their getaway at a local regatta, and were suspected of fleeing to the Moroccan port city of Agadir. What disturbed me most, I had to admit, was that in the photo of the rowing team, a gentleman seated directly behind Margaret looked suspiciously like one Stephen Roedde, M.D.

"Steve," I said—but before I could address the issue of his mad collusion with Command, he barked, "It wasn't me!"

And thus we entertained ourselves—fantasizing, kibitzing, swapping stories about our years as young dogs. And of course as old dogs too.

MEANWHILE, we rowed hard down the coast through that first official night of our bid to cross the Atlantic, sometimes hitting speeds of nearly six knots—all the while bucking and sledding and making the sort of progress that, had the wind continued, might have kept us in the race with *Hallin* and *Sara G.*

As always, we paid for our progress in bruises and soakings and exhaustion. By this time, I had worked out a crude system for rowing safely in a "following" sea, which is to say in swells that were moving in the same direction as the boat, as this night's were. If the wave alongside me was rising, I stuck my oar in; if it was falling, I kept it out. In that way I could hold my stroke, rather than distorting it to chase a wave as it fell away, leaving me vulnerable to getting my blade caught.

All of this was academic on moonless nights such as this, when all waves were invisible, and the ability to keep your stroke under control was a matter largely of experience and, to a degree, dumb luck. At one point on the 2-to-4 a.m., despite my system, a breaker caught my oar, driving the handle so hard into my shoulder that it lifted me off my seat, right out of my shoes, which stayed tight in the stirrups, and slammed me yelping into the trench wall behind me.

ALL TOLD, DURING our first twenty-four hours out of Tarfaya we covered a respectable ninety miles, pushed by the persistent northeast wind that we had picked up out of the harbor. But by the second night, the wind had turned and was now coming daggers out of the south, forcing us to veer west, a direction that, had we maintained it, would eventually have taken us into the vicinity of the Canary Islands. Unfortunately, we didn't want to *go* due west at this point, even though it put us on a direct path toward North America. In order to get into the trade winds—the "swoosh" as Sylvain called them— we had to go significantly farther down the coast toward the Cape Verde Islands.

By the middle of that second night out, Margaret, who had arrived without a proper seat cushion, had decided she liked my pathetic little ass pad and had commandeered it for use on the other watch. Thus, atop a few ounces of foam rubber and a few feet of duct tape, were our fannies wedded (minus the consummation, of course). However, she regularly gave me the goose over getting the thing back.

"*Margaret,*" I'd holler across the cabin to the other hull, where she'd be coming off watch as I was coming on, "where's the cushion?" Sometimes I waited two or three minutes for the thing to appear atop the bridge while those around me stewed about my delayed start.

When I suggested to Margaret that we make her an identical cushion of her own so that I could get more promptly to rowing, Ryan, who was within earshot, informed me rather testily that I should just start rowing without the cushion, and it would appear in its own good time. Which sounded reasonable, except that once you got your feet bound up and strapped into the stirrups, your safety line hooked, and your oar working, you weren't in the mood to get up, especially after six or seven minutes of grating your already tattered ass.

BY THE AFTERNOON of the third day out of Tarfaya, the wind had shifted again and was now coming sporadically out of the northeast, so that we were again headed in a more-or-less southerly direction down the coast. Twelve hours later it had turned again, this time almost 180 degrees, and was coming hard out of the south.

And twelve hours after that had turned again.

It was a pattern (or more precisely the absence of a pattern) that would persist through the first two and a half weeks of the voyage—as would the frustration of being knocked around by crosswinds and sometimes headwinds; being unable to get moving, unable to get into the trades and get properly out to sea. Margaret told me that on her 2009 doubles crossing in the Woodvale race, the seas had been a breeze compared to what we were seeing, the rowing far easier. Some boats in the race had seen no wind at all, sometimes for days in succession.

On our fourth day out of Tarfaya we covered sixty miles, which as the crow flies brought us just twenty-five closer to Barbados. On our fifth day we logged eighty miles, ending up closer to Barbados by forty-five. It was progress of a sort, although nowhere near the 105-mile daily average that would be required to get us to our destination in just over a month.

Steve was in a funk about it all—disappointed over what he called "the reality of things" (a reality of which I was probably about as grating and "real" a part as it was possible to be). Despite the all-but-absurd effort of getting out on watch on time in the middle of the night after perhaps eighty minutes of sleep—of having to waken out of something pretty close to a coma, pull on soaked clothing and shoes, and, in a sleep-deprived daze, negotiate a screaming wind on a heaving bridge in order to get to one's seat—I had, since Liam outed me in Tarfaya, been trying hard to be punctual. And had been succeeding, if at times resentfully. During the past couple of days I had shown up as much as five minutes *before* the actual watch change.

However, on this fourth day out of Tarfaya, cored by exhaustion, I had fallen into profound unconsciousness coming off watch at eight in the morning. I had entirely missed wake-up for the 10-to-noon, and by the time Angela shook me to life was already two or three minutes late. Steve was, of course, rowing as I took my seat and got my oar into the water. After a few seconds, he said quietly, "I note that able-bodied seaman Wilkins is losing his military discipline," to which I replied that able-bodied seaman Wilkins (not to mention his alter ego *un*able-bodied seaman Wilkins) had never had any military discipline to lose and that furthermore able-bodied seaman Wilkins considered military-type discipline to be a brainless derivative of the authoritarian priesthoods of antiquity—"Gimme ten push-ups!" I shouted in his ear. "Gimme ten Hail Marys!" We pretended we found this amusing, and I was five minutes early for the 2-to-4.

By now I had realized that both Steve *and* Angela were perfectly capable of applying their private obsessions to whatever ailed or affected the voyage. Indeed, in some surreal way it seemed to me that Angela's food fixations, which were weighing down the boat, had become a kind of gravy for Steve's disciplinary fixations, which were weighing down the zeitgeist. As far as I could see, what ailed us at that point had more to do with weather than with human lassitude or the possibility of malnutrition. What ailed me personally lay in their presumption that things were the other way around. Frankly, I was already fed up with being told, if indirectly, that I was a slacker (the whole Pharisee fandango) and could see that if I was going to keep my balance, going to cope in this environment and under these pressures, I was going to have to tune out some of the low-level coercion and anxiety and tune in to the sea.

Having arrived at this simple coping strategy, I was able immediately to expand my valences for the wind and water and, on that very afternoon watch (perhaps not coincidentally), experienced what I might presume to call my first "transcendent moments" aboard. The wind had dropped, and by three o'clock a run of gentle mountainous rollers, separated by vast sinking plains, had settled in behind us. At times, when you looked out from the boat, you were looking down a steep hundred-yard slope of water, a vision simultaneously of terror and vertigo and bliss. The sea was the color of Vicks VapoRub bottles, and the sun's rays, flaring off the surface, laid a silvery filigree along the long lower edges of the clouds. Taking his cue from the rollers, Liam settled into a measured, relaxed stroke, perhaps thirteen or fourteen to the minute—a dreamer's pace.

We saw a sea turtle, a yellow-finned tuna, a team of acrobatic dolphins—synchronized swimmers, five of which came out of a wave in perfect formation toward the end of the watch and kipped onto their tails in a kind of chorus line. I could swear they were wearing top hats and swinging canes, but I was perhaps dreaming or hallucinating by then—must have been, inasmuch as the objectification of nature was one of the tendencies I had persuaded myself I would try to put behind me out there on the Atlantic. As much as possible I wanted to renew a fundamental sense of the planet: clouds as clouds, water as water, wind as wind—dolphins and sea turtles and sharks for what they are, free of the fearful or fanciful identities we have ascribed to them and from which we are reluctant to allow them to escape. In this, as in other areas, I wanted to be able to see the journey as something more than was promised, whereas the pressure, already, was to see it as something less. And yet on such an afternoon, on such a watch, it was easy to believe that everything would be fine, that Aquarius would rise, peace descend, and that our eccentric little boat, with its unruly crew, would continue to get us from where we'd been to where we were, and perhaps eventually to where we wanted to be.

AS WE CAME off watch on that blissful afternoon, Angela brought me quickly to reality with news that there was no dinner for me, that nothing with my name on it had come out of the day's dinner pack. She said (a bit too matter-of-factly for my liking) that she had put together a "bowl of soup" for me, which turned out to be a half pack or so of curly little ramen noodles, which supplied maybe a tenth of the calories I craved.

Having by now strained her back and been reduced to rowing just an hour or two a day, Angela had compensated by taking on full-time responsibility for preparing meals. It was the second time in four days that there'd been no meal for me in the evening, and I was not happy about it, especially as I watched others sink their sporks, then their chompers, into lumpy but alluring rehydrations of beef stroganoff, Bulgarian goulash, and Etruscan lasagne. It was ironic, to say the least, that after the hours upon hours of obsessing over food—of buying and shipping and chop-licking, of provisioning the boat as if for the hundred-year run to Sirius—the crew's skinniest citizen (a groveling Oliver Twist to Angela's Mr. Bumble) was being told that he must do without his supper. I believed the problem went back to the boatyard in Agadir, where Louise's partner, Noreen, and I got working at cross purposes in an attempt to get my meals into the proper stowage bags. Obviously, we had missed putting a dinner into each day's pack—an easy mistake to have made with hundreds of coded meals and meal packs lying around in rather eccentrically organized chaos. (I must make clear that I do not for a moment blame Noreen, who was innocently helping me out—and who, besides, is not the sort of person you blame for things but whom you *credit* for good things happening.)

As it turned out, Ernst had drawn rice and beans for the sixth day in a row and, declaring that his "azz" was "all rize and beantz," handed me a full packet of Taste of the Islands Caribbean-style black beans and rice. But it was not the salty, lardy, peppery rice and beans—the yummy, disease-inducing version—that I remembered from my days in Nassau during the 1970s and now craved, but rather a "healthy" California concoction, low on sodium and other poisons and laced with agave nectar of all things, so that after six or seven bites its oppressive sweetness got the better of me, and I passed the container on to Dylan. Even at this point in the journey, Dylan was perpetually starved and hoovered up the leftovers, as one might with actual food, before digging into the remains of some vitamin-burdened gruel that Ryan Worth had slurried up and abandoned. Meanwhile, Ernst had passed me the leftovers of a container of Mary's Own Butter-Mashed Potatoes with Chicken Breast and Rib Meat. The dish, he informed me, was "a bit dry"—was so dry in fact that, had it been a wee bit less so, a wee bit more digestible-looking, it might have been mistaken for Poly Filla. It didn't help that I had attempted to soften it with a squirt from my water bottle, forgetting that an hour earlier I had loaded the bottle with a greenish potassium/sodium rehydration compound intended to replace salts during what the directions called "perspiratory activity." Nevertheless, I scarfed it all down, fell asleep for an hour, and was back on my oar at 6 p.m.

NINETY MINUTES later, at sunset, as we fought robust crosswinds, Steve turned and lamented above the howl that whatever weight reduction we'd achieved at Tarfaya "wasn't doing us one gawdam bit of good." Our real weight problem, he believed, was that there were simply too many people aboard, each of whom represented not just body weight but an additional two or three hundred pounds in food and kit, plus the requirement for an oar, a survival suit, a life vest, bigger life rafts, heavier solar panels, and so on. The original agenda had called for fourteen people, not sixteen, and had been altered only out of a need for more money to fund the voyage. Steve, suspecting that a number of crew members could do with considerably less food than they were carrying, felt another 500 pounds should be jettisoned. He also believed that all sixteen survival suits should be donated to the mermaids. Together, the suits, hideous red Teletubby costumes, weighed 300 pounds and were so deep in the storage holds that should the boat have broken up it would have been extremely difficult even to get to them, let alone get them on in time to make a difference.

Personally I hated the suits, found them smelly and claustrophobic, even deathly. This was in part because, years ago, while on assignment aboard the MV *Paterson,* a Great Lakes bulk carrier, I had tried one on in my cabin, had gotten trapped in it, and (embarrassing though it is to report) had been unable to free myself for more than an hour. During survival maneuvers at Shelter Island, we had put on the suits and jumped off a high jetty into the frigid North Atlantic, where we were sprayed with fire hoses to simulate rough weather. On that occasion, the cold of the late November day combined with the existing stress of the maneuver had caused my asthma to flare, so that when I hit the icy water I was working as hard as a guy in his early sixties can work but on about a third of my normal lung capacity. At the same time, the suit's neck, which fastens high across the lower face, made mouth-breathing impossible at a time when I needed drastically to increase my air intake. In all, it was the worst experience I'd had since joining the expedition and left me thinking of the suits as some rough coefficient of waterboard torture or burial alive.

Our inflatable life rafts, both of which were attached to the outer front slope of the cabin, represented the more obvious and efficient emergency survival plan. This was in large part because of their accessibility, but also because, with luck and one of the two portable desalinators we had aboard, as many as eight people could survive in each of them for four or five days or more.

At any rate, it was unlikely the survival suits would be ditched. For one thing they were borrowed and were worth $400 each, and David, who was already a hundred thousand in debt on the expedition, would be reluctant to burden himself with another six thousand in liabilities. Moreover, in a sport and on a boat at least nominally devoted to the ecological health of the oceans, it would have been profoundly hypocritical to be stowing our garbage in the holds (as we were), carting it all the way to North America in the name of environmental integrity, only to toss 300 pounds of polychloroprene into the water to be chewed up by the elements and eaten by sea turtles and whales. Such creatures, it should be said, are well known if inadvertent consumers of the megatons of trash that float in the Atlantic and Pacific Oceans. In April 2011, the stomach of a gray whale autopsied on the U.S. coast was found to contain significant quantities of duct tape and electrical tape, a pair of sweat pants, a bath towel, a rubber boot, a golf ball, a tennis ball, a deflated beach ball, hundreds of yards of monofilament and woven fishing line, a length of hemp rope, a plastic flower, a juice box, twenty-six garbage bags, a quarter-mile of rubberized string, and a surgical glove.

Every day, from our own boat, we saw floating drink cartons, old fishing tackle, loose net markers, chunks of Styrofoam and plastic, lengths of synthetic rope, clothing, food packaging, dozens of grocery and garbage bags. One morning, a half-dozen corn cobs, newly husked and ready for the pot, drifted past; on another, perhaps fifty rotten muskmelons interspersed with dozens of chunks of plastic crating. On yet another morning, at sunrise, 500 miles offshore, I spotted a white plastic chair bobbing along about twenty yards off our port hull. All of which is to say nothing of the more insidious contaminants, the heavy metals, the barrels of PCBs and jettisoned atomic wastes that are known to rest on the sea floor in parts of the North Atlantic.

And we chipped in our share. Pharmaceuticals and lotions and bits of food packaging were constantly getting washed out the scuppers. In addition to my gel seat cushion, I had already lost, among other items, my water bottle, my gray sweatshirt, one of my rubber Crocs, my food bowl, a container of sunscreen, and one of my baseball hats.

Late one evening, just a week out of Tarfaya, in plain view, one of the ostensibly committed environmentalists on the crew laughingly tossed a dysfunctional headlamp and battery overboard, with an exaggerated "oops!"

"Life's getting simpler," joked Steve in response to my personal forfeitures, blissfully unaware that he would soon suffer his own dire loss, one easily as agonizing as anything I had experienced to date.

Regrettably, our losses overboard were the merest beginnings of the voyage's ecological deficit. Notwithstanding the absence of motors and exhaust, our carbon debt would eventually include the contaminants from more than 140 long-distance flights (Shelter Island, Agadir, Barbados; crew, family, friends), the shipping of nearly a ton of food across the U.S. by air, and the shipping of the boat and supplies across the Atlantic on a container vessel, one of the dirtiest forms of transportation on earth. Even in Agadir, our comings and goings had required hundreds of cross-town rides in taxis whose exhaust reminded me of the apocalyptic tire fires of my youth. In all, the trip—a superficially eco-friendly journey by oar—was responsible for some 30,000 pounds of carbon emissions, a debt that would barely have been matched if we'd been burning a hundred survival suits a day on board, plus a ton of garbage. I mention all of this not out of my intrinsic skepticism about ocean rowing or other extreme recreation, but as a comment on the state of the seas generally, and as a reality check of sorts on the preposterous claim by some ocean rowers, as well as those involved in other seemingly planet-friendly travel and sport, that their pursuits are a testament to sound ecology.

That we still had too much food was made obvious over the next couple of days by the "reject" bags in the cabin—a pair of insulated picnic-style totes in which we could put food we didn't want and which were brimming, as always, with nutrition bars, fake-cheese packets, crumbled peanuts, squashed raisins, all manner of protein and electrolyte supplements, and candies, many of them conveniently pre-digested by the humidity. The new joke aboard was that we were on target to set a world record for rowboats carrying 600 pounds of dehydrated stroganoff and 200 Snickers bars.

Another knee-slapper had us arriving so hopelessly far into the future that, like Rip Van Winkle, we would be aliens in the places we once knew and among loved ones who no longer recognized us. That failure at humor had at least metaphoric appeal to me, including a hint of Paul Theroux's observation that "You go for a long time and return a different person"—return to people and places that, in your absence, have themselves often become unrecognizable.

A **PHONE CALL TO** the boat on the morning of day five out of Tarfaya brought word that we had fallen significantly farther behind *Hallin* and *Sara G,* which were apparently enjoying bumper tailwinds and were well out into the trades while we languished. On the 10-to-noon, led by Steve, our little sub-watch of four discussed in the gravest of terms what options there might be for improvement. Hollering back and forth above the crashing of the waves, we concluded, not surprisingly, that since we couldn't alter the wind direction we could at least *be more punctual.* I needled Steve by pointing out that punctuality, once achieved, cannot be improved upon—in other words that there is no such thing as being "less punctual" or "more punctual." At the same time, I acknowledged my regard for the advice once given by Lee Strasberg to Marlon Brando, another late-arriving reprobate: that if he couldn't show up on time, he might try showing up early.

"In your case," Steve said, "punctuality will be fine," confirming what I had already suspected: that since the others in our sub-crew were for the most part already showing up on time, the new commitment was largely for my benefit.

Steve's aim at this point, he said, was that we should get across at least fast enough that we didn't "embarrass ourselves." In whose eyes I wasn't sure, but I imagined he was thinking about his friend David Hosking, the venerable captain of our competitor *Hallin Marine,* and a couple of others aboard *Hallin* who, before the shake-up, had been a part of the *Big Blue* expedition. Hosking is a British ex-naval officer with little use for anything less than superiority in human endeavor, or at least a striving for it. In what little contact I had with him during our mutual involvement with *Big Blue,* it became clear that he is obsessed with mental and physical toughness, with a corpuscle-busting commitment to "the cause," whatever it might be. For me, the lot of it seemed exaggerated to a point where, by comparison, the cause itself had become a mere testing mechanism for competitive durability—for "spirit" in the sense that it was manifested by, say, Horatio at the Bridge or the legendary football coach Vince Lombardi, who when questioned about his belief that "winning was everything" responded, "Winning isn't everything; it's the *only* thing."

In some ways, Steve might have preferred to be aboard Hosking's boat—and could have been, were it not for his entanglements aboard *Big Blue.* At the same time, I have sometimes wondered if those entanglements weren't also a gracious convenience in that a part of Steve didn't want anything to do with *Hallin Marine.* Hosking's rallying cry for the *Hallin* endeavor, "One boat, one aim, one ocean," was all very much in keeping with an m.o. that even Steve realized would be a serious and hellish punishment for a middle-aged guy with back problems, Crohn's disease, and what he once described to me as "a bunch of other internal difficulties."

Steve often remarked that Hosking had ordered *Hallin*'s crew to "cut the handles off their toothbrushes" in order to reduce weight aboard (prompting Tom's speculation that they could have eliminated toothbrushes entirely by having their teeth pulled, another significant reduction in weight). At watch change, according to Steve, *Hallin*'s six rowers were permitted a total of twenty missed strokes between the six of them. One of the boat's youngest and toughest rowers, Chris Covey, another graduate of the original *Big Blue* expedition, complained lavishly on the boat's live blog about the pernicious conditions aboard *Hallin:* the cold, the poor food, the soakings, the pain, the exhaustion. Which in all but the toothbrushes and watch changes—and of course the skull-busting commitment and chain of command—sounded pretty much like life aboard our own little chamber of horrors.

From what I know of Hosking apart from his preoccupation with record-chasing, he is a thoughtful and generous guy who, when I joined *Big Blue,* emailed me almost daily to encourage me in my training and rowing techniques. Such considerations aside, I couldn't have cared less what he thought about our effort or progress. Or what those aboard *Sara G* might have thought. More than once I pointed out to Steve that *Sara G* had crossed just a year earlier, with a presumably decent crew, in a month and a half—more than a dozen days off the record. And that no one had held them up to ridicule. Hosking himself had crossed well above record time in the 2010 Woodvale race—poor boat, lackluster crew, undoubtedly some bad weather.

Back at the boatyard, when Margaret had asked how much importance I placed on setting a record, I had

responded honestly that I considered the attempt significant, that it meant something to me to do our best, and
that of *course* I'd be excited if we crossed in record time.
But that if there *was* no record I would not be broken-
hearted. What else could I say? That if we fell behind I'd
hold my breath till we caught up?

At the time, I had taken the opportunity to relay to
Margaret a comment by the writer Pico Iyer that travel
is most rewarding when it ceases to be about "reaching a destination"—much less reaching it in record time.
Really, though, I preferred Steve's question (the answer
to which he considered something of a deal breaker):
If we had a chance for the record with just days to go,
and needed to lighten the boat for more speed, would
I be willing to jettison the remaining food for that advantage? *Of course* was my emphatic reply. More than most,
I believed, I was willing to jettison another 500 pounds
right now (easy enough for me to say, since it wasn't
my food).

If I was feeling embarrassment of my own at this stage,
it was *not* for the pathos or dejection that was *Big Blue*—
to my mind a most humanizing funk—but because our
entire endeavor, and to a degree our civility, was being
sublimated to this absurd notion that somehow the journey was debased or even meaningless because we weren't
getting across as quickly as we'd hoped.

In Steve's eyes, different leadership from the beginning would have changed things. And he may have been
right. It would not have improved the weather or wind
direction, but it would have altered our focus and would
certainly have meant that Margaret was not aboard,
which would have pleased Steve immensely. It might
even have resulted in the boat being ready sooner, and
thereby an earlier departure and different winds. But
that was debatable. David had all the help he needed in

Agadir, and had worked like a peon himself, and we were still not ready to go until January the 11th.

One thing was certain: under a different captain we would have had less food and a lighter boat. We would also have been traveling under a lighter irony, in that it was Steve who, late in the game, on behalf of the expedition, had offered Angela the captaincy, and had persuaded her to take it.

I AM PREPARED to allow that I was wrong, that the true gist of the journey *did* lie in discipline and punctuality and a rejection of individual preference or interests. Certainly we had a varied crew, some of whom might have performed better if driven a little harder. At the same time, most of us were already at the limits of our capabilities and endurance—we were putting out; we were banged up; we were exhausted. It might have been different if, having risen from our bunks, we'd been able to go peaceably and quietly to our rowing seats, to have begun work in practiced meditation rather than under the relentless unspoken dunning, the nonstop pressure to wake up, to get dressed, to get out, to get down, to get rowing, get wet, get cold, get numb. There were nights when every wave that went over me made me want to scream, to throw my oar as far overboard as I could throw it, to crawl into the cabin and curl up in Eden's little sleeping bag (which in its suffocating dampness was itself these days enough to get me screaming).

Above all, it was fatiguing, both mentally and physically, and in the darkest part of my brain I began a private deliberation on who among us would be the first to break, to stand screaming in the trench or on the bridge, or to awaken from the nightmare cursing God—or crying quietly in the bunk. Out of perhaps necessary self-delusionment, I assumed it would not be me.

Which is not to say I was far from the brink, or in any kind of shape to feel confident. More than once during those early weeks, Steve told me that he had had to look twice at me in my bunk, where I lay dreamless, mouth-breathing, comatose, to determine whether I was alive. On Day 3 or 4 he observed that I had briefly stopped breathing during an afternoon nap but had shuddered to life with a snore when he nudged me. It occurred to me that I had indeed perhaps been Gone for a few seconds— had mistaken Charon's rough ride across the Styx for the nonstop Tilt-A-Whirl that was the boat.

Because our videographer, Dylan White, was under instructions from Kelly Saxberg to capture what he could of my anticipated disintegration (which I assure you would get worse), and because his bunk was next to mine, there is plenty of unauthorized footage of me doing a rather convincing impersonation of a cadaver. It is only in retrospect that it occurs to me how morbid it was that my projected decline should have been perceived as a central theme in Kelly's film. Had I died out there it would of course have been the ultimate boost to the film and to my TRAGICALLY ABBREVIATED SCREEN CAREER. Even my literary agent, Jackie Kaiser, had joked that my story would be worth more if I croaked (eliciting a promise that I'd go again when the manuscript was done, with the hope of raising its value).

As for discipline, I have no doubt about the advantages of prompt watch changes on a rowing expedition such as ours. Or that a high standard for effort was indispensible. While to my mind neither was as important as morale, it is here that my own debilitating pathologies become apparent, as does the shakiness of the lens through which I view the world. I can go long, can go lean, can discipline myself to sit in a room for 200 days and write; can drive a thousand miles at a stretch or walk 1,500 miles to New

York City. However, all my limited capabilities fall to ruin when it comes to having to get anywhere on time. Or perform a task on time. One of my modest distinctions in the writing community is that, during forty years of publication, I have never met a deadline for a piece longer than a few thousand words (although I have come close and am getting closer). As a kindergarten student, living on Parkdale Avenue in Deep River, Ontario, I would lock myself in the bathroom when it was time to go to school and embark on fake hour-long bowel movements, complete with vocalized sound effects, while my mother hammered the door, demanding entry. One of my sisters claims I once showed up a month late for Christmas dinner at her home. No question, I prefer the bendy road to the straight one, the late hour to the early. At the same time I do not believe that my battle with the clock was any more than the tiniest of factors in the evolving frustrations aboard, the impatience and pessimism, the festering sense that we must get in the seats and stay in them—*and don't get out of them until it's time to get back in them!*

If my perspective needed reinforcement, it received it on the afternoon of the sixth day out of Tarfaya, as I lay in my bunk reading Simon Winchester's *Atlantic,* a breezy natural history of the sea around us, cut with human maritime history and the author's own extensive experiences at sea. In a chapter entitled "Oh! The Beauty and the Might of It," I came across an account of the participation of the famous French sailor Bernard Moitessier in a round-the-world sailing race during the late 1960s. Moitessier was leading the race as he sailed north past the Falkland Islands, and it was assumed he would win. But as he continued on toward Europe he suddenly changed course and began sailing due east, eventually right out of the Atlantic via the Mediterranean and south into the

Indian Ocean. Weeks later, he squeezed a letter into a tin can and fired it with a slingshot over the rail of a passing merchant vessel. It said in part: "My intention is to continue the voyage, still nonstop, toward the Pacific Islands, where there is plenty of sun and more peace than in Europe. Please do not think I am trying to break a record [for continuous ocean sailing]. 'Record' is a very stupid word at sea. I am continuing nonstop because I am happy at sea, and perhaps because I want to save my soul."

Years later, in a kind of personal manifesto, he added, "I am a citizen of the most beautiful nation on earth. A nation whose laws are harsh yet simple, a nation that never cheats... where life is lived in the present. In this limitless nation of wind, light, and peace, there is no other ruler besides the sea."

The Italian filmmaker Lorenzo Fonda's declaration that "The sea will kick your sorry human ass" is a less eloquent, more fearful, consideration of the theme, or at least part of it. There is a dark side to our connections with the sea. However, to be out there in a boat that might or might not be equal to the relentlessness of the Atlantic—indeed in a body (mine) that might not be equal—had created a kind of suspension in my mind that could not be translated into the normal vocabulary of fear. This was in part, I realize, because for me fear too had been suspended—or perhaps merely subsumed into some seedling version of an addiction. T.E. Lawrence said that once a traveler had experienced the Sahara, "no other place was strong enough for him" or could offer what he called "the supremely satisfying sensation of existing in the midst of something that is absolute."

I believe now that, in my private way, from beyond the traumas of the voyage, I too was beginning to experience that sensation.

IF THERE WAS a more tangible mystery afoot during those first five days off the Sahara, it lay in the suspicion that somehow we were running heavier, that the shedding of weight in Tarfaya and the consumption by this time of ten days' worth of meals had not lightened the boat one ounce. The hulls seemed sluggish and were burrowing deeper into the waves and troughs.

Meanwhile, the rowing seemed harder by the watch. Or were we simply wearing down at an accelerating rate? Because of the constant chop, it was impossible to tell precisely where the waterline met the hull, although I was sure the water seemed closer than ever to the tramps and to the underside of the cabin. Some of the detonations of the waves against the bunk bottoms during the past couple of nights had shaken me awake expecting to see plywood shattered in the alley and water pouring in.

It was a matter of fortuitous timing that our first ten days' worth of "snack packs"—our personal daily bundles of raisins, nuts, cookies, candies, pepperoni, and so on (packs that had been stored in the captain's private pantry)—ran out when they did. And that some hungry soul opened one of the four hatches in the floor of the starboard rowing trench in order to get at the next couple of weeks' worth of same. Whoever did so on Day 6 made the alarming discovery that the hulls were sloshing with several hundred gallons of water—water that had washed over the gunnels into the trenches and, before it had had a chance to drain from the scuppers, had leaked through the hatches, which until now we had assumed were watertight.

Because Zach Scher and I rowed in the same seat (on opposite watches), our snack packs were bagged up together beneath the rearmost hatch on the starboard hull and, happily, had remained dry. But some people's packing had proven inadequate, and hundreds of pounds of both snacks and regular meals had been damaged, if not ruined.

Up it all came onto the tramps for assessment, the ruined stuff going into the sea, minus its wrappers, the salvageable stuff going into the cabin onto Angela's shelves. Meanwhile, we squeezed perhaps thirty pounds of crumpled cling wrap into the emptied garbage bags and rammed it all into the rear starboard hold, where perhaps a hundred pounds of rubbish, mostly food wrappers, had already accumulated.

As I was gathering up the trash in preparation for pumping out the hulls, Margaret clamped a baleful eye on me from the bridge and, surely able to see that I was engaged, said, "Charlie, I don't think you're needed right now—I'd like you to go into the cabin; there isn't room out here for everybody."

Not on your freaking life, I was tempted to tell her, and after a cartoon silence said, "Margaret, there may not be room for everybody out here, but I have a job to do, so there *is* room for me." If there was space in the cabin, I told her, she should go ahead and take it, at which point she shook her head in disgust and disappeared down the other side of the boat.

Surveying the losses as food went into the sea, and with no hint of irony, Liz made one of the trip's more memorable and endearing comments: "Boy," she enthused in her beaming, childlike way, "there's gonna be some skinny people around here!" While no one laughed or responded outright, Ernst could barely contain his delight in the comment, and I detected what I believe was a tremor of discomposure, perhaps mere amusement, on the face of one of several people within earshot who would have been quite happy to be among the "skinny people" of Liz's innocent foretelling.

What I liked best about her comment, however, was not its unintended or inferred humor but her assessment of the ever-moving boat as a locale, as a place, a "here." To this point in my life, I had too often thought of the Atlantic, its surface, as an expanse of infinite amorphous sameness, a place whose latitudes and longitudes, except in the extreme north and south, were more or less undifferentiable to a landlubber such as myself. But I had been wrong. Happily so. During the first ten days of the voyage I had been deeply impressed by the sense of identity, of locale, imparted to every acre of water by the positioning of, say, the sun and moon and stars, by clouds and horizon, and by our tiny vessel, invariably the center of the universe. Even the waves and whitecaps, always advancing and receding, permitted at least a fleeting sense of position and place. As did the horizon, which at sea level, seen from the boat, was never more than a couple of miles away, forming a visual partition separating us from the vastness of everything beyond.

The whales and dolphins too were in place in these waters, or were at least on their routes and rounds, guided by their own innate sense of global positioning. And we were now seeing five or six sea turtles a day, animals that likewise were on routes as specific as any flight plan from one continent to another. One had only to contemplate the sea floor, with its valleys and mountains and tectonic plates, to understand further that a sense of locale at sea, a sense of place, was more than mere poetics.

The sea turtles were a marvel: stolid and patient, working their fins in an endless slow-motion row as they stroked their way across thousands of miles of open water on their way to exotic islands and shores. From the boat, depending on the light, they looked yellow or rust-colored and, though they can dive to depths of up to 3,000 feet, were most often just an inch or two beneath the surface, sometimes with their snouts up. While birds are thought to migrate visually, and fish in response to water temperature and currents, it is said of sea turtles that their brains contain an iron compound, magnetite, and that this, in response to the earth's magnetic field, guides them on their routes across the planet.

What mystified us initially was what the turtles were eating out there—apart, tragically, from the plastic bags that they are said to mistake for food and which are ultimately fatal to them. Eventually I learned they eat everything from plankton to shrimp to the ubiquitous Portuguese man o' war, a neon-pink jellyfish-like creature that floats on the surface, dangling deadly poisonous tentacles as far down as thirty or forty feet. We saw hundreds of them, bright little sailing ships as alluring as crib toys, and only later learned that sea turtles, in eating them, undergo changes of body and stool chemistry that make them more detectable at a distance to sharks and therefore more vulnerable to attack.

A more persistent mystery, meanwhile, was what the turtles were doing out there at all—a mystery not just to us but to scientists through the centuries. What is known about those that live in the Atlantic is that during their early years, aided by the Gulf Stream, they migrate from the beaches of Florida and the Caribbean across thousands of miles of open sea into the coastal waters of west-central Europe, then south down the coast of Spain into the trade winds and, like ourselves, back across the Atlantic to the Caribbean.

Unlike writers, only turtles with a flawless inheritance of brain chemistry survive to tell the tale. During a leatherback or loggerhead's early years, if the brain's proportioning of magnetite is not infinitesimally attuned to the ever-shifting forces of the earth's magnetic field, the turtle on its initial passage east will drift too far north into waters that are too cold for its survival, or too far south, where there is too little food to sustain it.

While the first leg of a young turtle's long round trip between the Caribbean and Europe can be accomplished in some 240 days, the trip as a whole, it is now believed, can last for years, including long periods during which the turtles take up semi-permanent existence in the food-rich waters of that part of the mid-Atlantic known as the Sargasso Sea. They can live to be a hundred years old and in the years following their gradual maturation will often resume their trans-oceanic migrations, perhaps part of a grand mating or sustenance plan or some heroically protracted effort to sustain their worldwide range.

From the turtle's point of view, the mystery might well have been: what was *Big Blue* doing out there? What was any boat doing out there? Nothing in a sea turtle's deepest inherited memory could possibly explain to it— could *ever* have explained—the sudden appearance some five centuries ago of large wooden whales and, eventually, steel whales moving across the surface of the tropical Atlantic on more or less the turtle's own migration routes. From the human perspective, it seems astonishing that it *was* only 500 years ago that Europeans and Middle Easterners found the courage to venture out into the mid-Atlantic, which for centuries they had referred to as "the outer sea." The Mediterranean was the "inner sea," the safe one, a sea that had been enough for them for several thousand years—or at least until 700 BC, when the first Phoenician traders sailed west through the Strait of Gibraltar and down the coast of what is now

Morocco. They did so in search of a vivid purple dye that the coastal dwellers had learned to extract from the murex snail—an elegant, fist-sized mollusk that lived off the coast in the vicinity of what is now Agadir. The Phoenicians had long traded for the dye overland, creating a demand for it among the rulers and courts of Babylonia and the Middle East. But they craved more than could be brought back on the long desert treks. So they defied death at sea to get to it and are said to have paid plenty to the coastal dwellers for the right to harvest it directly.

During the ensuing thousand years, the murex trade became so important both to the suppliers and to the Middle Eastern consumers that the mollusk is commemorated to this day on the Moroccan 200-dirham note, one of the fundamental denominations of the country's currency, worth about forty dollars.

So the starting place for our journey was more significant to the history of Atlantic seafaring than we had known. And also to the broader coastal history of the Atlantic. For it was on the west coast of Africa, south of our departure place, that the earliest human beings first saw the ocean. During a period of hundreds of thousands of years, they had worked their way west across the desert and Serengeti Plain, arriving at the coast some 200,000 years ago. And from there had established the encampments and villages that are today some of Africa's foremost western ports.

What is commonly misunderstood about the ports and coastlines of the Atlantic is that they are anything but permanent fixtures. Because of the endless eruption and expansion along the Mid-Atlantic Ridge—in effect the meeting place of two great tectonic plates—the Atlantic widens by three or four inches a year, as it has been doing since its formation as a distinct body of water nearly 200 million years ago. When I mentioned to Tom one day that the ocean was at one time just a couple of hundred miles wide, he said immediately, "I could have rowed it by myself!" And he could have, except that until a few million decades ago it was a toxic stew of chemicals that would have immediately dissolved his boat. It is because of this modest annual widening that the Atlantic will, over the next 200 million years, evolve to where the world's continents are rearranged and the Atlantic will be reunited with the planet's other oceans as it was in the days when the earth's entire land mass was a single great continent, Pangaea.

The Norsemen, we now know, crossed the Atlantic as far as Newfoundland in AD 1100 but returned to northern Europe, leaving permanent settlement to a brace of colonial brigands such as Columbus, Cortés, de León, Cabot, et al. These legendary explorers were for the most part brilliant sailors but greedy and cruel men who brutalized the aboriginals and in some cases their own sailors and subordinates. Cortés in particular was a despot, as was Columbus who, despite his reputation as an American hero and champion of the New World, was known to beat his men for relatively modest offenses, even to blind them or cut out their tongues.

Amerigo Vespucci, the first explorer to touch mainland in the New World, was a talented scoundrel of another sort, reputed to have made his living as a pimp in Florence before setting sail and eventually lending his good name to what is now the Land of the Free. His publication *Mundus Novus,* written when he returned to Italy, enthuses over the culinary accomplishments of the New World aboriginals, over their immaculate anal cleanliness (always a plus), and over their lurid and joyful sexual practices.

The first rowers to cross the Atlantic, exactly four centuries later, were a pair of Norwegian-born fishermen named George Harbo and Frank Samuelsen, who during the early summer of 1896 rowed out of New York Harbor, heading for England in a custom-built open dory named the *Fox.* Their aim was to attract the attention of the world and eventually to grow wealthy on the returns they imagined would flow to them on an international lecture tour to be undertaken in the wake of their crossing.

Predictably, the trip was a nightmare. The adventurers had just one pair of gloves between them, had no seat cushions and no room to lie down or even take a step for fear of capsizing their eighteen-foot craft. Getting what sleep they could sitting up, they faced week-long gales, thirty-foot waves, severe headwinds, icebergs, fog, aggressive whales, boils, blisters, bad food, then no food at all after their provisions and fresh water went overboard just a quarter of the way across. Luckily, a ship came along and took them on board, fêting and dining them before sending them off with renewed provisions and water.

When they arrived in England fifty-five days after their departure, the skeletal and exhausted rowers were greeted by a few rubberneckers and were eventually presented with gold medals cast by the owner and editor of the *National Police Gazette,* Richard Fox, for whom they had named the boat in the hope that he would back them financially, which he never did.

WHILE RELUCTANT to claim kinship with those courageous and durable wild men, I suspect that life on our own rollicking vessel was pretty much as precarious and unforgiving as it had been aboard the *Fox.* But you wouldn't have known it on our eighth night out of

Tarfaya, as we slid across mirror-calm water beneath a panoply of rising and falling constellations.

On the 2-to-4 a.m., Steve and I had a long, humanizing chat about, among other things, his boyhood aloneness and insecurities. He had grown up on Toronto Island but lived winters in the core of the city, where his dad was a librarian and his mom a social activist who twice ran for political office under the banner of the New Democratic Party of Canada. As a kid, he had possessed little physical confidence until, one spring during the mid-1960s, in his eleventh or twelfth year, a neighbor showed him how to hit a baseball, which he learned to do with proud proficiency. However, he had few chances to demonstrate the skill until one day at Jesse Ketchum School, in central Toronto, he stepped to the plate in an inter-class baseball game, walloped the ball to the fence, and began excitedly to round the bases.

"I got close to first," he said, turning on the rowing seat, "and suddenly, as a joke, the first baseman yanked up the base, so that I had no place to go and they were able to tag me out."

No amount of pleading to the teachers overseeing the game reversed a prankish injustice to which Steve responded with what he described as "a frustrated, angry, tearful burst of profanity." The outpouring, aimed at everybody present, including his teachers, led to the principal's office, to the strap, to suspension, to his dad's intervention, to grudging reinstatement—all of this without any expression of understanding or compassion from the principal or teachers that might have restored an insecure child's faith in a cruel and unaccommodating world.

He recalled with equal solemnity having purchased an entire box of bagged potato chips to give to the island kids in the hope that he might find friends among them.

When they'd eaten the chips, he explained, "They tied me up, dragged me to my parents' home, and left me on the verandah."

In attempt to brace him, and as a bit of a joke, I quoted him the Robert Frost lines, "Better to go down dignified / with boughten friendship at your side / than none at all..." etc. He responded that the lines had been written for him—would I write them down? They were the first of several such quotations that I would scribble out for him: half-forgotten snippets of Auden and Eliot and Dickinson, and of the Winnipeg poet George Amabile, whose observation that "the heart of existence is untranslatable," became for us a kind of mantra, a recurring point of reference, during the long nights of conversation.

Steve married for the first time during his early twenties, and now, at 3 a.m., on the high Atlantic, he suspended his oar, turned to me on the seat, and with barely contained glee said, "This isn't for public consumption, but the day I got married I wore a baby-blue tux with wide velvet lapels."

I said, "No wonder the marriage didn't last!" However, it did yield a son, Jeremy, and eased Steve toward medical studies at McMaster University in Hamilton, Ontario, where he met his current wife, Janet.

Like Steve, she is a friend of mine, and as Steve and I spoke, the younger of their two sons, Nigel, was asleep within seven or eight feet of us, on the other side of the cabin wall. It was no secret that Janet had been anything but sanguine about Steve having drawn Nigel into this "crazy-assed plan" to row across the Atlantic. She said to me quite nonchalantly one day about a year before the expedition set off that it was "one thing for Steve to do something like this on his own," and that if the boat went down and he was lost at sea, she'd be able to handle it (he'd had a good run, his insurance was paid up, thanks for the memories). "But if Nigel was ever lost," she said, "I'd never get over it; I'd want to die myself."

What had become obvious by this time was that whereas Steve was generally perceived to be Nigel's support and guardian on the voyage, Nigel was at least equally Steve's anchor, and I thought went a distance to keeping his dad balanced with his unwavering equanimity and his refusal to get caught up in cabin politics. In this he was an example to everybody, as was his quiet companion, Zach, a muscular, understated kid, a non-complainer, with a kind of "configurative" habit of mind. "Got any riddles?" he said to me one afternoon when he was rowing and I wasn't. I had not given a moment's thought to "riddles" in half a century. However, as I was about to tell him I didn't know any, one of my great-grandmother's was suddenly in my head, then burbling off my tongue:

I'm the beginning of every ending,
The end of every place,
The beginning of eternity,
The end of time and space.

"What am I?" I said, and within seconds, everybody on the port hull was fussing with possibilities.

It was Zach who, perhaps five minutes later, as I scrubbed at a few clothes, said quietly, "The letter *e*"—the correct answer but one that relative to the eloquent expectations raised by the riddle had always disappointed me as a kid.

I had never heard anybody actually "get" the riddle, so that from that point forward Zach possessed for me a level of eminence as the guy who got the *e* riddle—connecting him of course to my great-grandmother, who would have been impressed by his sagacity, as well as by the fact that Zach's ribcage was emblazoned with a tattoo the size of a street sign. The image morphed a range of spiritual and cultural symbols into the word COEXIST and was perfect ink for a guy who got along with everybody and in the summer traveled deep into the forests of northern Ontario, fighting fires, preserving the ecological COEXISTENCE of timber wolves and black bears and bald eagles.

OVERALL, we were still attempting to move southwest toward the Cape Verde Islands, where our sustaining hope was that we would eventually find our way into the trades. Before sunset on the night of our conversation, Steve had familiarized himself with the boat's autopilot system, and in the middle of the 2-to-4 a.m. had gotten up and adjusted our bearing so that we were moving more directly with a westbound wind that was beginning to swell and to interfere with our rowing. The autopilot was straightforward: a compass with a digital readout, a handful of computerized electronics, and a rather frail-looking hydraulic arm that attached to a brace linking the rudders. The navigator had only to set a bearing (taken in our case from the GPS on the bridge or in Angela's hideaway) and the little electronic pilot did the rest, compensating constantly for wind and current.

To be clear, Steve's emergence as a navigator was his own doing, perhaps sanctioned by David, who as the boat's builder had access to the controls. But it was in no way approved by Angela, our official navigator, or by Margaret, who assisted her with navigation. When Margaret came out at 4 a.m., she assessed the altered bearing and, undoubtedly aware it had been changed, promptly changed it back, making the rowing more difficult again.

Steve, to his credit, was unwilling to see Nigel, Zach, and the others on their watch take the spanking we had avoided because he had adjusted the setting. As he rose from the trench, he all but leapt at Margaret on the bridge, challenging her on why she'd do such a thing.

"Because that's where David wants it," she said (the subtext of the remark being a rather hearty *So shove it up your kazuzu*).

Having come late to the expedition, Margaret hadn't a clue about the nature of some of the relationships aboard, in particular the ties between Steve and David, who at several points during the past year had worked with great determination and mutual respect to salvage the voyage when it had been about to tank. Margaret might better have invoked Angela. In citing David, she had played directly into the hands of Steve, who went immediately to David's bunk and got him to acknowledge that the new setting was fine, could stay where it was—which it did, to Margaret's annoyance and humiliation.

But the incident marked a change in Steve's gradual insinuation back into the running of the boat.

AS THE DAWN watch began atop a now-rolling sea, Steve, still in a mood to talk, initiated a memoirist's assessment of his complex marriage to Janet, who like him is a physician and, by his assessment, "the only person on earth" who understands him. In recent years they have taken different paths, Janet's into clinical practice in the little northern railway town of Bruce Mines, Ontario, Steve's into more-or-less full retirement from medicine.

Nigel's participation aside, Janet's quarrel with the voyage was that like many such schemes, it consumed the energy and time not just of its participants but of others, if not everybody, around them. "For over a year, Steve and I have both been *totally* sucked into this *Big Blue* vortex," she told me in December of 2009. "There's a real selfishness to these extreme commitments that I doubt many of you guys have thought much about."

She is no flannelmouth, and as expenses mounted, she told Steve at one point to "quit spending my money on this thing." But she was a collaborator too—had, for example, bought herself a rowing machine so that she could share in the experience. And thus they rowed together in the basement rec room of their rural home, in front of a television monitor, often watching reruns of the show *House,* which is about (wait for it) the private and professional lives of strong-willed physicians.

"It was a challenge," Steve told me over his shoulder, allowing that his marriage itself had been a challenge—more for Janet, he acknowledged, than for himself. Which is hardly surprising, given Steve's hard-driving ways—ways complicated, albeit, by nuance and doubt and perhaps more so by his sometimes disarming vulnerability.

As the watch deepened, Steve's voice dropped. Or maybe my ears were getting deafer, a result of the salt water that on some watches sloshed into them three or four times an hour. For a day or more they had been itchy and scabby, and I had noticed a reddish-brown discharge seeping from them. Initially, I had assumed it was a species of wax, a protection of some sort, and not the persistent and ugly bacterial infection that it turned out to be. (Sea water, while a purifier, is also a contaminant bristling with bacteria that tend to fester in warm, damp conditions, such as in an ear canal.)

About halfway through the watch I told Steve I couldn't hear him properly unless I quit rowing and leaned in toward him. I assumed, with regret, that it would end our conversation, and took it as a measure of his desire to unburden that he immediately urged me to go ahead. Which I did—and was rewarded. For during the last forty minutes of the watch, in the half-light of the coming dawn, Steve offered up a jeweler's portion of bright revelations about himself that I was still sifting several hours later as I went to my notes. He said, for example, that one of his frustrations in life was that he had never figured out what to do with the several great truths that had been revealed to him thus far: among them that he was alone (as both Buddhism and experience made clear); that he was not going to get the world he wanted (as experience had also made clear); and that he was thereby never going to get what he wanted from the world. He told me with a straight face (although with perhaps a twist of irony) that, much like his ambition on the Atlantic, his life's ambition was to get as "quickly and constructively as possible to the finish line and to check out, to have it done with, neatly tied off." My own ambition, I told him (also much like my ambition on the Atlantic), was to imbed as deeply as possible in the ride, to give to it what I could, and to deal with the messes as they came. "And to try not to be too big an asshole," I told him.

"Which must be difficult for you," he brightened, giving me a chastened laugh, not to mention a dose of perspective, as I returned to my oar.

Of the night watches, the 6-to-dawn was invariably the toughest. Not only did it explode any vestiges of the circadian rhythms to which we might have been clinging but brought with it an almost anguished anticipation of daylight—so painfully slow to arrive as the clock ticked to 7:30 then 7:45, and the sky along the eastern horizon turned from charcoal to gray to cobalt, sometimes to lilac or diluted blood.

Our little foursome rowed solemnly through the last quarter hour, until eventually the first tracer of fire came boiling across the water, and the sun popped out of the sea, as it does in the equatorial latitudes. Backlit by the sunrise, Sylvain appeared on deck, then the others, straggling out of the cabin. And thus the watch ended, and I tossed my cushion to Margaret, and in a somber mood went inside and attempted to get some sleep.

FROM THE BEGINNING I had been warned that of the
daily torments at sea, the sun would be the most
insidious. It could roast you, dehydrate you, give you
skin cancer, cause strokes, destroy your vision. When
Angela had vetted my kit, which contained three tubes of
45 SPF sunblock, she had virtually demanded that I go to
Marjane for at least three more.

So I was surprised after two weeks on the water that I
was one of just a handful of people aboard who seemed
to have any real apprehension about the sun. Steve and
Ryan were already "black" from it, and Angela was
"toasting up good," as I heard her describe her evolving tan when she was on the SAT phone with Deb one
night. Meanwhile, Zach and Margaret, and to a lesser
degree David and Aleksa, had endured angry sunburns
and seemed a trifle casual in their lack of concern over
the damage the sun can inflict at latitudes so close to
the equator. Indeed, that afternoon, four of the women
initiated a nude row on the noon-to-2, claiming the starboard hull for themselves and exchanging their already

infinitesimal skimpies for inflatable Mae Wests—worn commando, as Mae would have worn one.

It was not my watch, so I spent most of it inside, nibbling and note-taking, then catching a brief nap. When I stuck my head out at about 1:45 I was impressed to see the girls, full starkers, tugging away at a nice ocean pace of about eighteen a minute. I was more impressed yet to see that the third seat, where Angela had rowed briefly before succumbing to back pain, was now occupied by my Austrian watchmate, Ernst Fiby, even nakeder than the women in that he had no life preserver on and was shaved entirely of both head and body hair. He *was* wearing his iPod, reminding me of the old story about Marilyn Monroe, who when asked if she had anything on during one of her bathtub scenes, replied, "I had the radio on."

Ernst's compulsive attention to his anatomy was "very Austrian," I had been assured by Tom, who in his own steady exactitude was "very Swiss," according to Ernst. The two would eventually row with Steve, who referred to the three of them as the Squarehead Watch, although Tom was quick to remind anybody that Roedde was "the only true Kraut" and that a significant part of the Swiss and Austrian identity was that they were "*not* blockheads," as Tom put it, but "just the more regular kind of excessive fanatic." Ernst's flawless hygiene included a more or less daily shave, top to bottom, and a freshwater minishower after every watch, followed by a squirt of Givenchy cologne. He was not merely our sweetest-smelling crew member but was arguably our most talented athlete, having been both a competitive cyclist and a member of Austria's national junior soccer team, a feeder program for the country's highest-level professional club. In reality, he was from the old Czechoslovakia, but had left that country as a boy during the most oppressive days of Eastern Bloc communism and had fled to Vienna with his Czech mother, a bookstore manager, and his Austrian dad, now a Viennese railway administrator.

Like Steve, Nigel, Ryan, Liz, and David, Ernst's association with *Big Blue* went back to the original tryouts in March 2009—to which he had been attracted, he told me, by "an alwayz big interest in cracy adventure." Ernst was a far tougher rower than I but could be a trifle loose in his focus, especially with his iPod on. So, particularly in the early days of the crossing, he would occasionally clatter his oar off Liam's or Steve's, sending Liam in particular into exaggerated histrionics: *Fer krissakes, Ernst, what is the problem? Is this going to go on all the way to Barbados? If you can't stay in sync with me, YOU get up here and set the stroke!* Sometimes Ernst would do that, leading to new levels of rasping and gasping, as well as pleas from Steve that he speed it up or slow it down or even it out.

I knew that if it had been me in the number two seat (which it would never have been, given that the number two rower is a kind of sub-lieutenant who must be steady enough to hold the stroke and occasionally to set it), there would have been a good deal more rattling and prattling than there was. To his great credit, Ernst held both his tongue and his ground, never fired back, answering them rather with the unspoken message that he was doing what he could and that if it was not good enough for them they could (as I heard him say in private one day) "put it up thare arzzes." Which eventually they did, metaphorically, perhaps having come to an appreciation of Ernst's persistence and durability, not to mention his reluctance to spill, to sound off, to fall into the pessimism and nattering that too often characterized life aboard.

Ernst was not alone in elevating shaving to an extreme sport—or at least a twisted one, considering the contortions that must be required to shave one's upper back or, say, bottom end. Ryan too shaved his back and torso at one point, or had it shaved for him. And Margaret cut his hair—"Aussie style," she said, although I can think of other adjectives that might describe a cut whose chief feature was a three-inch-wide possum's back running from the middle of his forehead to the nape of his neck. The rest of his skull was a kind of goat pasture of tumbleweed and stubble, some of it half-an-inch long, some chipped hard to the scalp.

Unbeknownst to the happy hairdressers, Angela had, during Ryan's haircut, been in her bivouac stewing about the disappearance of her prized kit scissors (surgical steel, officially approved)—*where could they be?* She has a vulgar streak, bless her heart, and when she was informed that Margaret was cutting Ryan's hair with the cherished implements—repeat: *was cutting Ryan's hair, including perhaps his body hair, with her personal and beloved kit scissors*—it was too much for her, and she declared sarcastically that it might have been nice if they'd asked permission because just maybe she'd wanted to cut her own hair, if anybody cared, and that just maybe she'd wanted to cut her *pubic hair,* if anybody cared (the lot of these absurdist theatrics captured for the ages because Dylan just happened, at that point, to have his video camera rolling).

Meanwhile, Ernst and I were the only crew members who bothered shaving our faces—he for aesthetics, I because I didn't like the feel of the dried salt in even a quarter inch of stubble. Every second day or so, in the absence of a mirror and warm water, I would rub a little lubricant onto my face and go to work with razors that in the salty air were quickly rusty, corroded, and stubble-clogged. During the course of the voyage, invariably working blind, I experimented with a variety of "shaving creams," including sea water, Vaseline, sunscreen, argan oil, and "creamy" Vietnamese coffee (which, curiously, worked as well as anything). One night when sleep was difficult I sat up and shaved in the dark, dry, feeling rather proud of myself for this rare if modest accomplishment (especially under conditions in which I was at one moment tipping into the aisle, the next bouncing headfirst off the bunk ceiling).

Once finished I would solicit an assessment from Nigel, who more than some was sympathetic to the boat's resident Boswell—or perhaps more accurately because I trusted his judgment and tolerance not just in pointing out stray whiskers but in all the boat's business. Nigel had been a track star at Lakehead University in Thunder Bay and until recently had worked as a personal trainer at the GoodLife gym in Guelph. He shared his dad's sense of fairness and integrity but was "probably a better team guy," as he put it. He was certainly lighter of spirit—due in part, I suspect, to a contented and confident childhood, some of which was spent with his brother Zack on couches in the emergency wards of northern Ontario, when his parents were called to work and were unable to arrange care for their boys. It was Nigel and Steve's shared fixation with "excellence," as Steve called it, that the previous autumn had led the pair to Toronto, where they settled onto rowing machines at the Toronto Island Rowing Club and did not get off for more than twenty-four hours. By that time their backsides were pulp but they had set new world records for a day's distance on a stationary rowing machine (good preparation, joked Steve, for the effort they were now making on an all-but-stationary boat).

LATE ON THE night of the women's naked row, amid the usual high crosswinds and a light but persistent rain, I spotted a ship's lights perhaps half a mile away and clearly coming toward us. During daylight, you could see what you were up against with passing or approaching vessels—a tanker, a container ship, a bulk carrier. But at night, because you could not judge the distance, you could not tell how big a vessel was. A sardine trawler at close range made more or less the same impression as a major freighter a mile or two away. Admittedly, most of the really big vessels, the tankers or container ships, were floodlit and stood out. Not so every deteriorating little breadfruit or scrap carrier from Angola or Namibia.

This particular vessel seemed to be heading east, probably toward Nouakchott or Dakar, but so far had given us no indication of whether it would pass behind us or go across our bow—or perhaps come directly down on top of us, which for the past ten days, in the shipping lanes off the coast, had been one of my sporadic neuroses. Small boats had been hit in the past by freighters coming out of fog or darkness too late to avoid them, and I had only to think for a microsecond about an eight-storey-high freighter bearing down on us at close range to set me glancing around nervously in search of something as insubstantial as a sixty-watt running light on the fo'c'sle of some moldering Mauritanian scrap-bucket. I recalled from my days on the MV *Paterson* that small boats did not always show up very clearly on even a well-equipped vessel's radar or scanning system and did not show up at all (or at least to anybody) if the boat was on autopilot and the mate and wheelsman were plastered or asleep.

It was at night, too, that the specter of piracy tended to slither out of the darkness into one's skull. If we were to be taken, it would most likely be here off the coast of Mauritania or Senegal, two of the poorest and most desperate countries on earth.

"What have we got that pirates would *want?*" somebody had laughed in the cabin a couple of days earlier.

"Us!" blurted Ernst, who works in the shipping industry and can cite chapter, verse, and line on any number of contemporary high-seas crimes. One of piracy's commonest forms these days—a form that eliminates having to sell a tanker-load of oil or a couple of million pounds of ore on the black market—is to take a boatload of hostages and demand a ransom for their freedom. Which was Ernst's point. Americans are a preferred target. We had six of them on board—and the Stars and Stripes flying from the bridge. All of which gave me to wonder whether David, a guy who once routinely carried a revolver, had stashed any sort of weapon on the boat. I will say that he had both the wiles and the guts to take what measures might have been necessary to protect himself and the crew. Not only had he encountered his share of pirates in Tbilisi after the Georgian civil war, he had spent his early years in the U.S. playing and winning a high-stakes mind game with American immigration authorities. David entered the country legally via a farm exchange program in 1995, at the age of twenty, was given a one-year working visa, and went to work on a fruit farm in Hawaii. Unhappy with his prospects, he left the program voluntarily after a few weeks and took a job in a building supply store on Maui. Six months later, thirsty for adventure, he flew to California and from there, sometimes hitchhiking, made his way to Long Island to be with friends who had also come from Georgia on the farm exchange program.

Today, happily, David lives and works legally on Long Island. However, for several years after his arrival on the east coast he tiptoed around the authorities, working in marinas in Florida and New York, quietly learning the trade that would eventually make it possible for him to run Shelter Island Boats and to put our own audacious vessel on the Atlantic.

The ship that had originally set me guessing passed behind us—but too close, it seemed, for a ship that had properly seen us on its radar. An hour later, a mysterious red light came bobbing into view at some indeterminable distance off the port hull. It occurred to me that it might be an illicit vessel, although we ultimately decided it was the mast light on a sailboat whose hull was below the horizon line. As it blinked from sight, I heard a disturbance in the water about fifty feet away. Steve had been having trouble with his Crohn's and was up from his seat. I mentioned it to Ernst, and as we squinted into the rain we heard a lengthy whistling exhalation that I am certain was a very large whale, undoubtedly more aware of us, with its delicate sensors, than we were of it. Sure enough, a few seconds later, the musk of its immense breath, smelling more like a barnyard than the sea, was briefly in the air around us.

While I harbor no specific wariness of sea creatures, it spooked me to consider that intelligent mammals a hundred times the mass of our boat, some of them shepherding babies ten times our size, were cruising the surface waters within a stone's throw of us, or perhaps passing directly underneath, just a few feet beneath our rudders. If they had surfaced from there, either in curiosity or perceived self-defense, as whales have occasionally been known to do, we would have been immediately in the sea and swimming for our lives.

Through all of this the wind was picking up and the rain falling more persistently. During a downpour a couple of days earlier I had been razzed for taking sanctuary in the cabin, so was determined this time to stay put and row. Besides, I was caked in salt from a dozen good dousings earlier in the day and saw it as an opportunity to clean up. Often the rain showers were so brief that it wasn't worth taking your clothes off. And yet with a day of dried salt in your hair and on your back, you craved uncontaminated skin. Unfortunately, it could never quite be achieved, since the salt saturates the deepest levels of the dermal tissue. Eventually it pools into subsurface pockets that create little red bumps, some as big as watermelon seeds. After a day or two, these begin to leak, forming salt sores that can get infected and itchy before they eventually start to dry out—or not dry out, as the case might be. More than anybody, Aleksa was suffering from them—hundreds of them, covering her thighs and ankles and wrists. Before every watch, she dutifully anointed and covered them, sometimes with tubes of fabric cut from leggings or stretch pants, and out she went to row. I'd see her in her bunk after a watch—sometimes, it seemed, on the edge of tears—and while she was occasionally cited for her tendency to disappear for a few minutes during a watch (the idea was that we were to use the head *between* watches), I thought it commendably tenacious that she was out there rowing at all, and rowing well.

Irrespective of the sores themselves, there is a kind of agony that derives from salt crystallizing and accumulating on the skin, an occasionally crazy-making torment that sometimes at night would set me twisting and scratching, practically delirious for a bucket of fresh water, or even a quart or a cup. For that reason, when the rainfall persisted, I stood up and removed my jacket and T-shirt, then my slush pants and everything else and, in the warmish rain, enjoyed perhaps the best cleansing I had had since Agadir.

top Nigel and Steve Roedde (left and right) during training at Shelter Island, New York.

above The city of Agadir and the Atlantic Ocean, seen from Agadir's mountaintop kasbah.

top Outfitting *Big Blue* at the boatyard in Agadir.

above Launching *Big Blue*, Agadir.

top *Big Blue* leaving Morocco, the Atlas Mountains visible in the background.

above Crew meeting in Tarfaya, at the edge of the Sahara, while *Big Blue*'s rudders are lodged deep in the sand.

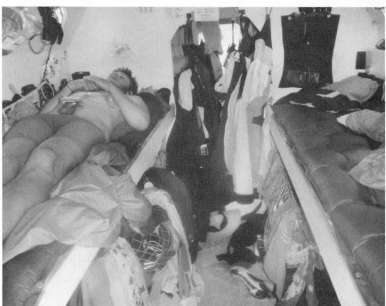

top Ryan Worth and Zach Scher (left and right)—big smiles, meagre meal.

above The stifling interior of *Big Blue*'s cabin.

from top, clockwise Captain Angela, Dylan White,
Tom Butscher, Sylvain Croteau, David Davlianidze.

top Steve Roedde and Sylvain Croteau (left and right) on a day when 40 mph headwinds made rowing impossible.

above Nigel Roedde concentrating on his oar on a rough day in the trade winds.

top Heavy weather: Margaret Bowling (foreground) and Sylvain Croteau struggle to control their oars.

above From left: Liz Koenig, Louise Graff, and Liam Flynn, looking into a mid-Atlantic sunrise.

top *Big Blue*'s arrival in Port St. Charles, Barbados.

above Safe across and celebrating. Top row (left to right): Ernst Fiby, Steve Roedde, Liz Koenig, Louise Graff, Dylan White, Liam Flynn, Ryan Worth. Middle row: David Davlianidze, Zach Scher, Nigel Roedde, Margaret Bowling. Front row: Angela Madsen, Tom Butscher, Sylvain Croteau, Charlie Wilkins, Aleksa Klimas-Mikalauskas.

WHILE WE DID NOT yet know it, the Cape Verde Islands would figure rather dramatically in the evolving shenanigans of the Little Big Blue Theater Company. For now, it is enough to consider that some of the worst tropical storms in the world develop in the area directly over that storied archipelago. Warmed by the tepid shallow water of the islands, rising columns of moist air can initiate immense atmospheric swirls, some of which eventually become hurricanes. Indeed, as many as fifteen times a year, such disturbances find their way into the trade winds and are pushed out onto the Atlantic, with hellish effects—or, in more severe cases, are driven fully across to the islands of the Caribbean and the shores of North America. Hurricane Katrina, which destroyed New Orleans, was just one of dozens of recent tempests that rocked out of the cradle off the western-most coastline of Africa.

Understandably, even the largest and toughest-hulled vessels stay away from the seventy-foot waves and hun-dred-mile-an-hour winds that are often the result of these storms; and no captain or crew wants to be in the vicinity of the Cape Verde Islands, or on the tropical Atlantic at all, when such weather is on the loose. But it was exactly where we happened to be at that moment, and for that reason I was jittery in the hour before dawn of our eleventh day out of Tarfaya as Steve and I watched a succession of bluey-green bolts of lightning split the eastern sky perhaps fifteen miles away. Around us, the wind began to drop, as it is said to do in the minutes before coastal storms begin to spin themselves into the vortices that can become hurricanes.

What we couldn't tell at that point was whether the evolving disturbance was receding or coming toward us, and I was reluctant to report my nervousness, for fear it would seem ridiculous or even cowardly when the others were clearly rather nonchalant about our circumstances. In theory it was not the right time of year for tropical storms; the meteorologists knew it, and so did we. The question was, did the lightning know it—and if it did, why was it pitching billion-volt teasers when it was supposed to be taking a few months off? We had carefully chosen our departure date so as to avoid storms and hurricanes, which in the northern hemisphere occur mostly between early summer and late fall. However, rogue storms have been known to blow well into December or even into the new year—more so these days than in the past, as the warming of the seas contributes to a more persistent rise of heated air and a less predictable season of gales.

The result was that despite my knowing better (despite my *wanting* to know better), it was storms—the *possibility* of storms—that more than any other threat to our well-being had galvanized my attention. During the earliest days of my participation I had meticulously assessed the increasing randomness of hurricanes on the Atlantic and had weighed the minuscule likelihood of their occurrence during the weeks we would be out there. I hasten to say that since childhood, storms at sea, or on any big water, had been one of the foremost of my images of dread, particularly where boats and sailors were concerned. For that reason, I did not like the movies *Kidnapped* or *Mutiny on the Bounty*. And when I read in my Grade 5 history book the story of Henry Hudson and his ten-year-old son being set adrift by mutineers, I took it personally, imagining myself as the boy and suffering an anxiety about it all that in a sense lingers today. I was haunted similarly by the sinking of the *Andrea Doria* in 1956, and still find myself in knots as I look out across Whitefish Bay on Lake Superior to where the *Edmund Fitzgerald* went down in 1975.

I suspect that a portion of my anxiety about ocean storms is my lifelong (largely secret) paranoia about drowning or being lost at sea, both of which hearken intimately to my childhood. When I was nine, in Deep River, Ontario, one of my dad's English students at the high school, Jack Foster, who was also a family friend, drowned in a duck-hunting accident. I knew him well; he played on my dad's basketball and football teams. He had been hunting with an older man and had attempted to swim to shore after their canoe capsized in the icy November water. Halfway to land, he stopped swimming and called out, "I'm going down!"—words that echoed in my head for weeks after I was told what had happened, and that still have the power to rattle me.

I was troubled equally by the oft-repeated story of how my Uncle Edgar, a kid of eighteen on his way to war aboard an English merchant vessel in 1943, was torpedoed in the North Atlantic and, on his way home a year later, broken by stress, was hit again. While the details are sketchy, he is said to have spent days alone in a life-boat (and spent much of the rest of his life in a psychiatric institution in London, Ontario).

My conflation of the family destiny with disaster at sea is perhaps deepest rooted, however, in the events surrounding my dad's birth the day after the *Titanic* went down in April 1912. On the night of the disaster, my grandmother, Birdie Wilkins, wrote a letter to my great aunt, in which she expressed a wish that what had been for her an uncertain and agonizing pregnancy could *please* now just be over. Further down the page she lamented the loss of "all those lives aboard that big ship."

Her own life ended the following day while she was giving birth to my dad. I was not told until I was nearly ten years old, at which point an aunt read me my grand-mother's letter. I was an impressionable kid, and from the moment I heard the words I equated my grandmother's death and my dad's birth—and in a sense still do—with the loss of "all those lives aboard that big ship."

I had been aboard 700-foot bulk carriers on the Great Lakes during bad weather, had seen furniture in the cabins and heavy equipment on deck tossed around like toys (I am tempted to say like words). Ovide, the naval architect in Agadir, had been discreet in his assessment of *Big Blue*'s chances, but had volunteered at one point that a spidery craft like ours would do well to stay clear of storms. The catch was that on the night of January 26 we were going directly into the area where the severest of Atlantic storms are born and live out their wrathful and violent lives.

With all of this either awash or buried deep in my skull, I was intensely relieved (although did not say so) when, after an hour, the lightning retreated and the wind returned to normal, signs that the storm was moving east onto the Sahara or farther south down the coast, rather than west into my nightmares and neuroses.

Given such apprehensions, it is paradoxical that, like Moitessier, I continued to view the ocean largely as a sustainer rather than a denier of life. More importantly (and despite my skepticism about aspects of *Big Blue*'s construction), I have an intrinsic, almost loving faith in small boats—far more so than in ships. It is a confidence that goes back to my Uncle Clive, one of the finest boat-builders in the world during the palmy days of inboard mahogany luxury craft. And to my Grandpa Scholey, who as a young man in Bracebridge, Ontario, worked with Clive and who if he had a mallet, a cross-cut, and a plane could, without plans, build a rowboat out of a pile of scrap pine and have it painted your favorite color by the next day. And to my Uncle Hunter, who taught me how to read the wind and sail.

I had considerably less faith in my anatomy, and during the previous couple of days had abandoned my rowing gloves in an attempt to strengthen my hands. The calluses that had formed on the pads of my fingers and palms during the first ten days were intact, but the interior of the hands, the tendons and muscles and joints, had begun to ache and cramp. Some watches left me with salt-shriveled claws that took me several minutes to straighten once I got to my bunk. However, there was little I could do for my feet, which in the past week, rather than toughening as I had hoped, had been scored into blisters and abrasions where my perpetually waterlogged shoes had scoured away the skin.

The next morning, I spent fifteen minutes cleaning and taping them, and then fell deeply asleep. I wakened with a start at exactly ten o'clock and was three or four minutes late emerging from the cabin for the 10-to-noon watch. As I stepped down onto the tramp, I was surprised to find Liam sitting rather smugly in my seat, Steve in front of him as icy as a day in the Arctic. As usual, Ernst was toiling away with his iPod on, as impassive as ever to the politics of the watch.

I said to Liam, "What's up?" thinking that he had perhaps needed a break from the rigors of the stroke seat, which demands of its occupant constant focus and a strong steady rhythm, capabilities that I manifestly did not possess. Indeed, I was constantly grateful that I was able to row from behind, tucked into the bow end of the rowing trench, and that the inconsistencies of my rowing affected no one but myself.

"You're late," he said.

"Yes," I said, "I'm sorry about that. I've been doing my best to get out promptly."

He said, "Charlie, I've decided that every time you're late from now on, I'm going to take your seat and you can row up front."

I thought about this for a moment and said, "*You've* decided, have you?"

"Yes, I have," he said, as if addressing a recalcitrant spaniel. "If you want your seat you can get out here on time."

I considered taking an oar and cracking open his arrogant English head and, in as calm a voice as I could contrive atop my wrath, told him I didn't think it was the responsibility of an obviously self-righteous, obviously callow crewman—*mere* crewman, I emphasized, and *newcomer to the expedition*—to be disciplining me personally or to be assuming disciplinary powers over the boat. I added that I believed there were other ways of dealing with such issues and that I'd be happy to subject myself to them (which was a bucket of rubbish, in

that truly I had no idea what other measures there might
be for spanking an aging delinquent, and would have
been vilely unhappy to subject myself to them if I had
known). I told him that if he needed a break from setting
the stroke, which I knew was both difficult and draining,
all he had to do was ask, and I'd change places with him
anytime.

In the meantime, I said, if he felt it necessary to continue humiliating a fellow rower in front of the crew, I'd
simply relax for a couple of hours, or until he got out of
my seat, and let the rest of the watch row on its own.

At that point, I asked Steve and Ernst if either of *them*
wanted the stroke seat, reminding them that they'd be far
better occupants than I, since they were both much stronger rowers. I had rowed in the stroke seat only once prior,
during maneuvers at Shelter Island, and had been awful—
too fast, too slow, too jerky. And on that occasion the
water had been sheltered and calm by comparison to the
open sea. It was only Liz's patient advice that I should
raise my "top" elbow and push off methodically with my
legs before getting my arms involved that saved me an
hour of amateurish embarrassment. I knew Steve didn't
like the stroke seat any better than I did, probably for
the same reasons; and Ernst, who was effectively setting
the stroke as we haggled, had taken a turn or two in the
seat but, as stated, had been harassed over his inability
to establish a satisfactory pace. It was Liam's seat, plain
and simple: he had, like Harbo and Samuelsen, rowed
in open dories in the rough seas off the south coast of
England—was talented and durable, was in short the perfect pace-setter.

Meanwhile, as I withdrew along the tramp, it occurred
to me that I couldn't exactly retreat into the cabin, where
Sylvain was in the bunk, and that I would be far too

much in evidence if I simply hung around the bridge or on the far hull. Such was my hypocrisy that I did not particularly want Angela to see me screwing the pooch, much less behaving like an unruly school boy (one inks one's own tiny resume on an endeavor such as this, and it can survive only so many smudges).

Instead, with the faint taste of crow on my tongue, I eased myself under the safety wire and into the stroke seat. Having spread sunscreen on my shoulders and chest and adjusted my oar, I began a protracted fuss of wrapping my right foot in bits of sheepskin that had been given to me by Margaret. I would row, I had decided, or would at least attempt to, but at a pace that was comfortable for me, however excruciating it might be for the rest of them. I would begin only when I was good and ready.

Still fuming within, I hollered over my shoulder at Liam, above the wind, that his disciplinary measures didn't jibe with his usual ethic of squealing to the captain.

A little arpeggio of laughter (Ernst's) erupted behind me, spurring me to wonder, at volume, if Sheriff Roedde approved of his young deputy's tactics in punctuality enforcement.

When he responded rather weakly that he didn't know, another domino went down, and I hollered over my shoulder that I didn't think much of his abandonment and that since it was he who had started all this cowboy jingoism I thought he should at least figure out where he stood on it. Besides, I told him, I thought it was ironic that someone who had been touting discipline all along was now backing some two-bit species of anarchy.

At this point Liam's somewhat emasculated voice, as English as Her Majesty's, sounded from the rumble seat. "Charlie, how old are you?" he chirped.

"None'a your fucking business," I told him.

"Well, grow up!" he said, a joke so lame in the absence of its setup line that I felt I really ought to give him my age, so that he could start over and perhaps salvage the put-down, not to mention his pride as a wag.

When I had come out at the beginning of the watch, I had hoped to row with just one foot in the stirrups, bound in sheepskin, while the other foot, with the worst sores, rested to the side. All of which I could have managed in the rear seat, where the demands of the rowing were less persistent. But in the stroke seat I needed all the support I could get from my legs. So I stuck both feet in the stirrups, the left one unwrapped and thus unprotected from the Velcro'd harness that had helped create the sores in the first place. It was uncomfortable, to say the least, and within minutes had reversed every bit of healing that had taken place during the past day or two. At that point, however, I thought it best not to address the fact that the cause of this new aggravation was the moral officiousness of a pair of medical doctors for whom behavioral curatives obviously fell outside the Hippocratic Oath.

The curious thing was that even in my discomfort and ineptitude, I soon found myself enjoying the more demanding rowing, in effect controlling the rowers who had forced me to be where I was and who I imagined were now chafing under my rather inept leadership.

At watch's end, as I lay in my bunk nibbling a freeze-dried ice cream bar (think vanilla sponge toffee between chocolate cookies), I forgave myself utterly for the morning's theatrics. And forgave Liam and Steve, although not to their faces.

Since Liam was not yet in his seat when I appeared on deck for the 2-to-4 p.m., I claimed the stroke position for the second time and took a perverse pleasure in the bewildered looks of the others as they came on deck and rather distractedly took their seats. But none of them said a word, and we embarked on another two hours of haphazard stroking (made more comfortable for me by a thick layer of diaper rash cream beneath sheepskin atop both my feet).

For the 6-to-dusk, Liam was on deck and in his regular seat by the time I cleared the cabin. "You sure you wanta sit there?" I asked him as I passed on my way down the tramp, "I'm more than happy to set the stroke." To punctuate the farce, I told Steve it was great to know that under Liam's new disciplinary strictures all I had to do to gain command was show up a minute past the hour, a comment that probably had him resisting an urge toward homicide.

On the 10-to-midnight, Liam himself was late appearing on deck, giving me the opportunity to remind him of his responsibilities as a yobbish and insufferable young prig.

And that was that.

Later in the watch, when he came up to the bow to pee (where we all peed, to avoid having to go off the bridge into the wind), he gave me a peace offering of acidic candies (Frooties) and we had a laugh at the absurdities of the afternoon and never again got in one another's way—in fact were friends from that point forward.

The conclusion, I guess, was that his little gambit had worked, and I was a more experienced, if not a better, rower for it. And was probably a better person. I was certainly a more punctual person and, more importantly from my point of view, a less vulnerable person aboard the boat. The whole ridiculous exercise had given me to remember that, at age sixty-three, I had reserves not only for physical effort but for psycho-emotional preservation, and that anybody who pushed me around could count on my pushing back. While the culture on board was at least nominally that of a "team," dependent on intimate and constant cooperation, it was, like marriage, not a culture in which you could go without defenses. I had recently read a book called *Maximum City,* about Mumbai, where the population density, the highest on earth, is a cause both of trauma and indignity, and of immense chaos and squalor. It is a place where people need endless initiative and inner resources to survive. I had already calculated that *Big Blue*—Minimum City—had more than eight times the population density of Mumbai, and a proportionate measure of squalor. Independent of the broader stresses produced by a tiny boat's endurance on the Atlantic, it was no wonder we had, each of us, to hold our ground and occasionally to extend our claws in order to survive.

That said, it seemed to me of late that I was provoking more than my share of antipathy: from Liam, from Steve, from Margaret, occasionally from Ryan or Sylvain. Even Angela had singled me out the previous day—unjustifiably, I felt—over the careless husbandry of my dishes and eating utensils. She had refused to prepare my noodles at lunch because she didn't have a proper container to put them in. I explained to her that I had left my big purple mug outside her bivouac, as she had requested, and felt aggrieved when she said she hadn't noticed it and had assumed I'd lost it overboard as I'd lost so many of my other items.

I am not overly concerned about how others see me, but nor did I want to become a pariah on a small, crowded boat where there was no hope of even temporary sanctuary. That afternoon, I asked Steve what he thought it was about my attitude that was pissing so many people off. In a sense I was setting myself up, but I trusted him. I told him I'd noticed that the more crap he threw at Angela regarding her captaincy, the more she seemed to cleave to him, to respect him.

"I think it's your arrogance," he told me, half joking, to which I responded that I couldn't think of one thing I'd done aboard, including showing up late for watch, that was inarguably arrogant.

He looked at me with a very precise Charlie Chan grin and said, "No, but writing about it is."

I thought about this for a moment and allowed that maybe it was true, but only in a sense so broad as to be almost meaningless. Deep down, I believed something less direct had raised Liam's hackles—something beyond the mere fact of my showing up late for watch or my intent to write about the voyage. If it had been Tom or Louise or David, he would not have reacted as he did. And he would not have gotten away with it if he had; no one would have tolerated it. If I were to guess, I'd say he had become emboldened under Steve's influence and, in that mode, had loaded up his side-iron as much for Steve's approval as for the collective well-being of the boat.

Liam would eventually fall into his own version of the Delinquent Life of Charles, evident to the rest of us when, a little later in the voyage, in the middle of the night, he began getting up out of the stroke seat perhaps once a watch and disappearing mysteriously beyond the bridge, sometimes for as long as ten or twelve minutes. One night on the 2-to-4 a.m., Steve asked me in genuine puzzlement, "Where do you think Liam goes when he gets up?" Out of respect for his rowing, nobody questioned his choosing to take a break in the middle of the night if that's what he wanted to do.

"I guess he's eating," I said. "He must be hungry." However, why anybody would be eating in the smelly blackness of the cabin at three in the morning, with no place to sit and nothing to eat but protein turds, was beyond my reckoning. And so the mystery continued, until one day, quite out of the blue, I heard someone from the other watch mention casually that Liz seemed to be exhausted—couldn't get through a watch in the middle of the night without a ten-or-twelve-minute break.

In retrospect, I am amused by my naïveté. The "friendship" so obvious between Liz and Liam during the daytime had clearly become a night-timer, and since they were hot-bunking anyway, it was but a trifle for them to timetable a bit of snogging during the wee hours.

In daylight, Liz would often sit for an hour on one of the stern holds in front of Liam as he rowed—talking softly, telling stories, or simply smiling or gazing (she had the readiest and most engaging of smiles). Or she would appear with her camera and take half a dozen close-ups of the young doctor from Norwich and his oar.

In the sun, Liam wore an unlikely black hat, a kind of Tilley affair, high-tech, that was a size too small for him, so that it sat high on his conk, giving him the appearance of a mad Jesuit or sixteenth-century Inquisitionist. I had been intrigued to hear that in his interview for admission to medical school at the University of East Anglia, in Norwich, near his home, he had, rather than wallow or fabricate when asked why he wanted to be a physician, recited the hoary old dick-tickler "Invictus," by William Ernest Henley, which for rhetorical extravagance puts even "If" by Rudyard Kipling in the shade. "I am the master of my fate, I am the captain of my soul." Beyond his poetical choices, I thought it bold of Liam to have taken the time off before his graduation exams, running the risk of messing up his career, to row across the ocean.

One terrible night, about two weeks hence, in heavy seas and hard rain, I stood up for a break at the end of the 2 a.m. watch, turned to the bow of the boat and

simply stared into the night as the hull rose and fell perhaps twenty feet at a bounce. For nearly two hours, I had
taken one wave after another, and was at the end of my
tolerance. Dylan, who had been rowing in front of me,
had retreated to the bridge, and Ernst was sitting with
his head between his knees as sea water teemed onto his
back. I didn't know where Liam was—didn't know much
at all at that moment, except that I was cold and cored,
and my hips and shoulders ached, and more than anything I wanted the watch to be over so that I could get
inside into the bunk where for two blessed hours I would
not have to row. As I stood in that benumbed state, a pair
of jacketed arms slipped in under mine from behind and,
before I had had a chance to react, gripped me in such a
powerful embrace that I could not move—and after a few
seconds didn't want to, such was the warmth and reassurance of this anonymous and welcome hug. As the seconds
passed, and the embrace held, I permitted myself a kind
of cottony descent into whatever vortex or rabbit hole
seemed suddenly to be opening beneath me. It was not
the first time, in the exhaustion of the wee hours, that I
had experienced some private level of transport, perhaps
even hallucination, but it was the first time under near-
torturous conditions that I had felt buoyed or comforted
by whatever forces were afoot within or around me. For
what seemed five minutes but was probably no more than
ten seconds, I indulged in the sensation of being suspended, then of falling, and on a whim reached back over
my shoulders, thinking to grip the head of whoever was
accompanying me down.

But there was no head. And now no arms. And I turned,
expecting to see Louise or Sylvain or Steve, all of whom
are huggy sorts of people. But it was slim Liam Flynn
who was standing there on the tramp, perhaps five feet

behind me, wearing a spectral grin in the shadowy red glow of the trench lights. We stared briefly at one another, and I said, "Thank you, Liam—I appreciated that."

But he did not speak, and in the seconds that followed, time collapsed, and I was asleep in my bunk and then awake again as the ten-minute call sounded, and we were up and frantic and scrambling to get out the door before the sea shaman snatched us.

Not everybody, incidentally, was enthralled with Liz and Liam's rather impressive abandonment of decorum. I heard one crew member say she "thought less of Liz" for keeping herself engaged on the night shift. But the comment may have been mere envy. Perhaps typically, any disapproval of Liam had more to do with his occasional shirking of responsibilities than being a bit of a sport. Personally, I thought *more* of Liz for her attitude and activities, whatever they amounted to. It does after all take gumption and imagination—not to mention a certain discreet athleticism—to enact a restrained pas de deux over a period of weeks in a bedroom the size of a steamer trunk shared with fifteen other people. As I told Liz during the weeks after getting back, I'd rather be in the *Guinness Book of World Records* for what she and Liam achieved than for getting quickly across the Atlantic (I doubt somehow that there were many romances aboard *Hallin* or *Sara G*). She responded rather coyly and with a trace of indignation, "Liam and I were very special friends, but we were just friends—there was no other stuff." She scanned my face, looking for signs that I was buying it. After a few seconds I said, "I'm sorry to hear that," and she busted a smile, and implored me to put in my book that she and Liam were "special friends" and there had been no "other stuff," and I assured her that I would pass the message along.

"**WEAR SOMETHING WARM,**" Sylvain told me quietly as he came into the cabin at 2 a.m. on our twelfth night out of Tarfaya. He had been so cold during the last half hour of the watch that he had taken shelter, briefly, in the port hold (along with a desalinator, a quarter ton of food, eight or ten survival suits, four inches of bilge water, and a few cubic feet of "air" that, while toasty in its mutant appeal, made the stench in the cabin seem a heady and welcome idyll). By 6 a.m., we were running heavy chop and twenty-five-foot breakers directly into our teeth. At about 7 a.m., still in the dark, a wave came so hard over the bow onto my back that it knocked my head forward into my oar handle, leaving me not so much physically as emotionally rankled, deeply frustrated with weather that had begun to seem irreversible.

Half an hour later, in the coming light of dawn, Angela stuck her head out the front hatch and announced that according to her GPS, we were no longer making headway but were moving farther from our destination, and that to everybody's relief she was shutting things down. There was no longer any point in expending our energy.

By 8:15 the oars were stowed, the sea anchor was out, and we had begun a day of shiftless, well-fed indolence. For the most part we continued to alternate watches, or at least shadow watches, half of us on deck, half in the bunks. However, as the day wore on and our indolence deepened, some chose to share their bunks, sitting sideways, or curled up lengthwise like strands of DNA, or head to toe, as we had done when we were kids—all amidst a proliferating mess of clothing, food, bedding, garbage, toiletries, electronics, not to mention elbows and knees and shoulders, sixteen people, all of them wrestling for space in a cabin that, by rights, was perhaps adequate for four or five crew members and no more.

It hardly needs pointing out that there was an intimacy to it, a compulsory familiarity with everyone's digestion and body chemistry and "table manners"—and breathing and spatial phobias and skin (in some cases far more of their rashes and scars and private dermatological wrinkles than even their doctors will ever need to know about). It was Facebook and Arsebook and Farcebook. At the same time, there was a kind of freedom to it all, the sense, ironically, of an open zone, beyond the orthodoxies of authority and confidentiality, where we felt safe to talk, to exchange otherwise unspoken chapters from our personal histories. For nearly an hour that afternoon, for example, Sylvain laid out the through line on his peculiar, sometimes cultish, boyhood in Montreal, where his parents had subjected him to an all but insufferable evangelical Catholicism. Week after week, rather than meeting in a recognized sanctuary, the family had trooped around to apostolic gatherings in private homes—to prayer meetings, to Bible studies, to discussion conclaves, often led by young and radical priests, although not nearly radical enough for Sylvain. He said to me at one point, "I'd ask them, 'But *how,* my friend—*how* do you know that what you're teaching is true? You were not there! You're telling us things that are scientifically impossible. What is the basis of your belief in all of this?'"

The result of his indoctrination—his "brainwashing," as he described it—was that by the age of twelve or thirteen he had grown to detest not only Catholicism and the priests but to detest Christianity. "I detested Christ," he said flatly. "The little bleeding figure on the cross." For a one-time Catholic, the admission was a daring flirtation with spiritual oblivion—or perhaps with spiritual certainty.

By his late teens, he had evolved a rigorously pragmatic skepticism, a kind of internalized screening lens through which he scrutinized every ideal, every person, every fact and fancy that crossed his path. Several weeks into medical school at the University of Ottawa during the 1980s, he openly questioned the need for professors, some of whom he perceived were going through the motions, delivering their lectures from old ward or diagnostic notes, in which he had no interest. He decided to kiss them off. And with a group of equally subversive fellow students proceeded to study medicine on his own. "We went to the labs," he told me. "We did the clinical work with the others. That was all." At the end of the term, he and his fellow irregulars wrote the exams and did fine and carried on, Sylvain into a career in the emergency ward, where for more than two decades he has stitched up knife wounds and brought heart attacks under control and flushed out poisons. Sylvain has rounded, Gallic features and speaks an inflected but poetic English. And when he was finished his story, he looked at me for several seconds with the sort of steady, reptilian gaze that a cobra might apply to a mouse before swallowing it whole. "Charles," he said with hypnotic solemnity, "what is the meaning of life?"

I laughed, and eventually quoted him the old standby about Truth and Beauty being all we have to know.

"Who said that?" he asked without relinquishing his gaze.

"John Keats," I told him, at which point his face softened, and he said quietly, "Who is John Keats?"

"An English poet," I said. "Early eighteen hundreds."

"And if truth and beauty are all we have to know," he now inquired, "what about ugliness?"

"I think that's in the truth part," I said, to which he nodded and, out of his own instinct for truth, revealed that as a kid he had thrown pepper in his brother's eyes and that his father, in a rage, had declared that the brother would go blind. "To prove it wasn't true," said Sylvain, "I got the pepper and poured it into my own eyes, so they were black with it, and I went up to my dad and looked at him through the pepper and I said, *"Et voilà, Papa—je ne suis pas aveugle!"*

ALL NIGHT we struggled to get and stay comfortable, or if not exactly comfortable at least positioned in such a way as to avoid extreme *dis*comfort, so that we could get some sleep. At a point just past 9 p.m., Sylvain, with whom I was inextricably knotted up in the bunk, said to me, "Charles, there's one thing troubles me."

"Only one?" I asked, raising my head, anticipating some complex reassessment of the meaning of life, or the nature of truth or beauty.

"Will you still respect me in the morning?" he said, drawing a laugh from those around and above us.

"I don't respect you now," I told him. "I might if you let me get some sleep."

But it was easier said than done. Within twenty minutes I was so appallingly uncomfortable that I squeezed out into the alleyway, where the space was equally crowded, but where I was at least free of the assorted lumpy dry bags at the bottom of the bunk and the net storage hammocks laden with food and kit and pharmaceuticals that were forever in the way of one's head or shoulder or knees.

At some point the previous afternoon, Ernst had compared our crowded vessel to the slave ships of the 1700s, adding that it stank like them too. While surely no match for the floating prisons of old (slave carriers are said to have announced themselves several miles off with their stench), *Big Blue* was stifling to the point where at perhaps 11 p.m. I was galvanized by a need to get out of the cabin, for fear the nausea I was experiencing was about to erupt into something more colorful. It is difficult to convey the near-panic, the nightmarish claustrophobia, that comes of being unable to stand up, even to reconfigure one's tortured limbs and hips, because there were simply *too many people* in too small an enclosure. Meanwhile, the boat continued to heave with unprecedented fury, the waves to explode beneath the cabin floor. One such blast at perhaps midnight had several of us convinced that the floor had been shattered and that at any moment in the darkness we would feel the ocean rising around us.

The space, I might add, was functionally lightless, except for a tiny green signal that blinked from Louise's EPIRB, which hung in the bunk she shared with Tom. The device's connection to a satellite service in the U.S., or perhaps Europe, was the sole means by which the boat was being tracked from land. Later that night, Tom, unable to sleep for the blinking pin light, and unaware of its significance (it was typical of *Big Blue* that no one had explained it to us), began randomly pressing buttons on the thing, succeeding not just in turning it off but inadvertently cutting ties with the rest of the world. For all anybody ashore knew, *Big Blue* had gone to the bottom, or had been seized by pirates, or by midshipman Wilkins fed up with the boat's divisiveness and turpitude and all-but-total disrespect for punctuality.

For my purposes at that point, it would have helped to have a flashlight. Perhaps typically, mine, a crummy little LED contraption with a battery the size of a sesame seed, had burned out on the fourth day. My headlamp, another Chinese *modeschmuck,* had burned out on the seventh. David had kindly supplied each bunk with a stick-on wall light a little smaller than a hockey puck, but ours had already lost half its power, and to turn it on would have awakened others. Not that I could have found it anyway when I was scrunched up in the alley. At such times, you literally could not rise and take even a baby step without crunching someone's fingers or feet. Nevertheless, I tried, and succeeded in raising myself at a strange angle, imagining that I could next take a step into a teensy but apparently unoccupied corner of the alley. As I did so, however, my foot fell not on plywood but on a lumpish ball, and I realized too late that my naked and salty toes were now splayed across Louise's temple and forehead. "Uhh... excuse me," she said as I whispered apologies and settled, chastened, into the torturous Plywood Maiden that was the rear alleyway of the cabin.

More than anyone, incidentally, it was Tom who was exercised about the lack of a proper light in the cabin. He had pointed out several times that the place was elaborately wired so that iPods and cameras could be charged at every bunk but that not a single reliable light had been set into the circuitry. If we capsized or wrecked in the dark, there would be chaos (and of course water) in the lightless cabin and nobody would get out alive. It was a harrowing thought, although at this point no harsher, really, than the thought of another night without sleep or another meal of semi-reconstituted macaroni. Or for that matter another rough watch in the trenches. During our last brief stretch with a tailwind, a wave had come through that for perhaps fifteen seconds engulfed both hulls, floating everything out of the trenches, including a couple of the rowers, who luckily landed squarely back on their seats. Such waves were felt almost as acutely in the cabin, where the roar left you holding your breath, unsure whether your bunk would be attached to the hulls, or to anything, when it was over. A few hours later Louise had said to me, half sincerely, that we probably needed life preservers as much in the cabin as on deck. Which was no joke. The problem, as I understood it, was that by that time at least one of the life jackets had gone overboard and a couple more were irreversibly inflated, so were impossible to row in, meaning there were no longer enough to go around.

Sometime after dawn, Sylvain gave me the bunk, and Dylan and I lay across the alleyway from one another discussing what the long-term lessons of an experience such as ours might be. It was unclear to either of us at that point whether the lasting effects would be invigorating or despairing, or whether our memories of it would in any way approximate our perceptions of the voyage as it happened. I had grown to like Dylan well, to enjoy his intellect and humor as well as the wildly erratic syllabus that constituted his interests and ambitions. At the moment, his creative and intellectual pursuits ranged from filmmaking to creative writing to music, from marine and mammalian biology to philosophy, ethics, and rhetoric.

But he was above all an artist—played stand-up bass in a little jazz combo in Guelph and was the boat's

designated videographer, working with equipment supplied to him by Kelly Saxberg, who had seen us off in
Agadir. Dylan's role as videographer went back to Roy's
days, when Dylan had been offered half off his fare to
take boat footage for what an independent television pro-
ducer in New York, a woman in cahoots with Roy, hoped
might eventually become a lurid reality TV serial (Would
Steve and Margaret find true happiness? Would Charles
curl up and die?).

Dylan's most persistent and intuitive art, I might add,
was that he could, as my grandfather used to say, talk
the leg off a table. Tell a story. Construct an argument.
Convince anybody of anything. Which endeared him to
me, in that I too am of course in a profession whose most
imaginative branches exist in the name of convincing
anybody of anything. Or at least somebody of something.

Dylan had spent the past couple of summers in the
Yukon, near Dawson City, by himself, climbing trees,
plucking baby squirrels from their nests and making
notes on their size, sex, and survival rates. In this connection, he told me one of the most twisted nature stories I have ever heard: that male adult squirrels will kill
their own offspring if they get the chance, the sole purpose being to get as much sex as possible via the mother's
desire to replace her brood.

Dylan spoke so often of his girlfriend, Zoe, an environmental activist and stage performer, that I felt I knew
her almost as well as I knew him. During that very week,
Zoe had embarked with Nigel Roedde's girlfriend, Kim,
on a snowshoeing and winter camping expedition across
eastern Ontario. Which I'm sure was no picnic. However, from the perspective of the boat, with its hector-
ing and dissatisfactions and exhaustion, it presented as
a kind of Christmas card, the loveliest little romp that

anyone could imagine. Zoe had written Dylan a series of thirty-three sealed letters, one to be opened on each of the days that it was anticipated we'd be at sea. In the end, he worked his way through them almost twice and was always the picture of ardor as he sat with his daily epistle, sometimes mulling its contents for fifteen minutes or more and then again later in the day. The crew's heartless and recurring joke was that the last letter would be a Dear John: Goodbye. Fare thee well. Be good. Boohoo.

As for our discussion, Dylan believed there were long-term lessons to be taken from experiences such as ours but for now was at a loss to articulate them. I believed so too but have tended as I get older to take experience for what it is and not demand of it some protracted instructional consequence or moral paddywacks. Picking up the theme, Dylan said it seemed typical of Western thought to want to measure today's endeavors by the value of their currency tomorrow. At the same time, one does not often get the opportunity to view oneself—to conduct or reconstruct oneself—in the context of such immense and eloquent forces as are present around a small boat at sea. Or, conversely, among a quorum of adults reduced to the social standards of Ralph, Jack, and Piggy in the fictional *Lord of the Flies*. Given the stage, it seemed entirely possible that one's inner compass just *might* be permanently reset, or even rebuilt, by an endeavor such as ours. For now, such a prospect only added to the weariness within me, as well as to an ever-evolving sense that if anything was ever going to mean anything, we were going to have to get moving, somehow to escape this awful trap of ill wind and ennui.

That night as we settled to our bunks and floor space, Sylvain organized a little restorative, an MP3 concert to which we each contributed one song off our iPods. These were broadcast through a pair of teensy, ineffectual speakers, hissy little things, owned by, I believe, Liz or Aleksa. But they were nonetheless a welcome lullaby as we drifted off to sleep, or into the torturous half-sleep that was the best some of us could manage under the circumstances.

Both Dylan's and Sylvain's contributions were gently abstract jazz pieces by musicians whose names I did not catch. When I suggested a few items off my own limited playlist, including a Sonny Rollins number and one by Van Morrison, Louise, who was beside me in the alley on the floor, said quietly, "I'd like to hear 'Tupelo Honey' by Van Morrison." I mention this if for no other reason than to make clear that when Louise Graff wants to hear "Tupelo Honey," or any other piece by any other musician, that is what Louise gets to hear. If Steve was the crew's disciplinary conscience and Angela its Victoria Regina, the unsinkable Louise Graff—"Louisville Louise," as I liked to think of her—was its heart and equilibrium. It is a description she would laugh at and reject, but this cultured forty-eight-year-old Kentuckian, with her mild southern drawl, all but breathed goodwill and empathy— and sensitivity and humor and durability. Even when conditions were at their worst and few of us had anything left with which to comfort either our crewmates or ourselves, she would invariably have a little joke or offer a word of encouragement, or would dispense a ten-second back rub or hug.

Louise's life back in Charleston was a bit of a mystery to me. She had grown up on a horse farm in the Bluegrass State, and I believe now owned and managed several properties that supplied her with a living. One thing she did make clear was that the best of her energies went into volunteer work bringing breast-cancer survivors to dragonboat racing, which provided social and recreational therapy as it raised research money.

Two afternoons earlier, with the Atlantic in chaos, the boat groaning, rain soaking what parts of us the sea hadn't reached, she had staggered into the cabin, ashen after two hours of dangerous and difficult rowing, but with a mischievous smirk on her face. It was during a week when twenty-five-cent packages of ramen noodles, which were in short supply and were popular because you could soften them in cold water, had assumed a boat value of perhaps a hundred times retail.

"Anybody with noodles need a blowjob?" she had said solemnly, throwing the surly caboodle of us into a gut laugh of the sort that helped keep us from going nuts.

Moreover, she had that rarest of gifts, the ability, under stress, to keep her pain and problems to herself. I never once heard her complain, for example, about her salt sores, some of which had eaten clear through the skin on her ankles or toes; or about the bruises she'd picked up when the breakers knocked her from her rowing seat, or when an unruly wave caught her oar, sending its handle like a baseball bat into her shins or midsection. She had crashed off her seat so many times that on Day 9 or 10 she had fastened a mat of sponge rubber against the steel stirrups of the seat behind her to save her back, which at one point looked as if a shark had taken a run at it.

It was Louise who taught the girls how to pee without getting out of the rowing trench; Louise who provided sunscreen and soap and duct tape when the rest of us had run out; Louise who when her wet wipes (which is to say her toilet wipes) were gone, rather than begging from the rest of us, as most of us had begged from her, simply ripped her cotton jacket into squares and carried on.

For the past couple of nights, in the mercilessly crowded cabin, Louise had given up her bunk to Tom, as she had done while he was sick. She was thus sleeping on the floor, her head banked against a five-inch plywood ridge—a kind of low dam that separated Angela's pint-sized quarters from the main cabin in order to prevent water from flowing around should it find its way in.

MEANWHILE, the evolving script around Margaret had taken a turn. At a point when I was off watch the previous afternoon, she had somehow slighted Sylvain, apparently demeaning his rowing or sense of teamwork while showing a preferential endorsement of Ryan Worth, a terrific rower and occasional loose cannon who had recently missed a watch or two because of some mysterious inner malady.

Sylvain was in a sense our Captain Trueheart, and Margaret's criticisms of him infuriated Dylan, who as I understand it backed Margaret off with a word or two, and then reported his displeasure to Angela, urging her to remove Margaret from her job as watch commander and allow each watch to elect a commander of its own. Which is exactly what Angela did, sanctioning a quick vote that saw Sylvain promoted on one watch (a job he held for mere days before realizing he did not have the attention of Margaret or Ryan, at which point the ever-equanimous Nigel took over). At the same time, Dylan began a judicious and chatty watch command with our own half of the crew.

I will say for Ryan that he had scored points with me a couple of days earlier when during the late afternoon at watch change I had fumbled my thermal mug, my one remaining food container, and had watched paralyzed as it bounced through the gap at the stern end of the tramp into the sea. Almost simultaneously, the blurred likeness of a human being (Ryan as it turned out) exploded from behind me, in full horizontal extension as if in the last instant of flight, and landed hard against the bridge at my feet. Almost before I realized what was happening, my quick-acting benefactor had hooked the mug with his finger and was back on his feet, smiling, as if to present me with an award.

That same night, I spent two hours on the bridge with Ryan, on watch, largely unaware until then that he was a talker on the order of Dylan White (who not surprisingly possessed almost reverential admiration for Ryan's lively, crowded, occasionally angelic brain). At one point, mid-watch, for twenty minutes straight, Ryan poured out a Vesuvial song of himself, details atop details: his ancestral home in rural Michigan (he could drive a tractor when he was six); his high school football career in Chattanooga (at the urging of his coach he had once ballooned to nearly 300 pounds), his rowing triumphs (including a first in Freshman Eights at the Head of the Hooch Regatta in Chattanooga, in front of 300,000 spectators); his Christianity, his conservatism, his liberalism; his fishing, his hunting, his year of art school; his self-acknowledged attention deficit. He loves beer (during a one-night stopover in Dublin on his way to Agadir, he had fitted in a two-hour tour of the Guinness factory—had in fact chosen his hostel nearby because it offered a free pint at the pub next door).

Toward the end of this mini-autobiography, Ryan addressed the successes and failures of his university career, pausing at a point to describe how what he called "the Hiroshima" had been deployed as a kind of ultimate collegiate infliction among his friends at the University of Tennessee. The gist of the punishment was that some gas-bloated undergrad would lower his naked hindquarters onto the face of a sleeping buddy so that a fart could be blown at powder-burn range directly into the sleeper's nostrils. The sting was that just as the fart was about to be applied, the sleeper would be roused from his or her slumber. Ryan reported all this quite lovingly—and then later to Tom, who wondered aloud if the gassy punishment might not be the perfect reprimand for those late out of the cabin to row.

Because of the watch system and because each hull had its own sub-watch of rowers, I had gotten to know some of those aboard far better than others. At this point, for example, I had barely spoken to Liz or Aleksa since Agadir. And I had little ongoing contact with Nigel, Zach, or Ryan—or even my dear pal Louise. On the other hand, Tom, Ernst, Dylan, and I had bunks within breathing distance of one another in the rear-cabin and thus ate together, snored in one another's ears, and yattered away constantly when we weren't out on deck. While I was rowing, my conversation was pretty much restricted to the rower directly in front of me—usually Steve, but occasionally Dylan or Ernst, both of whom tended to wear their iPods. Often, someone from the other watch would be out on the tramp during the day, particularly in nice weather, and you could chatter a bit with them, mostly about home or food or other travels, or salt sores or bruises, or sometimes the little fish that had just that second landed at their feet.

BY MIDNIGHT or so of that second night on sea anchor, the wind had begun to shift, and by 3:30 a.m. was raging down out of the northeast, giving us reason to hope we were at last coming into the trades. If we were, at the beginning of our seventeenth day at sea, our thirteenth out of Tarfaya, it meant that we were precisely where we had hoped to be ten days ago. And by 4 a.m., we were back on the oars.

By noon, alas, it was clear that we had not found the trades. The wind had swung erratically into the northwest, so that we were taking it against our starboard flank, making rowing as difficult as ever.

At about 1 p.m., Angela appeared on the bridge and, for a minute or more, above the wind, screamed her appreciation of her crew—WE WERE UNBELIEVABLE, WE WERE AMAZING, WE WERE THE REAL DEAL! Naturally, I read myself into this billowing flattery, particularly as Angela noted that she had not expected some of us to hold up under the battering. My unwarranted pride was of course tempered by the awareness that at my current age I was no longer the sort of person who people expected to "hold up" when things got tough.

BUT WE HAD! WE WERE AMAZING! WE WERE UNBELIEVABLE!

Late in the afternoon Angela appeared again, this time pushing her upper body out of the front cabin hatch, shouting to us that she was convening a meeting immediately, so to listen up, both from the bunks and from the rowing seats. First, she announced matter-of-factly that Margaret had been taken off watch command, which by this time we all knew anyway. For a couple of hours after the demotion Margaret had more or less quarantined herself in her bunk, hidden by a big Australian flag that she had draped across its open side. What we did not know was the degree to which revisionism had laid siege to the log and that the reason for the change was that Margaret "needed more time" to deal with what Angela referred to as "her duties as second-in-command."

In my opinion, what Margaret *needed* was to forget entirely about her duties as second-in-command, to be *allowed* to forget entirely; to be decommissioned, decaffeinated, gently encouraged simply to settle in as crew and get some rowing done. I believe that at this stage

everyone but Steve could have accepted Margaret fully
as one of them, as one of us, as just another stiff on the
oars—albeit a good stiff. After years of rowing in the Australian surf, Margaret could row like an Olympian; even
Steve conceded it. For her part, Angela had been well
intentioned in engaging her—had never dreamed of the
hassles that would ensue. That said, it is doubtful that
even a saint with a background in diplomacy could have
come in at the last second, with no investment in the project or the boat, no awareness of the complex history of
the expedition, and have successfully assumed the role
of the ship's jimmy. Perhaps if Angela herself had had a
longer association with the endeavor, there would have
been more respect for her choice of Margaret. However,
she too had but a pixelated awareness of how the core
of the crew had hung in, clinging to the wreckage, first
through Roy's travails, then through the reconstruction
of the boat, the near-bankruptcy of the project and, with
David's perseverance, the eventual revival of it all in this
glorious little voyage of the damned.

What might have surprised Margaret was the degree
to which her nemesis Steve had, in his sometimes ellip-
tical way, applied himself passionately to keeping the
expedition alive. Louise's contribution too might have
come as a surprise to Margaret. I myself would not discover till weeks after the fact that when the expedition
was at its lowest ebb financially, Louise had quietly given
David another ten grand to keep things moving forward.
Nor could Margaret have understood the sacrifices that
David and his friends had made in getting the boat ready,
or the contributions of David's parents, who had provided tens of thousands of dollars of their life's savings
so that their son could honor his commitment to the crew.
For Margaret, it was in many ways just a gig, a lark, a
line on her resume, made possible by Angela's last-minute

ambition to have another rower aboard who had success-fully crossed the Atlantic.

The second part of Angela's message that afternoon was more sobering than its prelude. Besides being ten days behind our own schedule, she reported, we were now a full seven days behind the pace of *Sara G* and were falling farther behind by the minute.

Whereas just hours ago we had been "amazing," we were apparently mere rowers again and were going to have to "PUT SOME EFFORT INTO THINGS," going to have to "TIGHTEN IT UP," going to have to "GET THE LEAD OUT AND PULL UP OUR SOCKS." Angela was "aware of some NEGATIVITY" aboard *Big Blue*—aware of "some TALKING BEHIND PEOPLE'S BACKS!" The time had come to "CUT IT OUT!" she now hollered. It was time "to REALLY GET POSITIVE around here!"

Did we UNDERSTAND? she wanted to know.

If we did, we were apparently keeping it to ourselves, because as the sun bore witness to the weltering after-noon, the only sound around was the bristling nor'wester as it whistled through the tramp, blowing us in the wrong direction, and the waves as they crashed into the transoms and hulls.

"Okay, then," Angela concluded, "from now on I don't wanta hear any more NEGATIVITY! From now on I don't wanta hear anymore BULLSHIT!"

In all, it was a strange little diatribe, a Bilko-like car-toon absurdly unsuited to Angela's mostly gentle and motherly personality.

Predictably, Steve was outraged by the speech. While he has been known to use the occasional blunt instru-ment in achieving his goals, he is not an overall fan of the disciplinary bazooka, and felt Angela would have done far better simply to outline the issues at hand and to discuss them with her crew, as she had reasonably done in Tarfaya. Plus, to suggest that the crew could somehow overcome the weather with harder rowing was nuts. And Steve knew it—could see it more clearly, I suspected, when it was postulated by someone other than himself.

More specifically, in reconfirming Margaret as her second (albeit relieving her of watch command), Angela had failed to address her subaltern's increasing redundancy on deck. We didn't need an extra level of command. The absurdity was apparent later that day when Margaret, who was standing on the tramp beside where I was rowing, said to me, "Charlie, would you go and tell Angela that it looks like the wind is going to get better for rowing and that maybe we should scrape the barnacles while it's not so good?"

My first and unspoken response was, *Well, since I'm rowing and you're not, why don't you just stick your head in the cabin hatch and ask her yourself?* But, rather than getting balky (as if we needed more of that), I quit rowing, unstrapped my stirrups, went into the cabin, spoke to Angela, and emerged to tell Margaret that Angela said it wasn't necessary.

Barnacles, I should explain, are stiff little crustaceans that attach themselves to the hulls of ocean vessels and have to be scraped off so that they do not create drag. Left to accumulate, they can form masses as big as flowerpots or basketballs, although typically we got rid of them when they were no bigger than fingertips.

In this case, as it turned out, Margaret was right. By the next day, when scraping the barnacles was suddenly a priority for Angela, the wind and bounce made it considerably more difficult for the kids who went into the water to do the job.

One thing Margaret grasped intuitively was that despite our occasional disagreements, I harbored no lasting antipathy toward her. I didn't care at all for her m.o.

as an "officer" of the vessel, but certainly did not view her as some sort of narcissist intent on manipulating or wasting her perceived antagonists. Some did. I would eventually gain confidential awareness that at least one of her adversaries on board was as intensely antisocial about her as she was reputed to be about others. During the weeks after the voyage, that person (who shall go nameless, and who is not as obviously identifiable as one might assume) told me privately that mid-voyage, when the wind was up one night, he had been so outraged at Margaret's attitude and arrogance that it had crossed his mind simply to bump her overboard when they passed on the bridge. I did not take the admission as seriously as I would have in mid-journey—indeed I suspect I passed it off a little too casually. I assume even now that it was a significant exaggeration. If nothing else, it was a reminder of how exceedingly raw our nerves had become aboard the boat, how primitive our responses had become—of how stress and exhaustion can impair, if not eliminate, one's judgment and sense of proportion.

12

---⚓︎---

ACCORDING TO THE adventurer Dervla Murphy, whose books are an all-but-howling subversion of common contemporary travel practices, the value and meaning of journeying are drastically eroded, if not destroyed, by our inability, even at the far edges of the planet and psyche, to rid ourselves of satellite phones, smart phones, dumb phones, laptops, iPads, iPods, and the like.

Dervla would not have been happy aboard *Big Blue,* or even among its crew, where the agenda from the start was a kind of post-vaudevillian absurdity of electronic devices and communication. Long before we'd even met one another, we were cluttering cyberspace with torrents of emails and retorts, proliferating muddles of information, much of it sciencey and argoty, addressing everything from nutritional chemistry to meteorology, to suitable sea clothing, to media coverage, to the evolving state of the boat, to commercial sponsorship, to the mathematics of navigation, to how the food would be packed for stowage, to dispatches from the training gym (where the contemporary vernacular is a battle-ready shorthand of "targets" and "loads" and "zones," of "setups" and "rips" and "reps"). The lot of it came with admonishments from fellow crew members urging us to "communicate," intensify our training, de-intensify our training, update our logs, identify our requirements, be more sensitive, be less sensitive. Or came with dispatches from Roy, demanding (sometimes after weeks of silence) that we look alive, smarten up, start acting like ocean beaters, prove our mettle, get our money in (the implied salutation invariably being *you dumb swabs*). There were attached essays and charts, links to more links, the great incorporeal bulk of it exploding from our inboxes with, at best, occasional human touches: bits of drama or humor, such as when Angela and Steve would get sparring (prophetically, as it turned out) over their sense of, say, how many calories constituted an adequate daily supply for the average rower, or whether Steve's insistence on "liquid" calories (protein and electrolyte supplements, necessary as a concession to his digestive difficulties) was a fitting approach to nutrition. "What would happen," Angela asked him at one point, "if the desalination equipment broke down, and we had to go on maintenance rations of fresh water?"

"I'd fix the equipment," responded Steve.

Angela is an intelligent woman, quick with a retort, and yet her emails as often as not read like alphabet soup or the random output of a bingo tumbler. A month before departure, in response to a dozen of Angela's food emails, each intended to clarify the last, Nigel wrote, "Ok. Shit. I'm sorry. I've re-read the emails a bunch of times. I still have a question, perhaps because what I THINK the process is just doesn't make sense to me." And so it went.

Our lives in Agadir had been similarly permeated by this bristling electro-profusion. Deb, for example, sat by the hour at her laptop in the women's apartment, writing emails, sorting data, fussing with photos—and I think even keeping up with her day job back in Bakersfield, California. In her off-hours, she gave up the computer to those of us needing to do our own emailing and Internet searches and photo organization.

So we were all part of the syndrome—especially Margaret, who from the moment she arrived stared into the screen of her laptop with the avidity of a bank hacker. Even at the boatyard and docks, amidst the dust and clutter, she walked around with the thing open in front of her, balanced on her forearm, tapping in the secrets of the admiralty, rustling up "to do" lists in an attempt to alleviate the chaos that was believed (if arguably) to be dragging us all down. On the night Margaret reached Agadir, she and her friend Tony, a British adventure tour leader (Dervla reserves her most withering broadsides for profit-inspired "adventures"), huddled in the shadows of Angela and Deb's apartment with their laptops and phones, absorbed to the point of ignoring not only the crew but a trio of amicable Moroccans—a Paralympic rower and his friends—who knew Angela and had dropped round to meet us and to wish us well. There the Moroccans sat, like lepers at the feast, attempting to be sociable, speaking French to one another and to Tom, who, with Angela (and briefly with Dylan and Louise), had separated himself from the reluctant Facebook addicts with whom he would soon be rowing the ocean. In the corners of the room, a quartet of laptops splashed their aptly kryptonic light onto the faces of those for whom e-gossip from the capitals of the universe trumped the measly matter of courtesy back here on earth.

I had left my cell phone at home rather than adding programming that would have enabled me to use it overseas. And I decidedly did not want an EPIRB that would, I became convinced, do little more than make my drowned corpse findable if after several days at sea it hadn't been eaten by sharks.

When Steve accidentally dropped his iPhone into the ocean during our last days in Agadir, I was secretly relieved, as I suspect he was, that another electronic tether had been snapped.

However, if I believed life aboard would be simpler, less "connected," I was (to utter a monumental understatement) mistaken. From the start, *Big Blue* was a veritable space garden of blinking lights and hourly recharges and digitized messages—of iPods and EPIRBs and satellite phones. Both Angela and Margaret owned phones and had purchased thousands of minutes of communication time. When they themselves weren't using such quota to gather weather reports or deliver "content" to their blogs, or to communicate with their associates or family, the minutes were enthusiastically gobbled by the crew, some of whom were apparently under compulsion, if not actual orders, to stay in touch with those at home. Aleksa, for example, made regular calls to Long Island, offering her folks a version of life aboard sufficiently sanitized not to horrify them, as well as explanations to her employer as to why she would be later in returning to work than anticipated.

Tom planned his calls across the time zones so that they reached the family kitchen on Toronto Island every Sunday morning, early enough that he would catch his wife, Luisa, before she left for other activities.

Steve, a reluctant user at first, began regular calls to Janet once he realized that with the help of a family friend, she could provide weather information as reliably as could the meteorologist who was supplying Margaret with her sometimes elastic forecasts. From the beginning,

Steve had been appalled that Margaret was receiving $5,000 in reduced fare for bringing aboard weather reports that he now proved, via Janet, could be taken off the web and phoned in by any intelligent amateur. It drove him almost to wall-pounding that the other half of Margaret's fare had been written off as payment for her by now discredited contribution to the command.

Like Aleksa, Sylvain was in touch with his employers about the number of work days he was likely to miss by being so long at sea. As was Ernst, who made increasingly abject calls to the international shipping company in Vienna that had hired him just days before his departure, on the understanding that he would be at his desk by mid-February to take up his responsibilities. With each distressed call, he added another few days to his projected return date, and as we neared the end of January was all but certain he'd be fired for his unintended delinquency. Beyond this, he had a new girlfriend who worked at the same company and whom he suspected would also deep-six him if he didn't get back to her and pronto. By the end of the third week, he had evolved a comic fantasy in which he eventually arrived at company headquarters, months late, limping into his boss's office, unrecognizable with his wooden leg, his eye patch, his missing teeth, *har har, matey*.

Liam, as much as any of them, was in trouble, having begged six weeks of grace before his final medical exams, which were to begin on March 12, so that he could row the ocean. On I think Day 18 he got a call from his mother explaining (in a mother's voice I can only imagine) that the dean of the medical school, with whom the family had been in touch over our delays, had called and was threatening to keep Liam from taking his finals if he was not back by such-and-such a date.

So the pressure was on, and the phone pulsed and beeped. Sylvain, I should say, quite quickly received word that his colleagues were happy to cover for him and that he should quit worrying and enjoy his time at sea. It was a vast relief to him—and to me as well. I had shared some of the stress that had crept into our bunk, and now shared in the unburdening.

Sylvain's more impassioned use of the phone, I might add, lay in his near-daily contact with his wife, Suzanne, and their school-aged boys. On the day mid-trip when he learned that the three of them would be coming to Barbados to meet the boat, he frolicked around the bridge, proclaiming the news with war-whoops and victory gestures, while the rest of us made dumb, or grinned dispassionately, attempting to celebrate Sylvain's moment as we swallowed our doubts over whether we ourselves would be met upon landing. Some of the crew—Ernst, Liam, Dylan, Margaret, Ryan—knew already that they would have no one there to greet them.

ON THE NIGHT of January 28th, as we rowed through a persistent cross-chop, Steve and I had an intense exchange about our relationships to our families and loved ones back home. If, as Janet said, there was a selfishness to extreme endeavors such as ours and that we were not aware of it, I would argue that based on the evidence, both Steve and I were very much aware of the imposition of our endeavors on everybody and everything around us. As were several other senior crew members. My personal problem was that I did not know quite what to do about it. Except perhaps to compensate those who were affected—or attempt to compensate them. When Steve asked what I thought he should do about his debt to Janet, the only thing I could think to tell him was,

"Pay it! Tell her it's her turn now; back her in anything she wants to do."

Steve, Sylvain, and Tom were the only crew members in traditional marriages, although Louise and Angela were in long-term same-sex partnerships. And half a dozen others aboard had romantic connections on one level or another. At the same time, it is not just the hours and domestic support provided by those close to us that must be compensated; it is their concern, their indulgence, their fear for our safety—the fear, for example, experienced by my children that I was going to be lost out there, or otherwise destroyed by the demands or privations of the voyage.

Meanwhile, if I so much as mention the intrinsic tortures of rowing the Atlantic—the salt sores and sleep deprivation and various mortal dangers—I am generally reminded pronto that I "chose to participate" and would be well advised to suck it up and keep my complaints to myself. Which brings me to a modest deliberation on the nature of choice, in particular on the Emersonian notion that we *choose,* say, careers and friends and recreational pursuits, but that we are *compelled* to endeavors more purely of the spirit and imagination—let us say to art and "belief" and quest. By these standards, my participation in the *Big Blue* expedition was a compulsion pure and without thought. *Not* going would have required a choice.

Certainly, when my engineer or teacher friends (all of whom have made career choices) tell me their professional lives suck, the last thing I do is remind them that since they chose their pickle they have forfeited their right to complain. My prescription for unhappy careerists is not that they shut up and quit wallowing but that they talk on and quit *working,* and quit *posthaste,* and go traveling, take up surfing, read the Complete Works, walk the

Dead Diamond River, build a boat, climb the Matterhorn as Geoffrey Wolff famously attempted to do in, I think, his sixtieth year. Read Geoffrey Wolff.

If you are really restless and nuts, go row an ocean— although I would not have been so pitiless as to drop any of my unhappy career friends onto the deck of *Big Blue* on the afternoon of our eighteenth day out of Agadir. For one thing, the sea toilet was plugged—at least until David succeeded in clearing out a wad of biodegradable baby wipes that had clumped in its innards. From now on, it was announced, we were to dispose of such wipes directly into the Atlantic, the "optics" of which are so at odds with the Homeric nature of our journey that I shall immediately declare them Too Much Information and proceed into details on why the sea toilet was a disgusting anathema to begin with: it stank, it was awkward, its seat was loose, its compartment in the rear hold was filthy; the floor around it was invariably aslop with brine (or worse); the hatch cover above it was inclined to fall on one's head. On perhaps my fifteenth descent into the aptly described "shit hole," I had finished up and was congratulating myself on having survived another evacuation—was attempting to yank up my skivvies (no easy drill while doubled over with one's elbows pinned to one's flanks), when a breaker came over the port transom, first drenching then humiliating me as I poked my dripping head above deck to the delight of my crewmates. From that point forward, when I settled onto the Tecma Hand-Pump EasyFit I snuggled in tight and closed the hatch over my head (indeed, from then on those in the rowing seats began issuing warnings to whoever was on the pot if they were about to be dealt an unscheduled bath).

But I must praise the loo, too. For I am sure there would have been casualties had we been required in its absence to suspend our collective recta above twenty-five-foot waves amid fifty-knot winds, in rain, at night, addled by sleep deficits that in fiscal equivalency would have bankrupted Bill Gates. It is a deservedly obscure fact that the majority of sailors lost at sea are claimed while urinating or defecating off the stern rail—a stern tale. As for *rowers* on the high seas, I have heard speculation that of the seven who lost their lives on the Atlantic in recent years, as many as three may have gone overboard taking a leak, which they would perhaps not have been doing at such risk had Cap'n Angela been along with her nasty little pump-action biffy.

None of which, I must say, was of any great concern to us as we settled to the 2 p.m. watch. What had us by the throats on that overcast afternoon was, rather, our ongoing and agonizing inability to attract some favorable weather, to get going, to get surfing, to get into the trades, those elusive easterlies that we knew were out there and that had pretty much defined our ambitions through two weeks at sea, not to mention the sixteen to twenty months during which our voyage was in the making. What we got instead were headwinds, crosswinds, ill winds, chill winds, l'il winds, no winds at all, the last of which made for calm water and exquisite rowing but slow progress.

I have been asked many times why it was so difficult to locate the trade winds, the assumption seeming to be that they are a fixed entity with precise spatial dimensions, like islands or a coastline or a highway. But they are infinitely variable from season to season, day to day, hour to hour. Like all winds they are mere air masses, arising and moving as a response to warmth, to cold, to rain, to high and low air pressure. They can be pushed hundreds of miles north or south by heavy crosswinds, or can be absorbed entirely into such winds. At times they may simply disappear. And no one from land, say at a map or computer, can tell you how to find them. What is constant about them, and has been over the centuries, is that sooner or later they resume their westward push, with great if unpredictable velocity, outward from the coast of Africa, somewhere north of the equator.

Not that my desire to get going meant that I had cast in with those "fast past the mast," as I had heard one of the women refer to any resolute souls still fixated on the discipline and self-denial that with a whale's helping of luck might once have carried us to an earlier arrival in Barbados. In spirit, I had become a walking Irish prayer—a plea, Loving Father, for just a *wee* bit of wind at our backs (an entreaty, Holy Mother, for just a wee puffa-weewee along our cracks). I don't think Dylan White and I were greatly exaggerating in our agreement that rowing at night in the crosswinds was the most difficult physical challenge we had ever faced—going hard all the time, on inadequate food and even less adequate sleep.

A day earlier we had received news from Margaret's parents in northern Australia that as far as they could tell we were somehow just thirty nautical miles off *Sara G*'s pace during our first sixteen or seventeen days. As it turned out, the math was off (never the mathematicians), and by the next morning we had word that we were actually a full five days off, which at *Sara G*'s hundred-mile-a-day average meant 500 miles. Our own average through Days 11 and 12 out of Tarfaya had been a mere fifty miles a day, most of it southerly—in other words still not in the direction of Barbados. Meanwhile, our weather reports suggested that our mileage (like our confidence) was about to collapse entirely.

Angela brooded. Steve chafed. Margaret pushed—particularly at Steve. I think sometimes it was her tone that grated more than her actual directives. The night before, when we were being bounced by forty-knot crosswinds, she had asked Steve (in a voice straight out of officer's training) to put on a life vest as he came out of the cabin for the 10-to-midnight watch. A day earlier, Steve had instructed Angela to call Margaret off, to have her desist from any attempts at managing or administering him. But apparently Angela's memo had not reached her, or had reached her and had been ignored. Whatever the case, Steve now invited Margaret (in precisely these words) to "fuck off" and pushed past her out onto the bridge.

The sequence and timing of what followed is difficult to know exactly. But it would appear that at some point later that night, or early the next morning, Margaret phoned in a report to her press agent and "bloggist" in the United Kingdom mentioning that the boat's "token alpha male" had told her etc. etc.

Such is the power of the Internet that no sooner was the post up than Steve's wife, Janet, had read it on the other side of the moral universe and, within hours, had spoken to Steve by phone, inquiring as to who the boat's "token alpha male" might be (just possibly suspecting it was someone to whom she had been married for twenty-five years). In no time, Steve had a sign on his bunk identifying himself as *Big Blue*'s "Token Alpha Male." And thus by the miracle of contemporary technology did one day's vituperation circle the globe and, with no loss of ill will, return to the vessel as the next day's hilarity.

Later that day, one of the instruments of these eloquent and cosmic exchanges, Angela's SAT phone, inexplicably quit working. For some, it was a significant blow. Sylvain perhaps felt it most, deprived as he now was of cherished daily contact with his family. For Steve, it meant the loss of communication with Janet and thus the daily weather information on which he and a few of the rest of us had come to rely. On principle, he could not ask to use Margaret's phone. And she did not offer it. A day or two earlier a warning had been issued that both phones were running low on minutes, even though thousands had been pre-purchased before our departure. Sylvain had offered to buy several thousand more, for the good of the boat, if there was any way to accomplish it.

At that point, David went to work with an old-world fixer's sense of wires and widgets. Over a period of twenty-four hours, with help from Deb in California (who fed him vital technological information via Margaret's phone), he succeeded in restoring the phone to use. Meanwhile, Deb was able to purchase several thousand more minutes, so that nobody needed to feel isolated as the sea pounded us, and our tiny vessel groaned and heaved, now nearly 500 watery miles down the coast.

13

THE FOLLOWING MORNING, a rumor crept round that there were crew members pondering the possibility of a landing at the Cape Verde Islands, which were just to the south and from which it might be possible to fly home and thereby call it a day and save face. I do not believe Nigel would have participated in such an action—he was too solid—but at one point I did hear him say to someone in the fore-cabin, "Is there even an airport on the islands?" Later I heard Angela refer to "this one last chance" to abandon the expedition. Such a move would have taken us several hundred miles out of our way in already unfavorable seas and would thus have ended the voyage both for the deserters and the loyalists. It would also have put us in danger along coastlines for which we had no charts, and might well have left the boat to be ravaged or destroyed.

To this point on the voyage nothing had truly outraged me. My disagreements with Steve and Liam had been yappy and confrontational, at least on my part, and born of very specific differences of attitude. But this was different. This was constitutional. No person or group had the right to terminate the expedition for everyone, to assume that their own selfish ends were somehow in everybody's interests. Even the thought of it, the discussion of it, struck me as a heresy—indeed, reminded me of why in the brutal armies of old even talk of desertion was often rewarded with a bullet to the head.

That day at noon in the cabin, I told Steve I'd overheard comments about going ashore at the islands, and wondered if he knew anything about it. He paused and said abruptly, "They're just joking," to which I responded that it was a piss-poor joke, and that if it was not a joke and they meant it, whoever *they* were, I believed they should get in a lifeboat right now, pack some food and water, and get lost. That was my opinion. I told him that those of us who did not believe quitting was a good legacy were still of a mind to complete this infernal crossing.

I do not know to this day what Steve's real thoughts were on it all. Over the previous few days, he had swung wildly from the position that we must get moving, must work harder, must apply ourselves diligently, to what in my view was a reckless announcement to several crew members that the only reason he was "bothering to row at all anymore" was so Liam could get back to take his medical exams. *Some crewmate you are,* I thought to myself (which was precisely what I imagine he'd thought about me on a number of occasions). However, I did not say it to his face, partly out of a reluctance to create enmity but also of an awareness that I could only raise so many hackles without beginning to cast myself as a mulish old fart.

Unknown to me at the time, Margaret, more pointedly than anyone, had considered cutting her losses and heading for Cape Verde—had in fact talked with Angela about attempting to contact a sailing vessel by phone, getting it to pick her up and take her to the islands, from which she would make her way home, or perhaps carry on as crew on a new boat. The plan would certainly have suited Steve and some of the others—but was a mere pipe dream, given the unlikelihood of Margaret persuading a sailboat to pick her up and transport her.

Perhaps Steve was right and the talk I had heard was just chatter—a "joke." I hoped so.

For now, Steve's concern for Liam went beyond just getting him home. Often on watch, to help him prepare for his exams, he would present him with a hypothetical sick person—liver failure, heart failure, kidney failure. As the rest of us listened, Liam would explain how he would respond to such a patient, what symptoms he would look for, what tests he would apply, what treatments and drugs.

"Okay," I overheard one of the kids say to another one morning, sending up the process, "you find a guy on an isolated roadside. He's unconscious, his vital signs are faint, he's a guy who stole your girlfriend and murdered your dog. He has a million dollars cash in his pocket. There's just the two of you. What treatment do you apply?"

It was an unexpected perk of the trip that by the time it ended, three or four of us on the watch were ready for the British medical exams.

Later on the day of the Cape Verde turmoil, Steve hit the low ebb of his journey to date when his beloved and splendid rowing cushion—an eight-inch-high par-fait of hand-assembled foam layers—got kicked accidentally into the sea. By Ernst. I will say for Steve that in the ensuing despair and tension he never once fingered our sweet Austrian crewmate as the culprit. He fidgeted effectively through the afternoon watch atop Nigel's pad, a lesser piece of gear. However, that night, on the 2-to-4, his lower back gave out on him, with the result that for an hour or more he alternated a few minutes of agonized rowing with three or four minutes of writhing around, wincing, and groaning on the tramp. Back and forth it went—from anguish on the rowing seat to anguish on the tramp. I won't say it panicked me, but it unsettled me. Steve is a tough guy. But with back issues. Janet once told me that at their home he had built the doors on their screened porch extra-wide to accommodate the wheelchair he expected to be in some day. With each new bout of tortured gyrations I begged him to *please* tell me what I could do to help him. Did he need painkillers? Could I get him the back support (an admittedly crummy little item) that I had bought at Shoppers Drug Mart in Thunder Bay for my own occasionally tricky lower vertebrae?

Blessedly, after an hour or so the groaning and writhing slowed, and twenty minutes later he was rowing pretty much normally. But just as I had recently glimpsed his emotional vulnerabilities, I had now witnessed his physical weaknesses. And I didn't like it, knowing well that if we lost Steve things could disintegrate more quickly than we might have imagined. The loss of his rowing was one thing; the thought of him aboard and *not* rowing, his energy festering, was quite another.

Beyond any of this, Steve's mere example was important to the boat. And he knew it. And in some ways it was a lot to live up to. I occasionally suffered pangs of regret that, at least on our watch, he was pretty much alone on the moral battlefield. One of his worst moments aboard had occurred a week out of Agadir, when he was a few minutes later than normal waking up for the 10 p.m. With a few seconds to spare, he exploded out of his bunk, haranguing the rest of us for not waking him when he slept through the ten-minute warning. He took it as a betrayal, and as he left the cabin made us promise we'd *never* let him sleep like that again. Or else!

"If I'm late even *once* out here," he scolded when I joined him on deck, "I've lost my authority." I told him I believed the respect for him aboard was far deeper than a minor breach of the timetable. But it was like attempting to convince a deaf man to listen.

I was relieved when Steve, using Nigel's seat pad, a decidedly lesser saddle, took a normal shift on the 6-to-8 a.m. As we talked in the hour before sunrise, the question arose as to why Angela's rules for stopping the boat—or not stopping it—were so absurdly inflexible. It was well understood that she couldn't be stopping every time somebody dropped something overboard, but surely some discretion was possible. On the night my own cushion went in, I had wanted to run to her, to dive at her feet, beg her for mercy, plead with her to stop the boat, just this once, to restore my hope, to give me a life. But like a craven sissy, I held my tongue, acceding to the sort of orthodoxies against whose senselessness I was now in outright revolt.

Since then Ernst too had lost his cushion, while others had lost jackets, shoes, sheepskin—forfeitures that brought with them not only discomfort but possible injury and, at very least, a diminished capacity to row. For obvious benefits down the line, it seemed a small price to pay to stop the boat for ten minutes and pick up what was lost, at least when the weather allowed it. But in this Steve was aloft on his own blown petard. As much as anybody, he had been a proponent of the view that we should drive ourselves to the limit—which is to say non-stop. That in torment lay the refinement of the soul. To stop the boat would not only cost us minutes but would deprive of us of the chastening opportunity to have our asses shredded, our spinal nerves crushed, our tailbones restored from Darwinian uselessness to scream-inducing torture mechanisms.

Whatever the case, nothing in the protocol for stopping or not stopping seemed to hinge on the fact that by this time, three weeks into our journey, we were already a mere footnote to the three-boat assault on the record. Ocean rowing doesn't deal in such subtleties. While its contemporary form is graced by electronics and computers and space-age materials, it is run at oar-level by a jumble of pre-Galilean stupidities. If there was an answer to the question of what items would have had to be lost overboard to compel a brief delay, it was not apparent, except that it was an easier choice if the boat was simply *never allowed to turn around.*

Coincidentally, Angela did stop the boat late that afternoon under a cloudless sky, on a glassy-calm sea, so that for half an hour she and several of the kids could enjoy a swim, more specifically a buck-naked skinny dip, the first and last of the voyage. As they horsed around, a sea turtle swam past, visible from the deck as a kind of hazy yellow bean bag, its slow fins churning, unseen by those in the water. A minute later I spotted a five-foot tuna about twenty yards off the port hull, but didn't mention it, as I thought it could be taken for a shark, which might have precipitated panic.

A few minutes later, as Ryan and Nigel scraped at the barnacles, we felt the first tickle of what seemed to be a change of wind and immediately began to speculate on whether or not we had finally come into the trades, or they into us. By 5 p.m. a steady succession of long gentle rollers was coming directly out of the east, pushing us decidedly toward Barbados. Slowly, the mood expanded. By the time the watch changed at six, the rollers had begun to break and we were running a steady three knots.

Throughout my adult life, I have maintained an ambivalent commitment to the meaning and power of prayer. And will say now what I could not have said to the platoon of atheists on my watch (but perhaps should have said): that that evening, on the twilight shift, as the sunset flared behind me, I closed my eyes, summoned the best of my energies, and pleaded long and hard with the Gracious Loving Spirit of the Universe—let us say, with God—to spill some of Her infinite loving blessings our way, to pour Her endless Imagination into the westbound wind, and to let 'er rip immediately if it pleased Her loving and capacious heart.

As I did so, *mirabile dictu,* I experienced for the first time on the voyage the distinct sensation of pulling away from Africa. By seven o'clock our speed had several times topped four knots, and was spiking at five. We were moving due west.

Angela's reporting of the speeds off the GPS in her quarters would become a familiar cry during the weeks to come—"Six point four!" she'd scream—or "Seven point eight!" When a monster came through, all but swallowing our transoms and then proceeding up the trenches at waist level, the cry would hit *Ten point six!... Eleven point two!... Twelve point five!*

While we had rowed a thousand miles or more during the seventeen days since leaving Tarfaya, we had advanced just 500 miles toward Barbados. The absurd part was that with the trades properly behind us, and with some luck, the mileage ahead—perhaps 2,500 miles—could be covered in just a little more time than we had needed to cover the mileage behind.

I FEEL ALMOST embarrassed to report that at about ten that night, without warning, the wind began to squall then swirl and, within an hour, had risen so hard out of the southwest that by the end of the watch, at midnight, we were taking a dousing every five minutes over our shoulders on the port hull.

At 2 a.m., as we were about to come back on watch, Angela stuck her head out the hatch and called for the sea anchor.

And so it was: another night of standing watches and crowded bunks and all but tearful disillusionment—made deeper this time for being measured against the optimism of the afternoon.

For a while, Sylvain and I tried sharing the bunk, head to toe. But he is a big guy, more than six feet tall and solid, and as soon as he dozed off his feet and legs began colonizing whatever space I wasn't in. Finally I was trussed up, as if by Torquemada, so that I could barely move a muscle, and was soon half nuts with it and was out onto the floor with whoever else happened to be scrabbling to protect their sanity in the narrow plywood passage. At perhaps 7 a.m., desperate to piss but unable to move in the darkness, I grabbed a steel water bottle that for several days had been rolling around the cabin floor without a top. I filled it to the neck and propped it upright between my legs, thinking to hold it there until daylight. What I had not counted on was the exquisitely therapeutic warmth that now emanated from its metal flanks. Unwilling to forego such a comfort, I began shifting it carefully between my thighs and finally onto my stomach beneath my T-shirt, a far-from-perfect little space heater, but still upright and dry when I woke at dawn.

As we resumed rowing at about 8 a.m., Margaret announced that since David was now in sick bay (he had injured his knee and would not take a regular turn again), we'd each have to row another hour a day to make up for the loss of power. Fortunately, by late morning the watch captains took charge and made the added hour optional, although not until I had put in my overtime, meaning I had no break before the 10-to-noon, which on this day was a dreamy, sun-bathed idyll.

While Margaret and I had never resolved our mutual claim on my rowing cushion, she had made peace to the point of offering me her spare Crocs when mine went overboard and a bit of sheepskin to protect my feet, and a water bottle when mine went into the sea. Later in the voyage, she would suggest that at some point we might walk the Spanish Camino de Santiago together. And we talked, if occasionally, about books (she had brought along a Jane Austen novel); about writing (mostly mine, although I had the feeling she had penned a poem or two); about her day job (as a production coordinator on BBC Television shoots); about her family (successive generations of Tasmanian farmers, although her parents were social workers who lived in Queensland, where they were handy to the Indian ashram at which they spent their winters).

By now, as I have hinted, I was developing a grudging appreciation of Margaret, who since losing her job as watch commander had shown an almost heroic fortitude in reasserting herself as someone to be reckoned with.

Late that afternoon, as Sylvain came on deck to row he said to her quite amicably, "Margaret, what is the weather report for tonight?"

She turned, glared at him and said, "Didn't I already give you the report?"

"No, you didn't," he responded with homicidal solemnity.

"Oh, well then," she brightened, "I've got us heading more south again."

"But what is the forecast?" he said.

"Well, I'm going to *keep* us heading south," she said, at which point he rolled his eyes, turned his attention to his iPod, and took his seat.

EARLY THAT evening, I watched a small school of dorado cruising alongside the boat, apparently curious about the oars. From time to time one of them would detour up to a blade as it entered the water and nudge it with its nose, perhaps testing its edibility. For me, it was a quite heady little intimacy, in that each time it happened a tremor of this wild creature's power came pulsing up the graphite shaft of the oar, like current in a wire, into my hands. Dorado are not pretty fish, but they are elegant: silvery, about three feet long, with blunt heads and underbites that (having seen three of my children through orthodontic reconstruction) I am glad I do not have to pay to resolve. Their showiest feature is their dorsal fin, a sapphire appendage that, extended, forms a kind of ripsaw or Chinese fan, as much as ten inches deep, running the length of their backs.

Even at night we'd see them ghosting along, often in schools of six or eight. At dawn, one or two of them would invariably come rocketing out of the water, hitting some helpless little flying fish or sardine. Or a shark would appear, and in an instant the hunter would become the hunted.

That evening, about twenty minutes before dusk, one of our silvery acquaintances came flaring up out of the ocean about a hundred yards from the boat and screamed toward us, leaping on its tail, bouncing off waves, ripping open the surface like a zipper until, at a point about twenty yards from our port hull, a surfboard-sized shadow settled in underneath it at speed. As in the panic sequence out of some Jacques Cousteau extravaganza, a shark's snout appeared above the waterline, mouth wide open, teeth on display, and in a last lightning plunge engulfed the fish, sending up a burst of pink mist and vanishing as quickly as it had appeared.

At the time, Dylan was rowing in front of me. He had stopped as the chase ensued, and now turned to me and, as amateurs will, we reviewed the performance in the sort of breathless overstatements I had once used to review plays for CBC Radio: *A splashy tour de force!... Oceanic in scope!... Sharkspeare at the height of his powers!*

"I think it was a white!" enthused Dylan (White).

"I think a Wilkins," I said, suspecting in reality that it had been a blue, because of its speed. I had learned to identify sharks during a year living in Nassau in the 1970s when I went almost daily to the harbor to watch the hammerheads and tigers and bulls—basically anything that cruised up to the docks, particularly in the lights at night, looking for a stray grouper or parrot fish, outside the Montagu Beach Hotel.

Dylan and I agreed that we had expected to see more sharks, especially off the coast of Africa. Previous expeditions had seen them daily, sometimes in pairs or schools. They are the governors of the sea, the top of the food chain, as well as the carrion sweepers, and are vital to a healthy marine ecology. But their numbers are down—some biologists say as much as 90 percent during the past fifteen years—due partly, it would seem, to their slaughter for the production of shark fin soup, which has recently become a kind of pop star among China's vast new population of tech wizards and entrepreneurs—and among expatriates as well. The result is that more than 73 million sharks were slaughtered in 2010 by fishing fleets worldwide, the most aggressive of which were from Spain, Norway, Great Britain, and France, not countries one would expect to tolerate medieval attitudes toward ecology. Such is the value of the soup's main ingredient (the dried fins go for $350/pound retail) that shark hunters will "fin" a captured shark, which is to say chop off its dorsal and pectoral fins, generally with a machete, and release the animal to bleed to death or to be eaten by its kin, which are attracted to the victim's blood in the water.

Dylan remarked matter-of-factly that there was a kind of justice in the fact that human beings are occasionally finned by sharks, or "limbed" by them, as the karmic case might be. His argument reminded me of journalist (and ex-seaman) Hunter S. Thompson's sage comment that "Civilization ends at the waterline. Beyond that, we all enter the food chain, and not always right at the top."

When the dorado weren't around, tuna would occasionally cozy up alongside the boat, gorgeous things, outsized, platinum, sometimes cruising to within inches of our hulls. Or an army of flying fish would slingshot out of a wave, spooked by a predator or perhaps a big blue rowboat.

While whale sightings were limited, we had while on sea anchor seen what I believe was a right whale about 300 yards off our starboard hull. It breached almost invisibly, blew perhaps a twenty-foot geyser, then five minutes later erupted out of the water, a pillar of black basalt, rising thirty feet in the air before crashing into the sea. On another day we saw a pair of pilot whales, the Potato Heads of the sea, a mother and baby, no more than twenty-five yards from the boat.

Our resident expert on whales was Aleksa, who had an affinity for a range of vertebrates but particularly mammals, large ones. She could not have seen many of them in the wilds of Long Island but lived just miles from the beach at Deer Park and had apparently spent enough time offshore to familiarize herself with marine species such as minke whales and fin whales, as well as pilots and rights and grays. She had brought along a bird book, which was quickly seconded by Dylan, who kept it in his junk hammock, from which I often snatched it to read about gannets and frigate birds and albatrosses—as well as our durable little storm petrels, which were forever around us, animating the wind, both riding and dodging it, like electrons in and out of orbit.

Whatever the stresses and pettiness onboard, and no matter what the uncertainties, the sightings were a constant and exhilarating reminder to me of the unabridged dimensions of the journey—the resiliency of a script whose margin illuminations were sharks and whales and dolphins; and sea turtles and flying fish and jellyfish. It was all of this, I wish to emphasize, along with the precious camaraderie of my crewmates, even those I have slagged, that kept me going, kept me sane, that in a sense kept us all going and sane. It would have been difficult, if not impossible, against a backdrop of such splendor and interdependence, of such unspeakable wildness, to give complete ascendancy to the grousing and griping and despondency, not to mention the exhaustion and physical discomforts, that tended to dominate our lives.

Amid all the perils and privation, and bad food and compromised ideals and doubts about one's stamina, there were mornings and afternoons in the trenches, with the sun blazing, the boat rising and falling like an elevator, the petrels diving, the flying fish soaring—mornings and afternoons when, somewhere deep down, sometimes for just a moment, I knew that as cheerless as I sometimes felt, I had never been happier; or that as skinny as I was getting, I had never felt more robust; and that as exhausted as I was, I had never felt more alive or invigorated.

As a kind of antidote to the hassles and despondency (and because I sat behind the other rowers where nobody could see me), I would occasionally quit rowing entirely and would simply lie back and gaze at the sky. Or I would get up out of my rowing seat at dawn to better witness the sunrise. Or would wait with my camera for the dolphins or whales, or for the occasional tuna or shark. Or in the wee hours, in the rain, would turn my tiny borrowed flashlight on a stray dorado that was cruising along by one of the rudders.

The water itself played a significant part in this rolling oceanic pageant. And the wind. And skies. One's connection to the stars on a dark night on the equatorial Atlantic—to Orion and Cygnus and the Southern Cross (barely visible above the horizon at those latitudes in winter)—is as alluring and uncontaminated as it must have been for the Phoenicians and Egyptians of antiquity. We were blessed equally by the sunsets and cloud formations, sometimes a thousand fine rills, like strands of kinked yarn, repeated in parallel from horizon to horizon. And by the power of the swells—by our immersion, day and night, in what I have come to think of as a kind of cosmological opera, replete with mysteries and melodrama and mercies.

On Day 20, in conversation with Liam, I mentioned my pleasure in all of this, explaining that despite the difficulties and exhaustion, I felt grateful to be out there, indeed felt badly for those who had been convinced it was all a pitiful disaster. He was in smart-aleck mode, and said immediately, "I hope you're being sarcastic," to which I responded that I hoped *he* was being sarcastic, because I was not; that I was in fact thrilled to be out here experiencing the Atlantic—its creatures, its rhythms, its vastness—in this immediate and exhilarating way.

I said it was "part of what I had come looking for," his answer to which was that he wasn't "into travel as Quest." I told him I wasn't either but that I thought one of the more useful delusions about an expedition such as ours was that at times it *seemed* like a quest, or at least represented one.

"It did when we were after the record," he said.

"To me it still does," I protested, adding that what bugged me about the journey was that as its original motivation had slipped away, and a need had arisen to create new motivation, some of our rowers had retreated instead into cynicism or frustration.

"Yeah, like me," he responded quite cheerfully, although he honored our conversation by saying he would think about what had been said. I told him I thought he'd gain more by thinking about the sea. There was a flippancy to the comment, and yet I believed it. So much of the planet is water—yet most of us know so little about the power and reality of the sea, or about our own intangible connections, some of them evolutionary, to its rhythms and draw.

Where ecology was concerned, it seemed that every mile we covered—the sea life, the water, the weather, the implied geography of the sea floor—was a kind of object lesson in planetary connection and history. At a rower's pace you're able to see, or at least sense, the intricacies of the connections, as you never can from, say, a jet or even a ship. As for human history, several times in recent days I had found myself thinking about the earliest Atlantic crossings, in particular the slave ships leaving Africa, as we did, with their wretched cargoes and crews. They followed our route exactly, arriving in the Caribbean, where we too eventually hoped to make land and where the ecology of that dire history is all still in evidence: the descendents of the slaves still bearing the names of their masters, still working the fields, still harvesting the flying fish that their forebears harvested in chains.

That night, toward the end of the 2 a.m. watch, the sea came alive with phosphorescence, billions of one-celled creatures, microscopic phytoplankton, ignited by our oars, blinking their tiny greenish lights among the reflections of the stars. These so-called dinoflagellates are said to light up when disturbed so that whatever fish or mammal might be grazing them will be distracted just long enough to allow the wee dynamos to slip away.

At dawn, a school of dolphins materialized, perhaps twenty of them, fishing and goofing around within forty feet of the boat. They are said to move in pods or convoys for protection, but when seven of them came out of a wave in a kind of syncopated choreography, I commented to Dylan that they seemed to get more out of their community life than mere protection.

"They communicate better than we do," he said over his shoulder, adding that each of them "has a completely distinctive voice—like his own FM radio frequency." The result is that when one dolphin contacts the others, they know not just that one of their own has located food or encountered danger, or has decided simply to have some fun, but precisely who it is, and where and with whom he or she is traveling. According to Dylan, they have more brain capacity than most primates and are one of few mammals that engages in sex when the female is not in her estrous cycle. "In other words for the fun of it," he said. Which is more than one can say for those psychopathic squirrels—or for the occasional human being I have met.

BY NOON that day, the wind had revived. And with it our sense of possibility. Our previous assumption that we had located the trades had been based on a rolling sea, long shallow swells that picked us up and drove us forward, then passed gently beneath the hulls. Today's wind was more aggressive, gustier, and the waves came higher and harder into the transoms and beneath the boat. And they were breaking, both beneath and around us, indeed sometimes overtop of our hulls.

The problem was that after so many false alarms and dashed expectations, nobody dared hope.

On the other hand, *something* was afoot, and by 4 p.m., when the powerful east wind that had been driving us forward for nearly five hours had neither shifted nor calmed, it did begin to seem that maybe, just maybe.

Just maybe.

By 6 p.m., the seas were the wildest we'd seen. Green water was rolling through the rowing trenches with such force that at one point Steve, who was rowing directly in front of me, was lifted off his seat, spun ninety degrees, and thrown hard into the trench at my feet. As I stood talking to Sylvain at the beginning of the next watch, holding tight to the safety line as the boat heaved, he too was lifted by a wave and thrown onto the outer gunnels in such a way that had it not been for the rigger, which took much of his weight and gave his ankle a good dig, he might well have been overboard.

The real problem with such weather comes at nightfall, when you can no longer see the waves arriving. Everything is a surprise, significantly heightening the chance of being knocked from your seat, or having your oar ripped free, or the handle of it driven into your sternum or teeth. However, Angela was insistent that we row. I was not sure she was the best one to make such a call, since she was not on deck but merely rocking around in her cubby hole. It is surprising how even a few seconds of exposure to high wind and flying spume, or to Poe-level blackness and rain, can clarify the hazards facing rowers on such a night. Perhaps the watch commanders should have been consulted. But Angela was determined that we not become "figureheads," as she put it.

As we went out onto the bridge for the 10-to-midnight, she informed us that this was "a rowing expedition, not a pleasure cruise."

"Make sure that's clear in your book," Ernst joked as we left the cabin with our life jackets on.

But there was little joking from that point forward. Within minutes, we were under such a heavy dunning from the sea that even Steve assessed the conditions as "pretty dangerous."

If I wondered at times who would be the first to blow, to rebel openly against the hazards that were occasionally imposed on us, I got my answer maybe ten minutes into the watch. At that point a fit of wild screaming erupted on the far side of the cabin, at first so much like an animal that it took a few seconds for me to realize that it was Tom. He had hit his limits and was now hollering above the wind that he couldn't row in this GAWDAM FUCK-ING WEATHER, that NOBODY CAN ROW IN THIS FUCK-ING WEATHER, that command could SHOVE IT UP THEIR ASS BECAUSE I'M NOT GONNA ROW IN THIS FUCKING WEATHER!

A minute later, when the commotion had died down, Tom appeared rather meekly on the bridge, ushered along by, I think, Sylvain or Louise, who quickly marshaled him into bed. And there he stayed until dawn, when he arose as hearty and energetic as ever. And not the least bit repentant. And why should he have been? Had he not declared revolt, we might have been out there all night. Indeed, any of the rest of us might have erupted five minutes later.

As it was, within ten minutes of his little blow-up, Angela, to everyone's relief, shut down rowing for the night. And some ten hours later had not yet called for a resumption. However, this time there was a difference in our inactivity. Rather than dragging the sea anchor, holding out against the gale, brooding on our lost progress, we were *riding* the gale, *surfing* it, borne along by what we were now convinced were the trade winds, as well as by the beginnings of the equatorial current.

I will pause here only long enough to restore Tom's potentially diminished reputation by making it clear that he is no softy and never has been. On the contrary, he was, at sixty-seven, one of the toughest guys I have ever met, with the toughest hide and sinew and the durability of a mule. He grew up in Switzerland, cycling through the mountains, developing lungs and leg muscles that served him well as a teenaged speed skater and, during the 1960s, as a Canadian champion. He has rowed the length and breadth of Lakes Ontario and Erie by himself and, once, having fallen through the ice of Lake Ontario while skating, resurrected himself without help, found a way of drying his clothes on a construction site at twenty below zero, and carried on with his day. A short film about one of his night rows across Lake Ontario begins with the eyebrow-raising credit "Tom Cruise." Then, as Tom puts it, "an apostrophe and an *s* drop into place," so that now it's *Tom's* Cruise, "and everybody's disappointed because it's just me and not the movie star." When he told me this story, he paused, reflected, and said, "What did they expect—that at the age of sixty-something I was going to be played by Tom Cruise rowing across Lake Ontario?"

As a young man Tom studied Berber carpet-making as it occurs in the Atlas Mountains, eventually became a carpet layer, and for forty years as such has spent ten-hour days on his knees, without pads, on concrete floors, often in Toronto hotel towers. One of the impressive results of this monastic-level self-torture is that he has developed a kind of natural knee pad, a callused thickening of the skin and bone, that reminded me of the knee pads of elephants and camels. One day in the boatyard in Agadir, while he worked on the tramps, I watched him kneel for three hours straight on rough concrete, in shorts, without flinching, while I lasted less than a minute before running for a knee pad.

Of all Angela's speeches to the crew, I most appreciated the one she delivered that afternoon, as the wind drove us with ever-destabilizing fury toward the west. We had resumed rowing—or rather poking our oars into the sea, hoping that somehow we'd be able to retrieve them without mishap. "OKAY, EVERYBODY!" she called from the bridge, where she could be heard both in the cabin and in the trenches. "It looks like we're on our way, that this is it! There's no turning back!" As far as she could calculate, we had a twenty-four-day supply of food for a journey that we should now be able to complete in twenty-two days.

The latter estimate sounded rosy to me, but right now neither I nor anyone else was of a mind to quibble. "As for rowing," she yelled above the wind, "We're gonna do it when we can! I don't wanta risk lives or injury! But with practice you're going to get better in these conditions. Some of you are already rowing better!"

She asked for questions, but with the exception of a comment uttered sotto voce about the weight of food still aboard, any of the dozens that might have been asked went unspoken.

"I'm proud of you all! You're an amazing crew!" she proclaimed in summing up. "It's gonna be hard! It's gonna be dangerous! It's gonna be tiring! But I know you guys can do it!"

At that point, as in a skit out of Monty Python, Angela called for "three cheers for *Big Blue*," drawing forth one of the measliest expressions of confidence I have ever heard, really less a cheer than a kind of discharge, a growl of the sort one might expect to be induced by an exorcist. Anyone who'd witnessed it would have been convinced that the boat's next solid landing was scheduled not for Barbados but for some spiny outcrop on the lightless floor of the Atlantic.

14

As **IT TURNED** out, Angela was not far off in her predictions: we did get better on the oars. And it was hard. And it was dangerous—more so than I had imagined. Indeed, from that point forward, for fifteen days straight, we were pushed—and pushed around—by winds as high as fifty knots and by rollers the height of houses. The onslaught at times bashed the boat so relentlessly that, particularly during the next few days, I had doubts, as did others, that our eccentric little craft could possibly hold together. It wasn't uncommon for a wave to roll right over us in the trenches or come up under the cabin and hit it with such force that from inside it sounded as if a grenade had been detonated beneath the floor.

One person I had not expected to blow under the pressure was Liam Flynn. But a few days into the wild ride, on I think the 10-to-midnight, he took several awful dousings and quite suddenly ripped his oar out of its lock and, with a scream, drove the end of its handle like a javelin into the cabin wall. And then did it again, then again, making a terrible racket and causing me to think that he was going to keep hammering till he broke through the wall. But instead, after the third convulsive pitch, he flung the oar onto the tramp, jumped out of the seat, beside himself with frustration, and disappeared to the other side of the bridge. Meanwhile, it was a tribute to the strength of the resin-coated plywood that the oar did not penetrate it and spear either Nigel or Margaret, whose bunks, one above the other, were immediately inside that part of the wall.

As the ride grew hairier, Dylan and I worked up a little exchange of gallows humor. "Isn't it great that the boat hasn't fallen apart?" one of us would say, to which the other would respond with vaudevillian gusto that for *sure* it was, that it was everything we could have hoped for—or we'd agree that *boy,* this ten-thousand-dollar cruise was good value, and we were just *so happy* we hadn't wasted our money on the deluxe cruise, the one with the toilet paper and the better chance of survival, and so on.

On the tougher watches, or in gloomy moments in the cabin, I occasionally found myself thinking about what lay below—mountains, valleys, impenetrable pressures and darkness; blind sea creatures so far down that they breathe sulfur gases instead of oxygen; and drowned seamen and the ships that took them to the bottom.

Such vessels are down there by the hundreds. Because of the trade winds they are concentrated on the very route we were traveling, a kind of sailing lane followed for centuries by the likes of Columbus, Vespucci, da Gama, Cortés, Pizzaro—and later Darwin and Maury—as well as by thousands upon thousands of now-forgotten trading, passenger, and naval vessels, many of which went to the bottom. There were some 40,000 slave-ship crossings alone on the route, carrying 11 million slaves, between 1550 and 1860.

IN THE GRIP of the trades, as Angela had mandated, we rowed when we could—essentially when it was safe. And as she had speculated, the periods of rowing got longer. By the third day of our new lives as swashbucklers, we were again rowing around the clock. And paying for it in bruises, battered backsides, and exhaustion.

The following afternoon, a day on which flying fish were in the air in battalions, as I stood on the bridge in a kind of trance, a pair of killer whales arced out of the swells fifty yards off the port rudder. I remember them because at that moment, behind me, there was a hammering from within against the sliding cabin door which was sometimes jammed and needed opening from the outside. I pried it back, and the captain, whom I had not seen upright for a day, emerged onto the bridge in a kind of duck squat. As always, to get around the boat, she was wearing her leg braces.

If she seemed distant or impassive it was perhaps the medication she was using to control her back pain, which had intensified with the increased pounding of the boat. Or perhaps for the moment she was simply floating free above her pain.

In her hand was a green nylon bag of a size that would comfortably have held a pair of shoes. Protruding from its puckered mouth was a foot or so of orange neoprene rope.

She looked at me as if at a rare insect and said quietly, "I want to review our man-overboard procedures," and she asked if I'd help her get everybody to the bridge. The word "review" was a misnomer, in that there *were* no man-overboard procedures. At least nothing specific. At Shelter Island in calm water, we had performed a mock rescue when Ryan, under instruction, had leapt into the channel in a survival suit. But his rescue was really little more than a charade, certainly nothing that could be applied now. The problem was that during the past few days, the likelihood that someone might actually *go* overboard had increased tenfold—as had the odds against their survival.

I summoned the crew, and a minute later a loose gaggle of them had gathered at the rear of the cabin.

"This," Angela said without enthusiasm, "is our man-overboard emergency bag." She held up the bag, looking at it not as if people's lives might depend on it but as if she couldn't quite remember whether she had packed the pastrami. "In the event somebody goes over," she explained, "all you do is yank the bag from the stern rail and let 'er fly."

The hope, she said, was that the rope inside, the near end of which would be knotted to the rail, would uncoil, all hundred feet or so of it, and that the person in the sea would be able to grab it and hang on. Suddenly, she was demonstrating—not with the bag, just with the coil of rope, flinging it into the wind in such a way that, at best, perhaps twenty-five feet of it fluttered off the bridge, settling in a loose tangle on the water.

"Well, so much for that," she said solemnly, adding that "everything flies better with the weight of the bag attached." In other words, even though there were difficulties enacting a significant life-saving maneuver under no pressure, in full daylight, it would all certainly work better in life-and-death circumstances, in the dark, in the cold, in a gale.

Almost as an afterthought, Angela informed us that the bag contained an EPIRB, which would, if activated, send a signal to people on land that a human being was in distress at such-and-such coordinates. The drearier awareness here was that in such a circumstance said human being would almost certainly be in the direst of straits, perhaps even without a life jacket, since he or she had been aboard a boat whose safety protocol could have been inked *tout complet* on a grain of rice or written out longhand on a three-mil chad.

"May we see it?" Ernst asked in reference to the EPIRB.

"Sure," said Angela, holding it briefly aloft and then tucking it back in the bag.

"How does it turn on?" asked Tom Butscher, to whom Angela responded that there was a button, "actually two buttons," and that it took both hands to press them simultaneously.

As she began fastening the bag to the rail, I said, "Wait, Angela! Hold on a second! Show us how it turns on."

"The two top buttons," she said.

"But you're in the ocean," I protested. "It's rough, it's dark, you're confused. Am I supposed to have a head-lamp and glasses on when I go overboard?"

"Only if you intend to do some reading," she joked. "There's a flashlight in the bag."

"A flashlight!" hooted Ryan.

"It's waterproof," she said. "It's one of those you crank."

"So you need a third hand to do the cranking!" he exclaimed.

"And one to swim," added Tom.

"If anybody wants to look in the bag," Angela said, "it's here on the rail. You can play with the stuff. Just make sure the rope's not tangled inside." And with that she ducked into the cabin and was gone.

That evening as we rowed, I asked Steve if he didn't find her evasiveness pretty bizarre.

"No more bizarre than most of what goes on out here," he shrugged.

I asked why he thought she wouldn't answer questions—or was it possibly just *my* questions she wouldn't answer?

He rowed a few strokes, hoisted his blade, and turned in the seat so that his voice wasn't lost in the wind. He said, "What you were asking was basically how any of us is going to survive out there on our own, in high seas, in the dark, with no help and no protection from either the elements or the sharks."

I told him I thought it was a good question—always had.

"The problem," he said, "is that like a lot of good questions it's one for which there isn't any answer."

I was thinking about this when he called over his shoulder, "At least none Angela can provide. Thank God she's honest enough not to try."

WITHIN FOUR hours, we were back on standing watch— at least through the wee hours. And the next day barely rowed at all. You couldn't get an oar in the water. The good news was we were rocketing toward Barbados. After five days in the trades, we had doubled our mileage (another five and we would be in the middle of the Atlantic Ocean).

Hard though it may be to fathom, one of the more compelling debates through these early days of transition and thrilling new progress was whether or not our rowing was actually doing us any good, was making the boat go faster. There was a smattering of evidence, or at least conjecture, that sticking the oars in the water was in fact impeding our progress as we plunged along on the surf. On I think the fourth day in the trades, Steve conducted some simple experiments, measuring our progress during a ten-minute period of rowing against our progress during a ten-minute period while we were not rowing—all of it at equivalent wind speed and direction. He did this three or four times in succession, and came to the enlightening if disheartening conclusion that under these preposterously favorable conditions, rowing added a grand total of 0.1 (maximum 0.2) knots to our speed—in other words 4 or 5 percent. Meanwhile, Angela, as skipper, with her reputation as an ocean rower on the line, declaimed that the rowing was adding 1.5 knots, or nearly 40 percent, to our speed.

I myself suspected that the tiny advantage of having rowers in the seats, oars engaged, was a matter more of "windage" or sail value than of the rowing itself—in other words that each rower, sitting upright, with oar extended, was catching sufficient tailwind to help drive the boat forward, even if his or her rowing did not.

Steve believed that on days when the wind was coming directly from behind, we'd get as much or more speed if, rather than rowing at all, we simply lined up on the bridge, joined arms, stood there in our appropriately named windbreakers, and together impersonated a sail. Which I hasten to point out we never did. Where the integrity of our row was concerned, we were impeccable Popeyes, interested in cheating only the Reaper.

The hard truth was that on our best day of progress—111 miles over twenty-four hours—no one rowed a stroke, or even got into the seats. It was simply too rough.

Months later, Roy Finlay, with whom I have kept loosely in touch, emailed me and suggested that because no one had actually rowed on our best day of mileage, the Ocean Rowing Society was considering denying us certification for an ocean crossing. Which did not surprise me, given the society's idiosyncratic and (in my opinion) rather self-serving standards. What did surprise me was to learn that the world record for distance achieved in twenty-four hours with a crew on the oars, full steam ahead, was just 117 miles, held jointly by the boats *La Mondiale* and *Artemis Investments,* both of which were captained by Leven Brown. When they set their respective records, both boats were being pushed by wind and waves approximating those that had been pushing us. Which is to say that some of the best rowers in the world were able to add just six miles a day, or 5 percent, to the speed we reached without oars. It was, as they say, a far cry from Angela's contention that rowing added 40 percent to the speed.

Not that I give a hoot about such statistics for their own sake. However, to suggest that the wind, with the waves it tosses up and the currents it generates, is not the most important factor in *any* ocean row is absurd. All crossings are current- and wind-aided. Or, alternatively, wind-deterred. Many ocean rowboats get hung up on sea anchor for several days, during which no rowing takes place, or get tossed around to such a degree that rowing can become impossible for periods of time. As it occasionally was for us.

Perhaps the classic example of the effects of wind and current on a boat's progress was reported by Ponce de León in 1513 off the coast of what is now Florida, when he found his ship moving alternately forward and backward, sometimes at significant speed, or sometimes standing still, under the influence of both a gale-level northeast wind and the varying strength of the northeast-bound Gulf Stream beneath him.

My point is that under such unpredictable forces, to penalize one boat for a day of unavoidably missed rowing and not penalize a boat on which the rowers were able to be in the seats but were perhaps doing nothing, is amateurish and prejudiced, and, to my mind, renders irrelevant any decision the rowing society might make about our crossing.

Fortunately, the temporal rewards of ocean rowing still amount to little more than a cheeseburger or two if and when you reach your destination—well, and perhaps half an hour of docking maneuvers if your sweetheart shows up to greet you. However, the moment any significant cash is offered to competitors, those in authority will almost certainly feel compelled to extend their paranoia about cheating into the realm of doping and urine testing and onboard surveillance cameras, and will eventually ruin what innocence might be left to the sport if they'd just leave it alone and let it breathe.

Beyond all of this, I might add, there was from the beginning a supposition among those who follow the sport that our cabin gave us a "sailing" advantage, which is to say it caught wind. And undoubtedly it did. And yet our true bursts of progress (like a surfer's) came not from wind directly but from individual waves, some of which pushed us briefly to twelve or thirteen knots, as Angela would invariably holler out.

I told Roy I thought the society's position was a steaming heap. Not that it disheartened me particularly. If anything, it made me appreciate our effort all the more. And our motley little crew. And our boat—our lovely ugly duckling of a boat, which, from the first time I saw her in the boatyard at Shelter Island, had possessed for me a kind of magic. Over the years, I had loved many: a seaflea called *Go Man Go* that as a kid I worshipped at a neighbor's boat slip on Clear Lake in Muskoka; a mahogany launch called the *Rocket,* built by my Uncle Clive in 1950 on the Muskoka River at Bracebridge; a Norwegian mahogany sailing dinghy with a blue gaff-rigged sail, given to me by my parents on my twelfth birthday and still in my possession; a twelve-foot Humber Jewel, the most elegant fiberglass runabout ever made, owned by my sister Ann and me and missed since the day I sold it forty years ago. I had loved them all. However, no boat of my intimate acquaintance had ever quite captured my heart like *Big Blue*—for its history and vulnerability and eccentricity; and for all it represented in terms of our commitment and effort and hopes. It wasn't just that our lives were dependent on this extraordinary vessel (as they are dependent on any boat that takes us away from shore) but that they were dependent on it in situations where they were genuinely and imminently at stake.

David told me that in the days before we launched *Big Blue,* people would come into the boatyard on Shelter Island and simply stare at it. Or would ask "What *is* it?" Or "Where's its engine?" Or "Is it modeled after a spacecraft of some sort?" At the risk of being taken for one of those people who wears a saucepan for a hat, I might point out that *Big Blue* is undoubtedly the only rowboat in history that bears a conceptual likeness to the ancient Ark of the Covenant, the mythic vessel of spiritual ascendancy. Indeed, if I were the Ocean Rowing Society and had half an imagination, I'd be far more concerned about the powers intrinsic to that likeness than about whether or not the cabin (where, like Moses, we stored the manna) was catching a little more wind than the society liked to see in a boat's sails. One day in Agadir I had mentioned the likeness to the electrical designer at the boatyard, who prayed five times daily to Mecca. "Yaz-yaz, I'm zee-ing it!" he exclaimed immediately. "Eet glow!"

And it did, in its way. As did its crew, to whom I have not always been either polite or kind on these pages. And yet I was conscious by now of the degree to which I was beginning to care, and care deeply, about these people— not (as the relativist might claim) in spite of their shortcomings and grievances (and chaos and liabilities and doubts) but in larger part *because* of all of these, and because of their nonstop reminders, both stated and otherwise, of my own rather glaring and artless deficiencies. It was *these* people and their improbable blue boat, not the record-breakers or rowing society or ethics inspectors, who were going to get me home and save my life and inhabit my story. And in some thorny inner part of me, I was increasingly reluctant to hear anybody call them down. Well, except for myself—or perhaps Steve, who, for all he had done, had in a sense earned the right. And the right to be dismayed. And be painfully, mortally disappointed. And be our token alpha male.

I should acknowledge while in the mood that even when I was livid at Steve, I still loved the guy—and in my way loved Angela and Tom ... and Liam and Ryan ... and all the rest, every one of them, for their humanity and fortitude and folly—and most especially, I want to say, for whatever mysterious compulsion had brought them, and had brought me too, to this curious little community making its way stubbornly across the Atlantic.

Meanwhile, there were nights in the rowing trenches that were so black and cold and lonesome that quite apart from my evolving affection for the crew, I felt redoubled in my love for those back home. My kids. My family. My old friends. *Where were they? What were they doing while I was out here on the ocean in the dark?*

"We'll rename it the *Love Boat!*" enthused Tom when I mentioned the fragility of my emotions, the affection I was feeling toward the crew and toward my loved ones back on land.

On a more immediate level, I continued to nurse a hope that perhaps Trish might come to Barbados to meet the boat. The possibility was increased somewhat by the fact that she had fallen in with Steve's wife, Janet, whom she had met for the first time during my reunion with Janet and Steve at Thessalon in 2009. Indeed, the two of them seemed inspired by each other on a level more intuitive and exhilarating than either of them seemed inspired by Steve or me.

15

THE BREAK FROM steady rowing, unfortunately, did not make the voyage any easier. On the twenty-third night, I went out on watch for an hour and—reluctant to go back into the cabin, which was as crowded and inhospitable as ever—scrunched myself into the port bow hold, where I hoped to sleep till dawn. There, below deck, the darkness was absolute, the air stifling, and the crashing and bouncing of the waves tended to bring on nightmares about the boat breaking up while you were more or less trapped in the hull. As I crouched, sweating, with my head between my knees, I was transported rather suddenly to a forgotten childhood dread that I would get imprisoned by bad guys in a space that was too small to allow me to move, and would be left there to suffocate. I emerged into the moonlight and, in my haste to get free of the hatch, tripped and tumbled into the rowing trench. I was not wearing my life line, meaning that if I had fallen in the other direction, I'd have been gone into the sea. As it was, before I could catch myself I had bashed my shin so severely that to prevent myself from screaming as I peered through the torn flesh at the bone, I settled onto the rowing seat, grasped my ankles in my hands and, for what seemed like half an hour but was probably ten minutes or less, rocked back and forth in a kind of rapture of pain as intense as any I have ever experienced.

Within forty-eight hours, the injury had turned ugly. Not only had it failed to scab over, it had produced an oval of angry-looking swelling as big as my hand. The pain grew so severe I feared having the lesion touched and took to wrapping it in a T-shirt and wearing long pants to protect it. Realizing it needed attention but not wanting to put pressure on Steve or Sylvain, who had enough to think about, I got up from my seat on the 10 a.m. watch on the twenty-sixth day, limped forward along the tramp and, raising my pant leg, asked Liam what he thought. "Good God!" he exclaimed and immediately demanded to know why I hadn't brought the injury to anyone's attention. "Show it to Steve or Sylvain immediately!" he said. Which I did when Sylvain came out at watch change. And I happily accepted his recommendation that I draw a ballpoint line around the swelling to gauge its progress over the next few hours. However, even touching the ballpoint to the skin was an exercise in acute masochism. Meanwhile, Liam mentioned the wound to Steve, who later, in the cabin, asked me for a look and with no hesitation prescribed an antibiotic and handed over a plastic bottle of pills.

I felt sheepish when an hour or so later Sylvain and Steve engaged each other briefly but passionately over their conflicting assessments. I attempted to explain to Sylvain that it was not I who had sought out Steve's opinion, but he who had asked to see the injury (and of course I was happy to show it to him and was grateful I had). I will say that at no point did the wound prevent me from rowing, one of precious few aspects of my physical performance on the boat in which I take any pride. That and the fact that I did not go overboard—or otherwise require burial at sea, which, among other insults to my self-confidence, would have been an indelible blot on my record as a seaman.

If I had a single abiding regret about the injury, it was that by a series of misunderstandings and misstatements, it brought a day of most excruciating distress to my children. I would not find out until weeks later that my hometown newspaper in Thunder Bay had carried a story reporting that I had been "badly injured" on my crossing of the Atlantic. I believe the report originated from a brief SAT phone conversation between Dylan White and Kelly Saxberg concerning the progress of Dylan's video-taking—a chat in which the state of my wounded leg was described by Dylan in perhaps overly vivid hues (rendered more vivid yet in their transmission to the newspaper, which was in regular contact with Kelly). The next day, one of my children was told at school that my injury was so severe I had been "taken off the boat." The supposition at home was that I was dying in some Senegalese hospital or had lost a limb and was lying comatose aboard some tramp freighter on its way to Kuala Lumpur. Only by a series of phone calls from my ex-wife in Thunder Bay to Trish in Toronto and to Angela's partner, Deb, in California was the matter cleared up—unfortunately, not before it had created a day of anxiety and fear for Eden, Georgia, and Matt.

FOR THE MOST part we wore safety lines clipped to various parts of the boat. When the seas were roughest, we wore life preservers. But even those precautions weren't "bombproof," as the saying goes; and on the afternoon of our twenty-sixth day aboard, as I lay in my bunk pondering the wildness of the sea beneath the cabin floor, it struck me with considerable force that there was a reason, a very specific one, for Angela's ongoing evasions about our man-overboard procedures—or lack thereof. In an instant of bleak insight it dawned on me that if you went into the sea under these conditions, even with a life vest on, you were gone, you were dead. That in the heaviest seas there was no possibility of turning *Big Blue* around, of rowing back upwind into the waves to effect a rescue.

Even if the victim was in possession of an EPIRB such as the one in the emergency throw bag, the efficacy of same depended on a ship or sailing vessel being nearby and being willing to seek out a swimmer who, in all likelihood, perhaps in the dark, would have perished by the time the vessel got there. As for helicopters—how many of them are there a thousand miles offshore? A good estimate would be none, since most have a fuel range that keeps them within 200 miles of the coast. Besides, who in, say, Mauritania (where life is cheap and citizens are routinely killed for crimes far less ostentatious than taking to the sea in a rowboat) is going to send one out?

Angela's ambivalence about addressing the dangers directly was, I should say, not an indication of ambivalence toward the dangers themselves. Several times during the days to come I heard her say to Deb on the phone late at night, "Well, another day, and we didn't lose anybody," or merely, "At least we haven't lost anybody."

Meanwhile, it was our remoteness and isolation that made ludicrous the notion of my being "taken off the boat" with an injured leg. But when I explained this to my daughter Georgia months later, she said impatiently, "Dad, that is exactly what scared us. We *knew* there was no way of being taken off the boat. So we figured if somebody'd gone to the extreme of actually doing it, you must have been in really rough shape."

That night, Steve told me he'd had a terrible dream in which Nigel had been washed overboard. He had awakened calculating what he would do if ever such a thing should happen, and came to the conclusion that his best bet would be to cut free and inflate one of the life rafts, jump into it and hope he could do what needed doing. Which I immediately adopted as my own dire plan should I ever need it. I asked Steve jokingly if he'd cut a raft loose if, say, an old writer went overboard. He assured me he would, that there was nothing he wouldn't do to save an old writer's life, and I thanked him and told him I hoped I'd have the chance to do the same for an old doctor or sugar bush farmer some day.

The new priority, needless to say, was to stay aboard, to stay alive. And immediately I became more fastidious about keeping my safety line fastened. Indeed, one night, alone, on standing watch, with the boat bouncing at wild angles, I fastened *two* safety lines, one from my wrist, one from my life jacket. As heretical as it might sound, we seldom actually *wore* life jackets—really only in the roughest weather, and sometimes not then. For one thing, they were hot on days of ninety degrees, and they were awkward. Besides, they were more or less redundant if you had your safety line on. The lines were heavy-duty surfboard tethers that fastened to the ankle or wrist with a double-wrapped Velcro sleeve. While they were theoretically strong enough to keep you attached to the boat if you went overboard, I sometimes wondered what the outcome would be if one of them was put to the test. Or, more specifically, if one of *us* was put to the test. Certainly it would have been anything but comfortable to be dragged along by the ankle, upside down, in high seas, battered by the oar riggers as those aboard attempted to drag you back into the boat. Steve mentioned to me that on their record crossing of the North Atlantic the previous year, Leven Brown and his rowing mates had at times been thrown from their seats and had saved themselves only by grabbing the riggers as they went overboard.

A couple of days later I had my own stark dream. This time it was I who had gone overboard and was watching the boat's lights recede into the distance. Such images tend to linger, and several times over the next few days I found myself pondering what exactly I would do with my last minutes of life out there in the water by myself. Would I have even the remotest semblance of composure or presence of mind? What, I wondered, would require the greater fortitude or courage—to dip one's face into the water and breathe in, filling the lungs (if that is possible) or to fight to stay alive? I had read Chris Beeson's book *Survival at Sea* and knew that to fend off a shark—the idea was to punch it or kick it hard on the tip of its sensitive snout as it came in to bite you in half. Which, if the shark was playing by the rules and didn't do something sneaky, like attacking from the rear or after dark, might get you through Rounds 1 or 2. I wondered if in the extreme I would be brave enough, imaginative enough, simply to throw my head back and laugh, and enjoy the heavens, a potentially impressive last sight, as I drifted toward eternity. (I am not so sluggish as to ignore that I am of course drifting toward eternity right now but lack the impulse to throw my head back and laugh.) I would, understandably, hope to die with a modicum of courage, thinking about my kids, perhaps praying for them, or for my tattered soul—all quite the tale as it evolved in my imagination, my regret as a writer being that if it did transpire I wouldn't be around to tell it.

For the moment, there were more immediate images on which to focus my apprehensions. On the twenty-eighth day, for example, two rather ominous-looking cracks opened in the front lower edge of the cabin, within plain view of my rowing seat. For twenty-four hours or more, I watched with spectral fascination as these ever-expanding lacerations, one on each side, opened and closed like crudely animated mouths. At about the same time, a clunking developed where the ten-inch carriage bolts joined the cabin to the frame. Upon examination by David, both problems were deemed "non-structural" (as indeed were the first fractured hull plates on the *Titanic*). Whether or not Angela believed the assessment is not clear, but a day or so later she had Margaret draw thick lines in indelible red marker around the cabin cracks, carefully noting and dating each crack's extremity. The ill-considered effect was that the already perverse-looking "mouths," constantly opening and closing, now wore a sort of whore's grin of creepy red lipstick.

Beyond these or any of my own lingering doubts, it was decidedly reassuring to have the boat's builder aboard. However, on Day 29, when I complimented David on how well the craft was holding up, he smiled wanly, advising me with a straight face that he wouldn't be accepting any congratulations or applause until we were safely in Barbados. By which time he would have new stresses, new reasons for deflecting accolades over his efforts. How, for example, was he ever going to repay the hundred thousand dollars that he had rung up in debt on the expedition? And what would he do with *Big Blue* in Barbados? One possibility was to dismantle and ship her to the U.S. But it would add another ten or twelve thousand to his debts. If he had time, he could put an outboard on one of her transoms and run her north to Florida and then up the Intracoastal Waterway. Or he could simply leave her at Port St. Charles until a crew could be assembled to row her back out to sea, or perhaps on a jaunt around the Caribbean.

For now, there were more pressing concerns. For example, would the desalinators hold up, thrumming away as they did, hour after hour, below decks? And would the rudders last? While they were well reinforced, one of their axis poles had bent a little too easily, I thought, during a brief grounding off Shelter Island during boat trials. Statistically, the most prevalent reasons that ocean rows fail are broken rudders and faulty desalinators.

However, it was the hatch covers and bilge pump that were perhaps our greatest vulnerability. The former, which opened into the hulls through the floor of the rowing trench, were brittle plastic wafers about six inches in diameter that seated poorly and might, it seemed, have snapped under any sharp or sustained pressure. When we had drained the holds and rescued our food nearly three weeks earlier, Steve had tightened the hatch covers in their frames by covering each with a sandwich bag (hurricane-grade) and had retrofitted the pump with a collar made of an old seat cushion held on with duct tape. The pump, it needs saying, was little more than a toy, a pair of four-foot-long plastic pipes, one inside the other (a chamber and a plunger), and an outlet spout, so that the water being sucked out of the hulls could be squirted over the gunnels when the plunger was thrust up and down (increasingly difficult to do now that the plunger's handle, which had broken off, had been replaced by a few rounds of tape).

IT WAS THAT very bilge pump and those hatch covers that during the mid-afternoon watch of our thirtieth day aboard triggered my most scathing and memorable conflict with Steve. I had been rowing behind him on the starboard side. The waves had been coming over the gunnels, leaking through the hatches into the hull. It was miserable; it was cold; the boat was being banged around. I was still limping and protective of the wound on my leg.

With minutes to go before the watch changed, Steve, on self-appointed command, enlisted Ernst and me to pump out the starboard hull beneath us. We were to do so with naval alacrity, so as to be done when the new watch came on. We were to begin on a signal from Steve, whose job, simultaneously, would be to lean out over the gunnels and to scrape the barnacles as thoroughly as possible from the starboard hull.

And so at his signal Ernst and I went to work—yanked the rear hatch cover, got the bilge pump down, and got the compartment cleared of perhaps ten gallons of brine. For reasons now forgotten, we were briefly delayed as we moved forward to the next hatch. And for a few seconds the pump stood in the rowing trench, squarely in the path that Steve chose to take as he repositioned himself on the gunnels.

In my peripheral vision, I saw him snatch the thing up, and turned in time to see him fling it toward the cabin. "Either get it done," he barked, "or get out of the way!"

I was immediately and crazily incensed that he would apply such pressure, essentially flip out, under difficult conditions, especially when so little was at stake (we were a thousand nautical miles behind our anticipated pace). There is an old aphorism, a favorite of mine: *It's not what I don't know that bugs me, it's when I forget what I do know.* In this case, I knew the proper course was to take a few breaths and reassemble my equilibrium—then to pick up the pump and carry on. Rather, I quacked back that

Steve should "quit fucking us up," that he should "get a grip," that it was time he "cut the He-Man shit."

We glared at each other for a second, and that was that. In no time, Ernst and I were back on the pump.

On the next watch, Dylan took Steve's seat in front of me, informing me that Steve had told him I was "tired" of him and that I needed a break. Steve had taken Dylan's seat on the catamaran's other hull, separated from us by the cabin.

That night, we did not row at all; the crosswinds were too high, the sea too rough. As usual at the beginning of the midnight watch, Steve brought a big mug of cold instant coffee onto the bridge, stirred up with Nestle's powdered cream. He and Tom and I slurped at it in the wind and chatted idly, and I thought about what I wanted to say to Steve by way of a truce. I was still running small talk when he spoke up, explaining that he was sorry for what had happened, that he regretted losing his cool, and that my "deftly chosen words" had hurt him deeply.

There was a silence, and he said, "You're a writer. You choose your words for maximum effect."

Under other circumstances, I might have taken this last comment as a compliment. For now, I attempted to explain that I had fired from the hip, with no deft choosing, and that I too was sorry for what had happened, for what I had said. Instinctively, we gave each other a hug.

But I knew deep down that he was convinced I had taken aim at his vulnerabilities, at his sensitivity about his image as a hard-ass, that I had done my best to wound him. Steve, I hasten to say, is one of the brightest, most capable, and impassioned people I know. He is a guy, like David, whom I would trust with my life. And in this case he may have been right: that on some level I had aimed to injure.

He told me he regretted the effect he sometimes had on people, and that he was attempting to be more aware of it—was attempting to change.

This impressed me. Perhaps I too should be attempting to change. I knew people who would say so. On the other hand, it had taken me forty years to locate a degree of contentedness with who I am: which is to say a cloud watcher, a storyteller, a rhapsodist—I like to sing the song. Steve prefers the chant, the lament; enjoys the north wind. During the past couple of weeks he had several times said to me, "Come on over to the dark side, Charlie!" Or "So you've finally come over to the dark side." Or simply, "Welcome to the dark side, my friend."

On other occasions, he had sung and sung again the chorus from an old Stan Rogers jeremiad about a "broken man on a Halifax pier." It was a line in which he had located a version, however transitory or cartoonish, of his conflicted and disappointed self. It was his story, as the saying goes, and he was sticking to it.

I regret to report that Steve and I never rowed together again. And yet I do not regret the spat. It was both inevitable and therapeutic. And occurred in a context where forgiveness too was inevitable and therapeutic. And both desired and desirable.

T OWARD THE END of his search for the snow leopard
in the Himalayan mountains during the early 1970s,
the writer Peter Matthiessen received a packet of mail
from home but refused to open it until his mission was
over. If the news was bad, he wrote in his journal, there
was nothing he could have done about it. "Good news,
too, would be intrusive," he said, "spoiling this chance to
live moment by moment in the present by stirring up the
past, the future, and encouraging delusions of continuity
just when I am trying to let go."

While I'd have welcomed good news from home, I
understood Matthiessen's rationale. A part of me, too,
was attempting to let go, to let be, to let happen. On that
account, for nearly four weeks out of port I had questioned the validity of using the phone, as most of the
others were doing regularly—of attempting to conflate
what was happening at sea (what was happening in my
head) with what was happening back home. Not that I
didn't want to speak to my children. I did, very much so—
indeed thought about them day and night, in particular

because they had faced some challenges at home in recent months. At the best of times over the years, I have felt a degree of remorse at having imposed upon them my uncertain, often peripatetic life as a writer. For that reason, I vowed years ago that I would do my best to show them a normal existence, to provide more or less normal comforts and securities, so that in one way or another they would not end up paying for my obsessions. Which to a degree was what they were doing at that moment. And at times had done in the past. Whatever the case, I dreaded finding them in anything less than good spirits when I was decidedly unable to be of any help or comfort to them.

Nevertheless, on Day 26 out of Agadir, feeling remote and exhausted and perhaps a trifle culpable, I did finally call Thunder Bay on the SAT phone and was deeply moved to hear the voices of my son and daughters so far away, and to attempt to allay their concerns about how I was doing.

"Are you safe, Daddy?" begged Georgia with a plaintiveness that I had not heard in her voice since she was tiny, and to which I could only respond that we had safety lines and inflatable life boats, and that the boat was doing well and had already ridden out some rough seas.

"I'm looking forward to seeing you soon, honey," I said at last, and she said quietly, "Please wear your life jacket and safety line, Daddy," at which point the phone crackled and we parted amidst the static with the customary expressions of love and concern.

When I called again a week later from the mid-Atlantic, I found Eden sullen and restrained, in part—if indirectly—over my absence from the scene. When the call ended on a low note a few minutes later, I spent the next couple of watches in a leaden funk, agonizing over my choices, in particular the current one, and what it meant to be out here, away, apart, gone, living out some skittish, perhaps selfish, variation of my private need to keep testing, keep exploring, keep escaping, keep stimulating and exciting myself, at the cost of my connections elsewhere.

Beyond getting farther and farther from a world record, what exactly *were* we doing out there, I found myself wondering later that day. Steve had a notion that the spirit of going, of taking risks, was of some intrinsic evolutionary advantage to us and was recognized by the human spirit as something best kept alive. Or was there something in the related notion that as descendents of our prehistoric past we have been deprived of the intensity of survival, the risk-taking and derring-do for which evolution has prepared us? "We are hunters," as Geronimo is reputed to have said, "and when the buffalo are gone we will hunt mice." He might as easily have said we are seafarers, and when the galleons have disappeared, and the war is over, we will embark on a thirty-eight-foot catamaran with iPods and EPIRBs and a GPS, and we will fight not enemy sailors but among ourselves.

Or was there something simpler at work here—perhaps merely an acknowledgment that life is short, death long, and that as Robert Frost said, "Earth's the right place for love"—which is to say for imagination, for possibility, for nurturing. I perhaps risk an impertinence in acknowledging that some ultimately practical fragment of me has always known that adventure is, deep down, about honoring and nurturing oneself. And passing the nourishment along—and the impulse toward adventure, too. In my own case, the latter has been well lodged in my kids, all of whom have since birth been irrepressible travelers, often on their own: by river, by air, by land; into the wilderness, through the backstreets. Was it ultimately less responsible to my children and loved ones to be out here, attempting to keep my spirit and sensibilities nourished, than to be depleting such spirit in whatever pursuits might have kept me in harness and in contempt?

In answer to the question of what one is to do with one's freedom, the Depression-era adventure writer Richard Halliburton (who, like Ryan, was from Tennessee) answered: "Certainly not squander its gold on the commonplace quest for riches and respectability, and then secretly lament the price that had to be paid... Let those who wish have their respectability—I wanted freedom, freedom to indulge in whatever caprice struck my fancy, freedom to search in the farthermost corners of the earth for the beautiful, the joyous, and the romantic."

It is lamentably worth noting that Halliburton's search for the joyous and romantic took him to the bottom of the Pacific Ocean in 1939, as he attempted to run a seventy-five-foot diesel-powered junk (built by a Kowloon cartwright named Fat Kau) from Hong Kong to the World's Fair in San Francisco.

MEANWHILE, if the phone played a significant role on the boat, it had nowhere near the minute-by-minute allure, the addictive authority, of the sometimes blessed, sometimes pestilential iPods or MP3 players.

One night in the mid-Atlantic, I tried to persuade Dylan, who was in front of me, to abandon his earbuds in favor of paying attention to the sea (if that failed, he could at very least be paying attention to me). I explained to him, as it had been explained to me, that in the absence of electronic distraction, which tends to do our inner living for us, our imaginations begin to breathe, to connect with parts of ourselves that are ancient coefficients of wind and water and waves.

"I can connect to myself through my iPod," he told me, adding that he was busy even now listening to one of his jazz influences—was working out some riffs and arrangements for his work on the stand-up bass. I wondered aloud if in the long run the waves wouldn't be just as good an influence, which at least gave him a smile.

Back at our adjacent bunks, I mentioned having read that the sound of a vibrating violin string has been found to resonate for nearly a minute in the human ear after the audible wavelengths have gone silent—evidence not just of the range and quality of natural sound, and the levels on which it invites human response, but of the broader allegiance between the planet and human senses. On the other hand, when a mere *recording* of a vibrating violin string is silenced, there is no resonance at all beyond the click of the switch, and hence no further response from the ear.

I took it as a harrowing symptom of the young rowers' addiction to their electronic devices that one night when the boat was rocking furiously and anyone without a safety line on was in imminent danger, one of the kids (who shall go nameless for his mother's sake), took his line off on the bridge and, balancing on the toes of one foot, leaned out recklessly above the abyss to ensure that the iPod he was passing to the other hull would safely reach its destination even if he did not.

Recalling my high school experience of the classics, I told Dylan one afternoon how Odysseus's rowers had packed their ears with beeswax so as not to hear the mermaids—the Sirens, as they were called—who were likely to coax them astray. "They were like you guys with your iPods on," I said, trying to convince him that it was only by listening, as Odysseus had done, that they could get a sense of what the sea and its mysteries might be about.

All of which was greeted rather skeptically—perhaps more so when I mentioned that Odysseus had considered the sea's message so compelling he had had his men tie him to the mast so that he could not be seduced away by what he was determined to hear.

On Day 28, Sylvain, perhaps looking to catalyze his journey inward or create at least a suggestion of privacy or sanctuary, announced that he was imposing a vow of silence on himself for twenty-four hours and that anybody else was welcome to do so too. Immediately several others, including Nigel, Liam, and Zach, joined him. However, no sooner were they out on deck in their new psychic harness than it became clear it was not silence or focus they were observing but merely another version of distraction—they had their iPods on!

During the course of our travels, Sylvain listened not just to music but to e-versions of some thirty books. Beyond inner nourishment, he may have been seeking to isolate himself from his watchmates, Margaret and Ryan, whose patter and attitudes and (real or inferred) antipathies toward him drove him deeper into himself and his recordings as the trip progressed. I know he was unsettled by Ryan's occasionally compulsive whooping and sometimes yowling accompaniment to whatever he happened to be listening to on his iPod. On perhaps Day 31, Sylvain said to me quietly in the cabin, "I'm going nuts out there. I can hear Ryan's singing even when I have my iPod turned up." For their part, Ryan and Margaret believed that the strain between themselves and Sylvain was heightened if not caused by Sylvain's wilful isolation of himself: "He's always got his iPod on!" Margaret complained to me one day.

Though there were times when it may well have been the best of possible worlds to escape into a trance of familiar tunes, there were occasions too when I wanted to stand on the bridge, facing the iPodders, and holler at them to *get the junk off their heads*. I told Dylan one day that I believed an encounter with the unrestricted planet was an encounter with the unrestricted self.

"In what sense?" he said.

"Because we *are* the planet. We're *of* the planet"—not of tiny electronic impulses emerging from an iPod.

Dylan, being Dylan, argued that just maybe we *were* nothing more than tiny electronic signals.

"But not from a machine built by Steve Jobs," I protested, having to acknowledge immediately (in the face of Dylan's persistent and free-thinking cosmology) that maybe we *were* mere electronic signals emitted by a machine designed by Steve Jobs.

In all of this, I have to admit, it was perhaps more myself I wanted to scream at and declaim to. For I too have been a non-listener, a self-absorber, as inclined as anyone to ignore what nature and the planet (and sometimes its human inhabitants) might have to tell me.

What's more, I am a hypocrite—I had my own little iPod aboard. My daughters, Georgia and Eden, had pooled their resources and had given it to me while I was in training, and I was grateful for it. Occasionally, on watch in the middle of the night, I would haul it out, start it up, and disappear into Bob Marley or Joni Mitchell or Sonny Rollins—or into Bach or Gershwin or George Harrison.

One night as I listened to the thing I got a most inspired and unanticipated lift. Over the course of our weeks aboard, I had rolled perhaps three or four times through the hundred-odd selections on my playlist but had invariably skipped past a certain unidentified piece because it began with an uninviting flurry of trumpets.

Then, one night, bored with the run of my tunes and too numb to work the microscopic controls of the machine, I let the unknown item run. Because of my upbringing in the Baptist Church, gospel music is deeper in me than bone. And here on a rough and rainy night on the Atlantic, when I most needed a boost, I was immersed unexpectedly in a medley of old standards sung by the Native American rhapsodist Rita Coolidge: "Precious Lord," "Peace in the Valley," "It Is No Secret"—hymns as comforting to me as a burst of serotonin, as reassuring as the simple truths of my childhood. And to this day, I have no idea how they came to be there.

Meanwhile, I should not be too critical of Dylan, who was at times as attuned as anyone to the messages and weirdness of our surroundings. On the morning of Day 33, as we went out to row in the pre-dawn darkness, we looked at each other in the faint glow of the running light on the bridge and, for reasons that I cannot now articulate, I knew what he was going to say. And he said it:

"Did you hear it?"

And I told him I had: a kind of howling through the wee hours beneath the boat, something neither of us had heard before.

"What did you make of it?" he asked as we Velcro'd ourselves into the stirrups.

I told him I had taken it as a warning.

"Of what?" he said solemnly.

"You *know* what," I said. "We've talked about it."

After a few seconds of silence, he said, "You mean paying attention?"

"Exactly," I said.

"But to what?" he wanted to know.

"To what requires it," I told him. Which at that moment was about as accurate an evasion as I could come up with in our little game, and about as close to the truth as either of us was likely to get.

WHILE THE iPods gave more or less what was expected of them, the phones seemed a perverse sort of denial of what they promised, which is to say direct communication, a version of the truth. In reality, little in the way of hard truth could be reported from the boat to, say, parents or children or partners in need of reassurance—to those who hadn't wanted to see their loved ones disappear over the horizon in the first place. What could you tell them? That the sea was so rough we couldn't row? That we were destined to run out of food? That if you went overboard you were gone? If you were Dylan, I guess you could tell them that the EPIRB you'd received for Christmas, while a reassuring gizmo, would be useless, or pretty close to it, if you were in the drink on your own in a storm.

Dylan had mentioned to me one day that his grand-parents had attempted to persuade him not to go—had even offered him a financial reward of some sort to stay home. I know that Zach's dad too was not entirely pleased with his son's presence aboard the boat (he did ultimately show up in Barbados to greet Zach but did not tell him in advance that he was coming, an omission he called his "revenge on Zach" for putting him through all this anxiety). For Nigel's mom, Janet, as I have mentioned, there was an all-but-paralyzing stress in seeing her son head off on an untried boat on an uncertain sea, with some decidedly untried crewmates. "Imagine if he and Steve were both lost," she had said to me at a point during the summer. "That's half my family!" There were days and nights, with the Sirens chanting, with the boat shipping water like a bathtub, when it occurred to me that if those who had feared for their children and loved ones'

safety had somehow seen us now, all of their darkest trep-
idations would have been confirmed. It *was* dangerous, it
was a flirtation with death, and if my own children ever
decide they want to do something similar, I will do my
best to persuade them to stay home, or to do something
less "beautiful and joyous and romantic," as the doomed
Mr. Halliburton might have put it. If they insist and go
anyway I will quite naturally urge them to carry an iPod,
the one item of survival gear apparently indispensible to
the contemporary global adventurer.

As the sun set behind us on our thirty-fifth day, Angela stuck her head out of her quarters to say again how proud she was of us all. "You've rowed through some of the toughest shit on the planet!" she proclaimed with the authority of one who had rowed through some large and sticky feces in her day. "I have no doubt at all you guys could row any water there is!"

The gist of her message was that whatever the weather or water, we were now going to row night and day continuously and that in so doing we could be in Barbados by February 28, two weeks hence. "You guys are building confidence in yourselves as rowers!" she hollered above the wind. "You're building confidence in the boat! You know you can do this!"

While all three of these last brisk endorsements were of dubious validity, none was as disconcerting as Angela's ensuing contention that if she didn't push us to the limit day and night until we got there, she'd be depriving us of our earned and rightful legacy as ocean rowers. "Part of the experience of rowing an ocean," she enthused, "is to get there looking like a bag of bones, to get there famished and wasted; to get there in a daze! It's all part of the euphoria of arrival!"

If it was true, I more than the rest of the crew was on target for some high times. Indeed, it occurred to me as she spoke that by extension, the ultimate euphoria would be to arrive having blissed off into eternity—yet a possibility. For now, I was reminded of what Steve had said when I had complained to him that I was sick to death of the exhaustion, sick of the hunger, sick of the "endless meaningless dousings in cold water."

"In ocean rowing," he had reminded me facetiously, "the meaninglessness is the biggest part of the meaning."

He was no less facetious (in fact was downright cynical) in his response to Angela's speech. When I mentioned it in passing the next morning, he said, "What speech? Did Angela make a speech?"

"Yeah, right," I said, unable for the moment to deal with his evolving scorn, especially as it spilled onto me.

But there was nothing sarcastic or facetious in his storming into Angela's little fo'c'sle at 4 the next morning and unloading on her for her delinquency in continuing to allow Margaret more or less free rein on deck. It seemed to me that as soon as Margaret perceived some stasis had been reached in her relationship with Steve, she would do some little thing, seemingly irrepressibly, to tip his wagon. For example, one day when my leg was healing she said to me—quite officiously and within earshot of Steve—"Charlie, I want to keep an eye on that injury of yours. If there's even the slightest problem with it, you must come and see either me or Angela immediately."

The next day on watch, I got thinking about a rather vicious book on pirates that I had enjoyed as a kid—in particular a passage in which it was explained that even bloodthirsty buccaneers needed a degree of coddling against the hardships of the sea. For that reason senior officers on their boats were generally chosen for their "decency" toward the men. The gist of things was that when the pirates weren't busy pillaging and cutting throats, they were treated with significant kindness and consideration. It seemed that Margaret did not quite grasp that her own job, like that of the pirate officers, should have been to charm, to invigorate, to assuage privation, not to aggravate it.

Meanwhile, Margaret's insecurities were beginning to rebound on her. Dylan, who had been videotaping interviews with the crew as he had the chance, had mentioned to me that Margaret now refused to be taped. In one brief interview, she had referred to herself as "the bitch" and had explained to Dylan that she felt humiliated about losing her role as watch commander and about being, as she put it, "disliked." My perplexity over the situation was that there seemed nothing Margaret could do to make things right with Steve or Sylvain, that she apparently had no capacity to go to those with whom she did not get along and broker a truce, ask if there was any way things could be made right. And they, in turn, seemed to have no way of setting things right with her, although I believe Sylvain had made attempts to engage her in conversation as they rowed, undoubtedly with a view to harmony. Where Steve was concerned, it seemed to me that it would not have taken a great deal of diplomacy on her part, or his, to improve the situation quite radically. I should say in fairness to Margaret that most members of the crew had no issues with her, that they more or less accepted her "edge" and did not take it seriously.

As for Steve's facetiousness, there was little of it on display a week hence when, to celebrate his birthday, Angela fired off a flare at the end of the dawn watch, led a chorus of "Happy Birthday," and prepared for him what was apparently her standard birthday treat—a kind of Snickers-bar pie, mixed up with candies, marshmallows, and chocolate sauce. Steve accepted it morosely, naturally rejecting any other aspect of Angela's m.o., even as a leader of birthday parties.

As was often the case these days, I felt aggrieved at him for being so grumpy. For Angela, birthdays counted—she was a mother and grandmother, with no defenses against anyone for whom a birthday cake was just the latest obnoxious reminder of compromised focus or disciplinary decline.

Liz's birthday five days earlier had been quite a different affair, with hats and bunting and a special meal, and Margaret dressed up as a sort of Chippendale girl, in sequins and a bow tie and skimpy black panties. Steve had been equally dismissive of those hijinks. I had witnessed it all from my rowing seat and had participated only later, when, in the claustrophobic bowels of the ship (party central), Angela gave me a few leftover goodies, including some fiery wasabi peas, harder than calculus, on which I promptly broke a molar in honor of Liz's twenty-fourth.

Tom and Angela celebrated with a brisk exchange of unpleasantries over a fishing rod that David had left on the bridge, in a holder, with its treble hooks exposed. Earlier in the day, Tom had asked Angela to *please* order it removed before somebody got caught on it and injured. She had either refused or neglected to do so, and it was of course Tom who eventually got the hooks entangled in his jacket—or more accurately a jacket he had borrowed from Ernst, an expensive one, which he had to cut with David's bowie knife so the hooks could be removed.

Tom's frustrations had been whetted a few days earlier when he had lost a pair of hundred-dollar slush pants lent to him by Louise.

How, you might wonder, could we just *lose* things, big things, in such a tiny cabin (the equivalent, one would think, of losing an overcoat in a hotel closet)? And the answer is that we *didn't* lose them, we didn't have to; they lost themselves! You couldn't *keep* them: your pants, your T-shirts, your socks, your jackets, your gloves, your hats, your shoes—all of which looked just like everybody else's gloves and pants and T-shirts! The more so because there was no proper light, and the stuff was soaked and black-ish and bunched up. In a heap. In a bag. In the hold. On the floor. In your bunk. In somebody else's bunk. On hooks or little bungee loops, some of which supported fifteen or twenty similar items. The only thing worse than this diabolical mess was the thought of anybody attempting to sort the mess out, which almost by defini-tion meant cramming it into dry bags or bunk crannies or net hammocks, or hanging it from bungee cords, or out the hatch onto the inflatable lifeboats, or bundling it into other clothing, from which it would never reap-pear. Occasionally those with a passion for something neater than a dumpsite in Lagos, which by now was what the cabin resembled, would take the heaps of shoes and clothes and push at least some of them out onto the bridge, or "hang" them outdoors on the cabin, which could mean anything from pinning them to the clothes lines in lumps or tying them in job lots around the vari-ous generator and antenna poles, to just dropping them on the tramps, where the wind and waves eventually car-ried everything away.

One evening I spotted my treasured gray sweatshirt on the tramp, soaked. I nipped into the cabin on other busi-ness and, by the time I returned to claim it thirty seconds later, it was gone. And nobody had seen it. Nobody ever saw anything. At least of anybody else's. In our exhaustion and ineptitude, it was all we could do to remember what our own stuff looked like. Dear Angela did some laundry for me one day. However, by the time I reclaimed it off the cabin wall about three hours later, three out of the seven or eight items had disappeared. All of which is to say nothing of our *tiny* items: our sporks and sunglasses and flashlights; and pens and nail clippers and duct tape; and razors and jackknives. I started the voyage with six good ballpoint pens, and by mid-Atlantic was writing with a pencil stub three inches long that I was sharpening with my thumbnail. If by some accident you came upon your folding scissors in your storage space or dry bag, you used them immediately whether you needed to or not, because the next time you looked they would be gone. Forever. Same with your Penaten or Sudocrem (I cannot, without sounding like a pervert, describe to you the satisfaction of smearing diaper cream on your bottom end and giddy-bits when you're itchy and squirmy and rashy down there from the dried salt).

On the morning of our thirty-fifth day aboard, I cleaned out the long net storage enclosure beside my bunk, which had begun to fester, and at the bottom, on the floor, in a puddle of sunscreen and argan oil, found my dad's graduation ring from Toronto Normal School in 1932 (which I had brought along as a kind of talisman and had forgotten was on the boat). Beside it, wet through and reeking, I found the little leather wallet in which I carry my credit cards and documents, all of which seemed accounted for, all happily useless out there in the middle of the ocean.

When our watch came on deck to row that afternoon, the GPS monitor indicated that we had covered nearly 2,000 nautical miles (1,400 of them since coming into the trades) and were quickly approaching the point at which we would have just a thousand nautical miles to go. The endless speculation, often pessimism, over when we were going to reach Barbados had been getting to me—like the harping of kids in the back seat, fussing interminably over how much longer we'd be on the road. For Zach and Nigel, it seemed to be a kind of game; I had heard them making bets on when we might arrive. It grated on me particularly when Deb had suggested on the phone the previous day that at our current pace we would not be in Barbados before the middle of March, nearly a month hence. She had measured our progress as an average of the thirty-five days thus far, including days of just a few miles, when for the past couple of weeks we had been averaging nearly a hundred miles a day, a pace that, if continued, would put us in Barbados within a couple of weeks. The hard part of it for me was that if we went much past the beginning of March I would all but certainly fade away from hunger, given my current state of provisioning and health. Up against the nutritional demands of the twelve-hour rowing day, the rest of the crew too would have trouble surviving much past the beginning of the month.

MEANWHILE, as the weather along the equator got hotter and more crew members got "right down to bare-ass," as Tom put it, I found myself increasingly out of sync with the evolving naturism of the boat. Not that I cared, except for an occasional inner sigh over my aging inhibitions. I was relieved that there were others who kept at least scraps of clothing in place—bandanas and bits of sheepskin and cotton skivvies. Angela had encouraged the men to bring "cock socks"—presumably to keep their brains from getting sunburned—although, happily, no one did, and we were spared the discomfiture that such wince-inducing finery might have brought to the boat.

Occasionally, in the dark, in the cabin, I would pull my shorts off and just lie there, stewing in the fetid air, sunny-side up, attempting to catch any whisper of sea breeze that might drift into the cabin when the door (normally closed to keep water out) was open for a few seconds as someone came or went. Not that it was always hot. Even at those latitudes, a windy afternoon could go cool with the disappearance of the sun, and nights often required a jacket and long pants.

On the afternoon of Day 36, as I shimmied up out of the toilet well (attempting to yank my shorts into place while I simultaneously got my safety line re-hooked and held the hatch open so as not to get skulled), Liz, who was in the stroke seat and thereby close enough that she could have leaned forward and peeked into the well, said quite jauntily, "Charlie, you're the only one aboard whose ass I haven't seen!"

"Yeah, I'll show it to ya sometime," I told her, adding that for now I didn't want to frighten the dolphins, a dozen or so of which were at that moment dieseling along beside the boat, rising out of the waves in syrupy loops, occasionally powering to within yards of the oars before diving out of sight. That morning, just after dawn, one had surfaced within a hundred feet of the port hull and kipped onto its tail and danced upright for longer than seemed possible given the roughness of the swells and chop. At first I imagined it was dancing for the joy of it, or perhaps as entertainment even for a comparatively festered audience such as ourselves. But when a few seconds later it rocketed straight up out of the water, to a height of eight or ten feet, presumably nabbing its breakfast en route, it occurred to me that its tail-dancing was more likely a kind of reconnaissance, a rise to max elevation so that it could survey its surroundings for prey, as the early hominids rose on their back legs to better case the savannah in the pursuit of game.

My resistance to exhibiting my sorry ass might have been trumped in the name of comfort. Certainly there was intelligence in avoiding the constriction of one's "junk" in the sea-soaked innards of a pair of shorts—or avoiding the crazy-making friction of a salt-thickened waistband or seam. Or in a simple desire to stay cool in the equatorial sun.

However, by this time I had grown so skinny that, besides everything else, I felt entirely too wasted and pitiable to hang around naked. Whereas I had spent months building up a modest reserve of muscle in my arms and chest and had arrived in Agadir at nearly 170 pounds, I had since then been dropping nearly a pound a day, as Angela had predicted, and was by now down pretty close to 140. My knees, the part of my anatomy most in evidence to me as I rowed, bore a distressing resemblance to doorknobs, my stomach and chest to a kind of rumble strip of old chicken skin. Worse yet, my hindquarters and thighs had begun to atrophy. Normally, the legs thicken with rowing. But in the heavy seas, with our quick and truncated strokes, we were not using our legs to push off as one does in more orthodox versions of the sport. Out here, as in the nightmares of Walter Gropius, function trumped form—"core strength" was what counted. There were times amidst the heaviest seas when it was all I could do to get my oar in for a fraction of a second, yank my torso around for a touch of propulsion, and get the oar out before its blade got trapped and its handle became a potentially lethal distaff.

Besides, I was not putting enough protein in my stomach to maintain muscle. By Steve's account, my carcass had consumed any spare fat and was now cannibalizing muscle in the interest of ongoing metabolism. He had a theory, undoubtedly valid, that the muscles most vigorously in use would be the last to deteriorate. Sylvain had warned us months ago that in the absence of full sleep cycles (which can require as much as 110 minutes and are indispensible for tissue restoration and growth) we would forfeit muscle at a far faster rate than would be caused by mere lack of nutrition. Whereas in the early days I had been sure-footed and quick in getting around the boat, I was now hesitating as I moved from bridge to tramp or hull, making certain I had a handhold for support. The others were graciously, diffidently concerned about me. Tom said to me one day, "Charlie, I think maybe you're getting just a wee little bit *too* slim." And Louise commented that I was "certainly keeping trim."

As an antidote, I had been attempting to spend a little more time in my bunk. Plus, every time I thought of it and could tolerate the prospect, I stuffed in a protein bar, grateful for the existence of these propitious turds, and even more so for peristalsis, given that there was little I could have done voluntarily to get one down. I had also been eating raisins and almonds and peanuts, which though healthy were a poor substitute for the gooey fats and carbs—the noodles and meat and eggs—that by this point I craved twenty-four hours a day.

On perhaps Day 37, as I lay in my bunk after the noon watch, I mentioned aloud (in what I hoped was a casual voice but was probably recognizable as something close to prayer) that if anybody had a spare pack of tuna or salmon I'd happily relieve them of it in exchange for a package of dried mangoes as soon as one came up in my snack packs. Immediately, a hand (Liam's) shot around the bulkhead and dropped a six-ounce foil pack of bluefin on my pillow. Later, when I opened the day's snack pack, I was elated, all but tearful, to find not just a package of cheap shortbread biscuits, which I inhaled on the spot, but one of the five-ounce tins of sardines that, way back in Agadir, I had secreted among my treats. I quickly drank off the heavy oil (which might as well have been sewing machine oil after the weeks of heat in the hold), then gobbled the bony carcasses and licked out the tin, at the risk of cutting my tongue. In the rank air of the cabin, I didn't have to worry that anyone would suss out my peccadillo on smell alone and, on the next watch, dropped the tin quietly into the sea. There, I believed, it would be at least less harmful than, say, the fishing tackle and Styrofoam and plastic bags that we saw strewn on the water, mile after mile, all the way from Africa to the Caribbean. In the most childlike part of my imagination, I saw my smelly little can, a wee golden coracle, sinking languorously over a period of hours to five miles' depth. Or settling atop the Mid-Atlantic Ridge, where monkfish and other prudent species would deconsecrate it, scorning it in pilgrimages as a monument to the folly of humanity.

What impressed me, meanwhile, was that everybody else aboard seemed to be flourishing. The women had certainly lost weight but were nonetheless robust-looking— muscular and ruddy and full-chested. Only Angela was something of an anomaly. While ample in the shoulders and thighs, she had, a few years earlier, lost much of her chest tissue to breast cancer. Which didn't stop her from pitching about the boat on hot days clothed only in her scars and tattoos—and in her estimable self-possession. Her poise may have evolved gradually and at a price (it had taken some punishing blows since Agadir and would take a couple more before we reached our destination), but she conveyed the impression that it was holding quite nicely in the continuing jostle of egos and was

unlikely to be further eroded by the occasional splash of
flying venom. One of her tattoos was a bracelet, a dolphin-
hibiscus motif around her upper right arm, the other an
immense cartoon zipper (R. Crumb meets Marilyn Man-
son) running from her tailbone up the heavy vertical scar
left by her catastrophic back surgery of the early 1990s.
The latter seemed a lurid if imperfect metaphor for her
achievements in keeping her fragments together—her
family, her self, the patched-up ambitions of both her professional and athletic careers. There were days, she told
me, when the agonies of her wrecked back made everything, up to and including breathing, difficult. Sleeping
pills got her through the night, painkillers through the
day. And yet when duty called at mealtime, she rallied
her energies, rising from her bed of nails, lurching up and
down the alleyway between bunks, lumping along on her
prosthetic leg supports, dealing lunches, collecting dirty
dishes, delivering clean water bottles, picking up garbage,
not always with a smile but invariably without complaint.

Until one day when, as she sloped into the little fo'c'sle
that was her stateroom and asylum, she said quietly to
no one in particular and with just a hint of irony, "As far
as you guys are concerned, I'm nothin' but your cabin
bitch—I know what you think of me." It was a joke, but
wasn't a joke, and was greeted not so much by silence as
by an echoing absence of response as the waves crashed
off the cabin floor, and our reluctant commander van-
ished into the hidey-hole from which she would eventually emerge with the next meal.

Or would not emerge.

On the thirty-sixth day out of Agadir, perhaps de-
pressed, perhaps zonked with pain, Angela had disappeared for nearly thirty hours, making no attempt to
communicate with her crew, sending the meals out with

an extended hand and a request that somebody, anybody, take them from her and pass them along. When
she did eventually materialize on deck, it was not with
news from home, or of our projected bearing or anticipated weather—or of the continued fine-tuning of the
admiralty. It was, rather, to announce a more important
development: that we were running short of dehydrated
entrees and that today's lunch would be "desserts only."
The word "cheesecake" figured prominently in the message, amidst a reverential cataloguing of the available
"crumbles" and "jubilees" and "chiffons."

I got a quite edible chocolate mousse out of the deal
(rehydrated of course), and would be a hypocrite to suggest that I did not benefit significantly from Angela's
obsessive gastronomic ministrations. I had by this time
become so devoted that I had reconfigured her com-
pulsions into an entirely new model of leadership—
"feedership," I called it, a concept well understood by, say,
the early traveling circuses, whose daily priority, *always,*
was to keep their workers fed; and by the North West
Mounted Police, who on their long march west across
the Canadian prairies in 1873 put the food on the lead
wagons, knowing that with dinner out front, the shoeless
and bone-weary stragglers, often miles behind by the end
of the day, would keep on trudging until they caught up
and ate.

At night I could often hear Angela on the satellite
phone, just inches from my bunk, in hushed conversation with Deb in California, offering up espionage-level
reports, gustatory intelligence, on what she had eaten
that day—"noodles Roma," "shrimp Rivoli," "shortcake
à la crème,"—and what she had prepared of any special
nature for the rest of us. During the course of the voyage, perhaps my favorite sight from the bunk was that of

Angela, on Day 30 or 31, extracting a mini-Snickers bar, her fave, from among her goodies, peeling it, holding it in tender anticipation before her face, and then biting its li'l head off.

IF ANGELA had one notable area of culinary insufficiency it was breakfast. From the start her intention had been to prepare it every morning for her crew—a sort of commander's noblesse oblige. If I had better understood the degree to which sugar had insinuated itself into her dietary choices, I would have brought better breakfast foods for myself. When in her early communications she spoke of "cereal," however, I inferred something dense and oaty, even porridgey, perhaps with raisins and nuts. I could live with powdered milk and was buoyed by the promise of added protein powder—all outlined in her original prospectus. So I had been surprised, to say the least, when on the second morning out of Agadir my twelve-ounce thermal cup was passed to me from her galley containing something resembling porcupine turds afloat in a watery gruel. I spooned a few of these slimy brown balls into my mouth, suffering at first a kind of gag reflex, then a compulsive reprise of a long-standing distaste.

"Cocoa Puffs!" I exclaimed across the alleyway in Dylan's direction.

"Yeah, Cocoa Puffs," he said distractedly, spooning them in, while Tom did likewise on the upper bunk.

"These are Cocoa Puffs!" I said again, finding it impossible to believe that everybody wasn't as impressed as I—and, more so, that anybody considered sugar-laden widgets, devoid of *all natural food value,* to be an even remotely plausible breakfast for people rowing twelve hours a day and in acute need of proper nutrition.

The next week brought Sugar Pops (Moroccan version) and the next Frosted Flakes, which I would eat in desperation as I came famished and exhausted off the dawn watch. Steve and Nigel, meanwhile, were eating the gourmet granola they had baked for themselves, submerged in the Nestlé's powdered cream they had bought in Agadir, perhaps without realizing what a godsend it would turn out to be.

I asked about the muesli that I knew had been purchased on my phantom shopping trip the day before our departure and was told it had been destroyed in the hull flooding. It was not until another two weeks had passed and I was ravenous that I ventured one day into Angela's tiny pantry and rustled through the bundles and packages until I located a one-pound bag of U.S.-made granola. And stuck it under my T-shirt and stepped back to my bunk and stuffed it into my dry bag. It was the sort of maneuver that 200 years ago, aboard any trade or naval vessel, would have earned me a flogging or perhaps a day upside down in the rigging (and then a flogging). Which occurred to me on every one of the next four or five mornings as I surreptitiously poured a few tablespoons of the lumpy mixture into the sugary sunrise soup that continued to come out of the galley.

Not that I blamed Angela. I appreciated that at heart she was a kid, a candy lover—sugar made her happy. In her way, she was just passing the pleasure along. Indeed, acting on my dad's reasonable principle that one should always compliment the cook, I would thank her, if hypocritically, for the breakfast.

NOW, ON DAY 40, alert to my weight loss, Angela "overruled" my prescribed meal of rice and beans, treating me instead to a steamy double bender of chicken à la king.

This paltry poultry was lumpy and rubbery and salty—was in fact so delectable in every way that I found it hard to stop scraping with my spork at the folds in the bottom of the pack, on the chance that I had somehow missed a molecule.

At sunset that evening, as Angela was engaged with David on deck, I stepped into her quarters to spring the fore-hatch, which had been closed at dinner because of a few drops of rain. I opened it three or four inches and was about to extricate myself when Margaret's voice sounded behind me. "Did Angela say you could open that?" she demanded in a tone that suggested both the meddling afoot and, somehow, the fate of continents.

I did not even want to begin. However, infuriated by the notion that I should need Angela's permission to attempt to get a lungful of decent air, I said quietly, "Yes, she did," preferring the lie and its consequences to some dreary plea for breath in a ninety-five-degree cabin that, from dusk to dawn, was variably a steam cabinet and a fart-ridden tomb.

From Day 2 or 3 on, I had done my best to initiate a moratorium on farts while people were eating. But at all other times the smell was a mere symptom of cabin life and lassitude, a processed derivative of rehydrated tamale pie or Hoho's Szechuan chicken or Maria's campfire beans. It was mushrooms; it was gull poop; it was the tire fires of my youth. It was sweat and foot fungus and sulfur gas.

We endured such impositions with a wince, and grew inured to the salt-swollen raisins or decomposing chicken bits or bacteria-ridden socks that had accumulated in all but the tidiest bunks; or the lumps of sea-soaked clothing that sat for days beneath the air mattresses or in the corners of people's cubby holes, or even under their pillows. By mid-Atlantic, I myself had a welter of wet T-shirts and socks moldering at the foot of the Croteau/Wilkins bunk. There they sat, stinking, undoubtedly offensive to Sylvain, awaiting the moment when I felt motivated to stagger out on the tramp after a hard shift of rowing, carrying a bottle of sea soap and a leaky bag of fresh water, so that I could knuckle my stinking garments into a less odious version of their current sliminess.

There were days during those later weeks aboard when even the rowing trenches carried a low-level pong, emanating from the toilet hold or the accumulating garbage bags below deck. Or from We the People, surely including myself. Not that anybody was deliberately letting his or her hygiene lapse—we brushed and flossed, lathered our pits and crevices. Curiously, we did not actually sweat, not very much; it was as if our bodies, our skin, like that of desert dwellers or the surface of cacti, had adjusted, had closed its pores, in order to preserve moisture (could this have been why the sea salt was getting trapped in the dermal tissue, having to force its way out as salt sores?). And yet we were grubby—or at least salty from the dousings. On the afternoon of Day 39, seated behind Dylan, who was busy shooting video and had been avoiding soap and water like a cat, I mentioned to him as discreetly as possible that I'd developed a kind of mini-method of lathering and rinsing my armpits and undercarriage, requiring just a few seconds and a mere cup of fresh water or even sea water—I had a little bottle of sea soap right there in my pocket.

"I guess I stink, eh?" he said brightly and, in the politic delay that preceded my response, was up off his seat with my soap in his hands and in no time had gussied up and was back on his oar.

On watch, in the middle of the night, Tom or Steve and I could invariably locate a laugh in the notion of our jaunty little stinkbox making its way laboriously through the night, beneath the heavens, hermetically sealed off from infinite volumes of the purest, the breeziest, the least contaminated air on earth.

There was literally not a molecule of dust out there, and no pollen, at least once we were clear of the African coast. I have mild asthma and bronchial allergies and had three or four salbutamol inhalers aboard. But despite the bad air in the cabin, I never needed a puff.

Nor, apparently, were there any viruses once those we may have been carrying when we set out had cleared our lungs and digestive tracts. Consequently, we had no colds or flu bugs during a period when our immune systems must surely have been at their most vulnerable with the exhaustion and limited nutrition.

More surprisingly to me, there were no insects out there—except on perhaps the forty-first day, when, miraculously, a house fly appeared in the cabin, more than 2,000 miles from our starting place and still hundreds from our destination. Preposterous though it might seem, when one of the kids whacked it with a rubber Croc, leaving it aquiver on the floor and then dead, I felt a genuine pang of sadness that so persistent a bit of life, such an obvious contender, could be so easily and arbitrarily wiped from the agenda. A day later, when a tiger shark whacked a dorado off our starboard hull, leaving the front half of the victim swimming gamely for the roundup, I felt no such regret—it was nature on parade, whereas the killing of the fly was no such thing.

GIVEN MY accelerating loss of weight, my hip bones were ever more vulnerable on the rowing seat, and even on the bunk, where Sylvain's bulky sleeping bag provided the only padding we had. On Day 40 I had a dream in which I looked down to discover that my entire pelvis had somehow been transformed into a brittle six-quart basket of the sort in which my mother bought fruit when I was a child. Rolling around in it were what I first took to be plums, reddish-purple things with strings, but what I quickly realized were testicles, each bearing the name of a crew member, male and female. I shall leave the interpretation to those who might dare, while adding that as always my discomfort necessitated regular infusions of 222s. My problem at this point was that I was running out of them faster than I had planned. I'd brought 280 in all, a supply plentiful for a journey of thirty-five days but inadequate for the fifty or more that were now being projected.

On the afternoon of Day 41, protective of my grubby little secret, I hung a towel from the storage hammock between the alley and bunk so that no one could see what I was up to, and poured out my stash, the entire precious motherlode, onto Sylvain's sleeping bag. I divided the heap into islands, each of a half dozen tablets, representing a day's intake, and realized with dismay that if we were even ten more days aboard, I was not going to make it. I would compensate, I decided, by cutting back to five hits a day, and that afternoon, for the first time, consumed just a single tablet, rather than two, to get me through to sundown. If the new economy went well, I'd cut back to four a day, perhaps three.

As I squirmed on the next watch, frantic for a little help from my friends, Dylan and I discussed the addictions of the jazz trumpeter Miles Davis, who in order to quit heroin during the 1960s went out to his father's farm in Illinois. There, he sequestered himself in a bedroom, which was nailed shut from the outside, and sweated it out, screaming. If all else failed, I thought, I'd beg a painkiller or two from Angela or a Tylenol 3 from Steve or Sylvain. "Or I could quarantine myself like Miles," I said to Dylan, who was aware of my habit and responded that in case I hadn't noticed I was already in the middle of the Atlantic Ocean, where I was as likely to kick an addiction as I was in any cell or straightjacket on earth.

THAT NIGHT, ON the 2-to-4, under a desolate full moon—a kind of Grimshaw painting come to life— a school of perhaps 400 flying fish, a host of tiny Celtic crosses, was suddenly in the air, surfing moonlight. At that moment, Aleksa and I were on the starboard hull on our own, and before we knew it the fish were bouncing off the boat, thumping into the cabin. By the time the mass of them had disappeared, a dozen or so lay senseless or flipping on the tramp, their "wings" now compressed to their flanks so that they looked as plain as sardines, except with an eye the size of a dime and a snout as hard as a car bumper. Aleksa has great empathy for animals—was incensed, for example, by David's continuing and futile attempts to catch dorado, which she believed mated for life—and was immediately on the job picking up the eight-inch flyers and depositing them back in the sea. They are a most astounding little creature, whose greatest survival mechanism is that their pectoral fins have evolved into wings, so that when they are threatened they can simply fly away, soaring across

150 yards or more of ocean. When a predator approaches, they drive toward the surface, thrashing their tails some seventy times a second (faster than a hummingbird's wings), propelling themselves from the waves at speeds as high as fifty miles an hour. Though beautiful, they are such gristly little missiles that it did not occur to me until we got to Barbados, where such fish are a delicacy (pretty much the national dish), that in a pinch I could have been eating them as my food ran out, although we had no proper frying pan or stove on which to cook them. At worst, I could have chopped them up as ceviche, with a little hot sauce or a sprinkling of citric acid, of which we had plenty in the form of vitamin C supplements.

A week earlier, Angela had enlisted Steve and me to pull every bit of cargo out of the port front hold "just to see what was in there." And in what condition. Out it all came onto the tramp, beginning with the survival suits, which were sopping and moldy, almost petrified in their sea-soaked condition. At this point it was impossible to imagine what level of effort would be required to get sixteen people into them in an emergency, particularly if the boat was in turmoil, given that it took us ten or twelve minutes just to drag them up out of the bilge water and slime and even to *begin* to unpack and open them. The smell alone would have been sufficient to send a drowning man swimming for the bottom.

Just as I was beginning to wonder what reason Angela could possibly have for this apparently pointless effort, a pack came out of the hold that I could see contained the familiar Ziploc bags that indicated food—apparently uncontaminated food. And then another. And *another* as we probed deeper into the hull. While the survival suits lay scattered on the tramp, the vittles flew *tout de suite* to Angela, who leaned from the cabin hatch to receive them, as hardy as a stevedore where the handling and stowage of food was concerned. Five hundred pounds of it, Steve estimated, lamenting again the vast load of calories aboard, and speculating on where the next secret stash would be unearthed. It was never quite clear to me whose food it was—probably Angela's, David's, Margaret's, maybe breakfast stuff, some of which might find its way to me.

Now, on the afternoon of Day 41, as we plunged along, Angela appeared on deck to announce that by her latest calculations, the food aboard, including what Steve and I had unearthed in the front hold, would get us to Barbados only if we limited ourselves to one meal a day—this plus our snack packs and the "breakfasts" she continued to provide. My own snacks were at this point a desultory assortment of peanuts, raisins, dates, protein bars—nothing even remotely appealing, since I had already raided them for their shortbread and dried mangoes and digestive biscuits, basically anything that made them worth opening in the first place.

As it was, I felt like a farm goat, an animal whose instincts for "selective grazing" attract it first to the tenderest grasses and vegetables, then to chewier greens, such as asters and chicory; and so on down through what's available in the pasture to the tougher stuff, until finally it is eating thistles and burdock and even tree bark.

While not literally eating thistles (I'd have been happy to get some), I had hit a new low the previous evening when what came out of the galley for me was a packet of Sicilian polenta that had not been rehydrated. At all. With the boat rocking as fiercely as it was, there was simply no way of heating water. Thus, rather than the enticing mushy cornmeal I had anticipated in reading the "heirloom recipe" on the packet, I was faced with a kind of sand soup, grittier than 2-grade aggregate and about as tasty. I chewed down a spoonful or two of it, went out, sent the rest of it to its reward, then, as usual these days, went scrounging through the reject bag for granola bars or packets of peanut butter, or odds and ends of candy or cookies. You never knew what somebody might have thrown to the bottom feeders while you were out keeping slim.

A few seconds later, as I was about to quit my excavation, I was astounded to come across a commercially foil-packed chicken breast, realizing only as I pulled it free that there was a small tear in its packaging. A warning that included the minuscule icon of a skull said DO NOT EAT IF SEAL HAS BEEN BROKEN. I stared for several seconds at the forbidden fruit, reluctant to ask anybody what they thought; if they advised me not to eat it and I did anyway, and died, I'd look rather silly. *He knowingly ate rotten meat.* Even dogs know better. In a curious inversion, perhaps known best to the very desperate or hungry, I found myself asking not *What if it's bad?* but *What if it's good?* Therein hung the risk as I perceived it; I could be missing out. I read the warning again, looking for loopholes, then read the small print, and realized the package contained nitrates, preservatives, at which point I ducked into my bunk and opened it, convincing myself that the slight garbagey smell and the bluish pallor of the chicken was just the poor cabin air and light.

Using an old trick of my dad's to test wild mushrooms, I placed the teensiest of fragments on my tongue and determined that at very least a molecule wouldn't kill me. And took a wee bite. And waited. And then a bigger one. And then engulfed the thing almost without chewing. And promptly fell asleep. And woke up... alive! At least alive enough to go out and row. Which is what this sport is all about. That and world records. (Never has there been a sport so obsessed with world records: for rowing across the Atlantic from the east, for rowing across the Atlantic from the west, for rowing across the Atlantic from all other directions... in a pea-green boat, etc.)

It is with restrained pride I report that while one record eluded us aboard the boat, we did claim another, or at least I did: for speed and distance in the projection of a chicken breast out the esophagus west of the Mid-Atlantic Ridge.

I will not linger on the feat, except to say that about twenty minutes into the evening watch I was gripped by a brief but intense nausea, followed by a rumbling in the stomach. I barely had time to link these to my big score of two hours earlier when my throat opened like a birth canal, my abdomen contracted, and a somewhat molested-looking loaf of greenish yardbird shot out of me at the speed of a Katyusha rocket and disappeared over the horizon—all of this so noiselessly and delicately as to go unnoticed by those laboring in the trench before me. Actually, Dylan did turn to me about thirty seconds later and said, "Did you hear something?"

"Like what?" I said.

"I thought I heard a kind of *whump*," he said—probably the chicken hitting a cargo vessel somewhere off the coast of South America.

BY THIS TIME, I was happily and shamelessly accepting gift rations. From Louise, from Ernst—perhaps most notably from Tom and Steve, the latter of whom occasionally slipped me a wallet-sized slab of his homemade fruitcake, from a recipe out of *The Joy of Cooking*. Tom's wife, Luisa, had sent aboard several puck-shaped ingots of *panforte*, an Italian spice cake, which Tom dispensed to

me in molecular portions when I was starving and which
I installed on my tongue with the care and anticipation of
a scientist placing fuel in a reactor.

And did I give back? Of course. Having realized that
the 7D-brand dried mangoes I had brought were much
prized, I would eat a few pieces from a new pack and
then pass along the rest to whoever seemed most in need.
On other occasions, I simply traded whole packs for, say,
jerky or cashews or granola.

And did I feel sorry for myself? Not at all. If anything
I felt grateful for the support I was getting as my food
dwindled. Less happily, I considered the fact that I, more
than some, had at one time been committed to traveling light, to getting across in thirty-three days—to doing
what we'd set out to do. Now, ironically, I was all but an
ambassador for those comfy with the fact that we were
nearly two weeks behind schedule. The double irony was
that I now had to rely on crew who had perhaps not initially believed as I had. Occasionally I wondered what
the most lavish of our self-provisioners had been thinking. Surely not that we would be rowing for seven weeks!
Their capacious stowage was more than just insurance—it
was a self-fulfilling prophecy: we must insure ourselves
in case the trip goes longer than anticipated, and by
insuring ourselves (significantly increasing the weight
of the boat) we increase the possibility we will require
insurance!

During my rare pangs of despair, all I had to do was
look across at Dylan, who, like me, had not brought
enough food—largely, I suspect, because he was a student
and didn't have much to spend, rather than out of faith
we would arrive in a jiff. When I had mangoes, I gave
him some. On other days I'd look over at his pathetic little bird meals and would have to look away. On I think

Day 42, nothing came out of the galley for him at dinner. I later saw him eating what I believe was a smear of peanut butter on a half piece of U.S. Air Force soda bread, a kind of biscuit that came foil-sealed, as dry as plaster, one of the most dispiriting items on our increasingly dispiriting menu.

An hour or so after Angela's announcement about rationing, Liam came forward in the cabin and, standing between Dylan's and my bunks, told Angela he thought a meal, not rationing, was in order, and pretty much pronto. While grateful to Angela, I was with Liam on this: eat now, deal with hunger when it comes (as for some of us it already had). It is apparent to me in retrospect that those with a mind to do so could insult Angela openly over her navigational or administrative choices, and that through her general grace and tolerance, they were more or less forgiven immediately. Had it been otherwise, Steve would long ago have been buried in durance vile. However, to question her decisions about food, about meals and their presentation, was a more personal and intimate offense.

Liam had no sooner departed her bivouac than Angela erupted in rage over our ingratitude—and undoubtedly over a dozen other stresses, the lot of which had been nudging her toward the boiling point. It was awful. We didn't appreciate her attempts to keep us fed, to keep order—didn't realize how hard she was working.

Dylan, who all along had been a kind of ombudsman for the crew, immediately reminded her that just the previous day she had told us how wonderful we were.

"I guess I was wrong," she shot back.

"Maybe so," agreed Dylan, who suggested now that she had "misunderstood Liam," whose "communication skills" were "not what they might be."

"I'll say," said Angela, who took the opportunity to slag those on the crew who she believed were undercutting her authority. Her example was directed anonymously but clearly at Steve, who she said had "pretty much decided he could do whatever he wanted with the direction of the boat."

"I think there are some misunderstandings about people's intentions," said Dylan.

"Maybe there's gonna be a mutiny," chirped Angela, almost hopefully.

"Or maybe you'll come to understand that much of the problem here is not insubordination but simple miscommunication," burbled Dylan, to which she uttered a soft, derisive laugh. "Oh, you're good," she said.

And he was good. Was a kind of diplomat. With teeth. And thus he talked her down, leaving her brooding in the little stall that was increasingly a kind of symbol of her life aboard, particularly of the limits of her authority.

I agreed with Angela, at least to the extent that too many of us didn't appreciate her considerable skills in nursing the expedition along, or staying out of its way when required. One of her biggest problems lay in having to accommodate everyone from hard-dieseling middle-aged men—men unaccustomed to being told what to do, in fact accustomed to doing the telling—to wilful boys (in some cases more judicious than the men) to restless young women who, despite their independence, needed her occasional nurturing and reassurance.

Angela's genius for the latter was most evident with Aleksa, a strong rower and a good kid, temporarily burdened by her thousand salt sores, her scrapes, her sunburn, her injured ankle, her homesickness, her loss of closeness with Liz who by this time had partnered pretty much exclusively with Liam. After each tough shift, day and night, Aleksa would rock forward through the cabin to tell the captain how it was, to partake briefly of her company and receive her blessing. What she received almost as an afterthought was Angela's considerable experience in dealing with the hundred nagging ailments that can befall a rower at sea. I'd hear them talking softly, mulling every lump and lesion; and never once, in weeks, did Angela, who was often tired and in pain herself, deny Aleksa the support and comfort she needed.

She showed little such patience for Ernst that same night when he mentioned to her that to save his job, he might attempt to get a helicopter to pick him up off the boat as soon as we were within helicopter range of land (about 200 miles). We were still nearly 700 miles out. I'm not sure the plan ever got parsed into specifics. However, it was quickly clear that Angela had little sympathy for anyone who wasn't willing to blow off a mere job for the satisfactions of adventure at sea and in particular of completing a tour aboard *Big Blue*. "One thing goes, another comes along," she called from her hidey-hole, assertively including everyone in the cabin in what might otherwise have been considered a private conversation.

"I don't live that way," objected Ernst (who manifestly *has* lived that way through much of the adult portion of his forty years on the planet).

"Take the risk!" she goaded, to which he responded that he'd already taken too many risks that didn't pay off.

She said, "I don't understand what kind of a company wouldn't cut you some slack in your current situation."

"They'll consider me unreliable," he said. "Shipping's a small industry. Everybody knows everybody."

Clearly, Angela's perspective was angled to the interests of the boat, to keeping a good rower aboard. At the same time, I appreciated the broader rattle of her argument, or at least part of it: that the corporate world could dance in hell, which, in reverse, is what she perceived it had been telling the rest of us for years.

Meanwhile, feeling badly for Angela as her argument with Dylan wound down, I scribbled on a scrap of paper that there were "lots of us on board" who appreciated what she was doing, and how she was doing it. I handed it through to her, wishing (perhaps pathetically) that I was someone from whom such an endorsement would mean more to her. But from the beginning I had been on the periphery of her sense of who aboard mattered. The journey quite simply was about those who could make a difference in the speed of the boat—or those she sensed might be a problem for her (who were in some cases the same people). So remote was my relevance, indeed, that Angela never seemed to give so much as a thought to how she might be depicted on these pages. And more power to her. Why should she care? In her world, writing was promo, not revelation, and certainly not inquiry. As her blog entries about the trip eventually made clear, the story of Cap'n Angela existed not in the assessments of some scrawny back-country scribbler but in the jargon and butt-polishing of "professionalism," the truisms of self-advertisement: *The Big Blue experience was amazing! My crew was amazing! The expedition showed what people can accomplish when they work together.*

But I liked her anyway—all the more for her perceived apathy toward me, because it gave me added freedom to come and go (it is so much easier to insinuate yourself into whatever's going on when nobody's paying attention). Months ago, I had, at her request, sent her one of my books so she'd be able to see what I did—had in fact offered to help her edit her autobiography, which she said was sitting drafted but unedited in California.

However, she never mentioned either again, leading me to suspect that her own writing may well have been as tedious to her as mine would undoubtedly have been. The one book in the women's living room in Agadir was an uncracked Harlequin about three inches thick, whose embossed cover showed a pneumatic young belle in a mauve gown, a gal with a foot-long neck, gliding purposefully into the antebellum mansion where all such stories invariably achieve their loin-chafing denouements. It wasn't that Angela didn't have an imagination. On at least a couple of occasions, onboard or in Agadir, she made fond if oblique references to sexual practices that, it seemed, involved leather and handcuffs and (because it was Angela) quite possibly whipped cream and chocolate fondue. And she sustained a vision of herself that, against the indignities of the past, invariably included at least a fretwork of optimism and reinvention. It was always a pleasure to see her sitting in a kind of lotus position on the starboard bow, eyes closed, hands extended and upturned, as if to honor the water and receive its blessings.

OTHERS WERE more curious about what I was up to. At one point, David, bored by the inactivity forced on him by his injured knee (he had at this point played a thousand games of solitaire on his iPhone and had read everything on the boat, including the toilet manual), asked me rather plaintively if I had any of my books with me; he wanted to read them. On another day, Margaret said to me, "Charlie, about this *book* you're writing," and she tendered a few questions, aimed at discovering, I suspect, whether she might have to murder me. Steve, dear chap, had already read most of my books, and I was flattered to know that Louise, of her own accord, had sent for a

U.S. edition of a memoir I had written about working in a cemetery as a kid. Sylvain had peeked into my opus, as had Tom's wife, Luisa. And Ryan told me outright that the book he'd asked me for had been passed along immediately to I think his mother, an English teacher, who was on orders to let him know if it was any good.

In the meantime, I plugged away at my diary (with my two-inch pencil), filling it up with lurid assessments of everything and everybody, until one day I took it from its pouch beside the bunk and, in one of those "uh-oh" moments, knew immediately that it had been disturbed, that somebody had been reading it while I was out on watch. Which changed things for me. It would be so easy for someone who did not care for the way in which I had depicted them simply to toss the diary to the dolphins. I considered whether I should start taking it out on deck with me. But how? In my pants? Plus it was probably more vulnerable than ever out there in the weather, and would be sea-saturated within a day. So I simply pushed it deeper into its cradle of junk and carried on.

BY THIS TIME, the great leap forward had begun to lose its engine, the winds their consistency. More and more the waves were coming out of the north, pounding our starboard flank instead of our transoms. The result was that we were being pushed farther into the tropics, farther south, where we did not particularly want to be.

The mood too had turned. The discipline and sense of order that were a kind of sub-clause of the consistent weather had begun to fray. Routines drifted. Normally, as I have mentioned, we switched sides every watch, in order to even out the strain on our bodies, mostly on our shoulders and abdomens. But because of a shift of weather and seating arrangements on Day 43, I rowed twice in succession on the starboard hull in a heavy cross-wind that pushed an endless assault of breakers into our laps, chests, and faces. By the end of the second of those watches, at dusk, the ribs on my right side felt as if someone had taken a tire iron and pried them apart and driven wedges into the gaps. The only way I could get to sleep afterward was to take four 222s, thirty-two milligrams of codeine, which metabolized down into a soothing itsy-bitsy of morphine.

Three days later, during the evening, the waves were as high as any we'd seen, driving down on us out of the northeast, as tall as the *Lusitania,* some of them bringing screams from the crew as they appeared out of the rain or darkness, throwing the boat briefly into chaos. Just after dusk, one such wave yanked Dylan out of his seat and stirrups, spun him like a break-dancer on his back, and dropped him, briefly stunned, against my shins. At some point over the past few days he had developed a habit of frantically shipping his oar when he saw a dangerous wave coming, then jumping up out of his seat so as not to get walloped. All of which was understandable, except that in doing so he would leave the oar unattended, a potential flying battle axe if the oncoming wave happened to pick it up. For the most part, I had little to offer in the way of rowing advice. However, in this case, because I was the likeliest victim if the oar flew, I caught Dylan's attention early on the 10-to-midnight and implored him *please* to secure the oar if and when he got up, at which point he turned to me and said quietly, "I'm sorry, I wasn't thinking," and never did it again.

Throughout the night, Angela did everything she could to keep us rowing under conditions she knew were beyond most of our capabilities. "Just a little wee stroke when you can," she urged me at one point, aiming a flashlight at me from the fore-hatch. At another point, she passed me out an insulated mug of the sweet, creamy Vietnamese instant coffee that she knew was pretty much a craving for me and of which there was very little left aboard.

Toward the end of the 2-to-4 a.m., having had all we could take, Dylan and I simply abandoned our seats and huddled against the cabin in the rain, unable to see each other in the darkness, though we were just a few inches apart.

After perhaps five minutes of squatting with our windbreakers over our heads, Dylan said in a whisper, so as not to wake those inside, "What do you take on your cheeseburgers?"

Immediately and with no intended irony I laid out my preference for tomato, dill pickles, onion, relish, mustard, a bit of hot pepper, a slice of bacon.

Did I like the tomato sliced thick or thin? Had I tried cucumber? What about fried mushrooms? Fried onions? Vidalias? Sourdough bun? Toasted? Blue cheese? Hot mustard?

The symposium turned to fries, to sweet potato fries, then to what Dylan called "condiments for fries"—chipotle mayo, green chilli sauce, sour cream. By this time, I was craning my neck to hear every gripping word. He knew a place called Dangerous Dan's at Broadview and Queen in Toronto that served a "kahuna" burger, with pineapple and peameal bacon, and a "McEwan," a bun-encased heap of ground sirloin, exotic mushrooms, and soft French cheeses, topped with a grilled lobster tail—all of this discussed with great ardor as the Atlantic raged around us and a more persistent rain than we had seen for days ran off our noses and chins.

The topic was decidedly less funky the next afternoon, when, as if to celebrate the return of the sun, Dylan embarked on an all-but-heroic monologue—on evolution, on scientific modeling, on correlatives for human intelligence in the animal world. At one point he wondered aloud whether altruism had "an evolutionary purpose." In other words, did extending oneself to others advance the species in any Darwinian sense? Was the Golden Rule a scientific as well as a moral tenet? To my mind it most certainly was; it ensured community survival, kept populations at a level where they were big enough both to breed and to withstand catastrophe. None of my crewmates considered anything as banal or folksy as the Golden Rule to have any connection to the evolutionary well-being of the species. When I asked one of the kids if he even knew what the Golden Rule was, he said: "Don't let them piss on your fire," then "No smoking within ten feet of the pumps"—both of which, it occurred to me to remind him, possess at least a smidgen of Darwinian validity.

AT SOME POINT during our forty-fourth night aboard, the mileage counter on the GPS slipped below 500 miles. And was at 360 by sunset of Day 46. Our navigational challenge as we entered the voyage's unforeseeable final week was that the winds were driving us ever-farther south. In order to make land at Port St. Charles, on the back side of the island of Barbados, we absolutely *had* to keep a course that would take us north of the island's most northerly point. Had it been possible we would have landed on the island's near or east coast, the windward coast. However, that coastline is rocky and mountainous, subject to heavy surf, and there are no suitable landing spots (which is why crossings sanctioned by the Ocean Rowing Society end at Port St. Charles). The difficulty was that we could not *get* to Port St. Charles by going around the south end of the island; the currents and winds would not permit it in a rowboat. A Russian solo rower had gone south of Barbados some years ago, hoping to travel north up the back side of the island to Port St. Charles. But as he passed the island's southern extremity he was swept hard to the west by current and wind and ended up in South America.

On that forty-sixth evening, the GPS indicated that we were latitudinally just six or seven miles north of the northernmost tip of Barbados. In the mid-Atlantic we'd been a hundred miles north. In the event that it became impossible for us to get around the north tip, we could call for a tow into Port St. Charles. If we did so, however, our crossing would not be recognized—or would be designated an "assisted" or "incomplete" crossing. Skeptical though I was about the designations of the Ocean Rowing Society and the world record, I was at least determined (more determined than some, it seemed) that we be credited with a "completed" crossing.

I report all of this both for its own sake and because on the next night it precipitated a yowling quarrel for which I have to take a certain amount of responsibility. Our course by this time was a mere two miles north of the island and we could allow ourselves to drift no farther toward the equator for fear of getting swept south of Barbados. With the wind still coming steadily out of the northeast we were resigned to taking a beating from the crosswinds through the night. And indeed were taking one.

The problem started when Margaret came on watch at about 3:55 a.m. and, for a few seconds, raised the Plexiglas cover on the instrument shelf atop the bridge and fussed briefly with the GPS, which sat within inches of the autopilot controls. Aware that we had zero margin for going farther south, I said to Steve when I came into the cabin that maybe somebody should check with Angela or David to see what bearing we were supposed to be on, and make sure that we were still on it. Dylan overheard me, burst forward into Angela's quarters, and reported that Margaret had been at the autopilot, reminding Angela not just that we had no leeway for any further movement south but that Margaret had at times adjusted the boat's bearing to facilitate rowing on night watches involving her half of the crew.

"I've had it with these fuckups over the bearing!" somebody bleated from the fore-cabin.

As the clamor rose, Angela, spurred to duty, lurched through the cabin and out on deck, returning minutes later to report that the bearing was acceptable—and that Margaret was most indignant at having been suspected of boat crimes that she did not commit. While I felt somewhat badly that I had asked about the bearing in the first place, and badly to have added to Margaret's ever-shifting burden, I (like the others) felt a great sense of relief that we weren't about to lose another couple of miles and perhaps the entire battle to stay north of the island.

ROUND 45 of the Rowing Knockouts took place the following day when Steve, offended by yet another of Margaret's intrusions on his sense of self and decorum, walked into Angela's quarters—or stuck his head in—and in a stage whisper that could be heard from one end of the boat to the other, told the captain that he had *had* it with her pathetic evasion of responsibilities (chiefly her inability to "control" and muzzle Margaret), had had it with the insufficiencies of her leadership, had had it with her avoidance of command—she had failed him, had failed him big-time, and he wasn't going to take it anymore.

It was a grim and irrevocable flaying, and when it was done Steve informed Angela that he would finish the row as an independent contributor to the effort but that from this point forward she was to consider him off limits to her authority.

I have occasionally wondered why Angela did not strike back, as she had every right, perhaps even a responsibility, to do. She could have ordered him to shut up, or off her boat, or to menial labor, and might well have received some support from the crew. But she was intimidated by him, and for that reason she failed to respond—as well as for all the other reasons Steve gave in defining the inadequacies of her captaincy.

Rather, she endured the keelhauling with a shrug—a kind of ho-hum retreat both into her strengths (her capacity for stoicism and self-sufficiency) and into all of the aforementioned weaknesses.

The lot of it left me not only distressed over the state of the boat's politics but annoyed at Steve, who I thought could have held on another few days without having so thoroughly to denounce Angela's failures and to separate himself from them in such an open and scornful way. What's more, his withdrawal came at a point in the voyage when it was of no conceivable benefit to anyone but Steve (and then only in that it drew a line between him and the flawed universe in which the rest of us were bound and doomed to exist). What would Steve's boat look like? I thought later—and had to admit that while there might be just one person on it (Steve), it would look a lot more seaworthy than mine or that of anybody else aboard. Which is fine if pure seaworthiness is the goal.

Later, I felt obliged to tell Angela that obviously not everybody felt the way Steve did about her. From within the recesses of her cramped berth, she looked out at me and said softly, "I guess ya gotta do whatcha gotta do."

Certainly Sylvain did what he had to do late that night when Margaret and Ryan joked openly about his being forced to retreat briefly into one of the holds because he was bare-legged and on the verge of hypothermia. "You two wouldn't know about cold legs," he told them in response to their needling. "You're both wearing an extra pair of pants made out of half an inch of fat"—which as I understand it brought a quick end to the discussion.

The following morning, when Margaret advised Sylvain that he should stop rowing when she and Ryan arrived (late) on watch, so that they could all row in sync, his response was less a protest—a doing-whatcha-gotta-do—than a sort of laryngeal explosion, an alarming and profane yowl, that brought an immediate silence to the boat, and a new respect for the man who, for weeks, had been a model of restraint and self-control. Later, however, when I told him I knew how upset he was because of his unprecedented deployment of the F-word, he said, "Oh, no, I'd never do that—I don't use that word." I let the matter rest, and for several hours entertained doubts not only about what I was sure I had heard but about the broader validity of my recollections as a memoirist and storyteller. The doubts were allayed that evening when I mentioned the incident to Nigel, who assured me that Sylvain had "definitely lobbed a few F-bombs" and that I wasn't "the only one who was surprised."

At this stage, I confess, I found it curiously reassuring that I was not alone in finding something comically inspirational, something borderline poetic, in the thread of absurdity that ran so persistently through the *Big Blue* saga. Ernst told me he thought our story might best be told as a kind of 1930s-Berlin-style cabaret: the gentle captain, the cunning first mate, the hard-driving lieutenant, the loud-singing but frequently discordant crew—the lot of it framed by a sub-cast of mermaids and sea gods, with perhaps a cameo by Zeus or Poseidon.

Steve had been incensed a day earlier when Ernst had referred to the expedition as "a little bit unprofessional"— had taken it as a strike against David, toward whom he was infinitely sympathetic. I took it as fair comment by a guy whose English is a trifle uncertain. I think he meant "rough around the edges," and am ever loath to imagine what a more austere or *Hallin*-like "professionalism" might have looked like aboard *Big Blue*. (Would the absence of toothbrush handles and a more military attitude have improved matters or simply brought us closer to a parody of professionalism, made of us a sort of contemporary HMS *Pinafore?*)

As for my own gaunt professionalism, I was by this time almost pathetically thin and exhausted. The night rowing got harder as my strength drifted. The daytime rowing, at least under favorable winds, was more than ever a kind of meditation—on sun, on sea water, on sky, on the dorado cruising endlessly beneath our oars. The record by this time was so far in the past that no one even thought about it anymore.

The hitch on the gentler afternoons was that with the languorous progress of the boat, people often got grousing about how slowly we were moving, how much time it was all taking, how the world was moving on without us. For some, this degenerated into obsessive calculation of what our arrival date might be: the twenty-ninth, the first, the second.

On the afternoon of our forty-seventh day out of Agadir, as Sylvain relieved me on the afternoon watch, I made the mistake of saying to him that I felt badly for those who could not enjoy these last days at sea and that I wasn't going to let anybody's impatience taint my own final hours of satisfaction in this most powerful of my planetary experiences. He was immediately onto me about my responsibility as a writer—to see their problems, to empathize with their stresses, to try to see all sides. This I explained to him was a generous ideal from a writer's point of view, as long as you didn't mind spending your life trapped in Journalism 101 or its moral equivalent in the wider world. I assured him that I understood well the pressures various crew members were under. Ernst and Liam, for example, had booked flights out of Bridgetown for March 4, desperately hoping we'd be in port on the third. Others had jobs to find, courses to take, money to repay, partners to placate.

In the face of it all, the cabin politics crashed back and forth between the usual appalling pettiness and the heights of generosity and goodwill. The next evening, for example, I got fed up with Sylvain, who for a day had been advising me almost hourly on the state of our shared quarters. "Charles," he'd say quietly when he saw me coming on or off watch, "—about the bunk." Surely I could dry my sleeping bag a little better, pick up the peanuts that someone had spilled on the adjoining floor. Had I seen his lost sweatshirt? Moved his shoes? Was the food wrapper beside the bunk mine?

As a matter of fact, *no... no I hadn't,* and no it wasn't (or maybe it was). I cared about Sylvain—in many ways loved the guy. And, while I acknowledge that the bunk could have been improved (and that I am at times an incorrigible slob), I also knew, at heart, that at that moment his pleas and complaints were less about a few peanuts or a sleeping bag than about exhaustion, about the very stresses we had been discussing, brought to bear on one of the few tiny facets of our lives aboard that he felt he could influence or control.

Nevertheless, that night, at 4 a.m., when he arrived to relieve me in the rowing trench, I crouched beside him as he lowered himself onto the seat. I was about to launch my reproach when it struck me that I was entirely on the wrong track, that by pressing my own perspective I was merely perpetuating the sort of grievances that had too often gotten out of hand during our weeks aboard. As if cued to my micro-satori, Sylvain, rather than addressing cabin issues, asked a simple question about the night sky. Immediately, I began describing to him what little I knew of Polaris, the North Star, the seaman's navigation point, which at that moment was visible off our starboard hull amidst an avalanche of constellations cascading into the sea. Our conversation led to poetry and philosophy, eventually to Galileo and on to Descartes and the Age of Enlightenment.

For half an hour or so, we enjoyed our own little enlightenment, and in this way were able to reroute our frustrations with each other and with ourselves amidst the ongoing chaos of the boat.

I should add that the next night, when I was hungry and every bit of my clothing was soaked with sea water, Sylvain, having assessed my situation and wanting to do something to improve it, hauled out his special fine-wool pullover, his mystic cloak, explaining that it possessed something akin to special powers and that if I put it on in the bunk between watches, my entire mood and perspective would be elevated in its warmth. He said he himself liked to put it on when he needed a boost. So I did—donned the thing after the 2 a.m. watch and crawled in under the blanket I had borrowed from Steve to replace my wet sleeping bag. And indeed felt better—felt *good*—partly because of the garment, no doubt, but also in the glow of my bunkmate's care and concern.

My own biggest stress by this time was of course food—I had run out. Angela continued to supply me with bits from her excess provisions—a few noodles, a scoop of beans and rice. But at this point she too had pretty much run out of grub. As a means of redistributing what food was aboard, Angela gathered up everybody's snack packs, emptied them into a pile on the floor and re-cut them into sixteen bags, so that we all had an equal supply of candies, nuts, protein bars, and the like. I was ecstatic to get a couple of packets of "real juice fruit gums" and a lemon Builder's bar, and was impressed at how much better some people's snack packs were than mine. Meanwhile, I was aware that perhaps half a dozen of our crew members possessed quantities of a product called Squeezers Cheese. As I understood it, they had fallen for the manufacturer's pitch that the stuff was "real" cheddar, which it may once have been. However, by the time it came aboard in its one-ounce plastic packets, it was an acrid, off-putting paste that for the most part had been sampled and abandoned as inedible. Nigel, for example, had stuffed sixty packets of it to the bottom of his net hammock. The reject bags had been awash in it for days, untouched even by those who were starving.

Now, on Night 49, as I rummaged through the rejects in search of stray calories, it occurred to me with a curious dispassion that if I was going to avoid fading away entirely during our last couple of days at sea, I was going to have to do so on a diet of Squeezers Cheese. And I proceeded to lay claim to every last packet of the stuff aboard—ending up with well over 150 of them, which I began eating immediately. One after another, I ripped open the little envelopes and squeezed out the odious orange goo, running it south over my tongue without mastication. By ten the next morning, I had eaten perhaps seventy-five packets, well over two pounds, and still I was as ravenous as a shark.

At about noon hour, on the bridge, I spotted Liam gnawing at a fist-sized chunk of some nondescript yellow solid and demanded to know what it was.

"Emergency rations," he said brightly, explaining that it was "a sort of dense lemony shortbread."

Exactly the meal I had been craving, and within minutes I had cadged from Louise Graff a foil pack of Mainstay, as it is called—generic nutrition, a product with a shelf life of five years and the specific gravity of potter's clay.

Within minutes, for the second time in sixteen hours I was in my digs, chowing down on preservative-laden gunk the likes of which I had never eaten before and hope never to eat again. And was grateful for every morsel of it. And for most of the other things that happened to me during the last thirty-six hours into Port St. Charles.

At about 11 a.m. on Day 51 the GPS dipped below a hundred nautical miles—which is to say miles from Port St. Charles, on the far side of the island. The near side was no more than seventy or seventy-five miles away, and during the next hour or so I was not the only one who stood on the bridge staring briefly at the numbers and then directly off the prow at the western horizon.

In the cabin, talk had begun of steak dinners and warm baths and real beds. And long nights of sleep. At that point, most of us hadn't felt a drop of hot wash water for more than seven weeks. For a while, off Africa, we had had a cheap "portable" shower, basically a suspended plastic bag in which water absorbed the heat of the sun. However, it had quickly sprung a leak and had been junked.

For several hours during the late morning and early afternoon, we rowed through a persistent mist, managing in the light crosswind to stay comfortably north of the northernmost tip of the island. At times there were a dozen or more immense dorado either beneath the boat or alongside it, nuzzling at our oars. They do a dazzling trick—swim lengthwise along the crest of a wave, just beneath its summit, so that you can see them in the translucent peak, moving at fantastic speed, perhaps just for the joy of being up there, as much as twenty feet above their surroundings. It is also possible that they elevate themselves to better see their prey. David, who had been fishing unsuccessfully for weeks, made a final day-long attempt to catch one—but didn't get a nibble. During the second or third week, I had given him fishing tackle that had been assembled for me by my friend Jake MacDonald, a one-time fishing guide. However, nothing in the way of Hoochies or Buzz Bombs or live bait had worked.

Just after 6 p.m., I looked up from where I was rowing on the port hull and saw a frigate bird perhaps a hundred yards above the boat. And twenty minutes later a gannet. They were the only birds other than storm petrels that we had seen since the coastal waters off Morocco.

The sky had cleared, and at about 7:30 p.m. I got up out of my seat and, for the last time, at least from the boat, watched wistfully as the sun threw a spray of soft gold from behind a distant bank of clouds and then cannonballed into the Atlantic.

In the cabin, Angela had cobbled together a version of chicken soup made, I think, of an envelope of powdered stock and a few packaged chicken breasts that she had kept squirreled away in the recesses of her pantry. When I had eaten mine, she stuck her head out of her quarters and, as she had done so many times during our weeks aboard, informed me quietly that she had a last cup of hot water if I wanted it for coffee. Which, as always, I did. Alas, I had already consumed the last of the fifty or so packets of Vietnamese instant that, with a titch of codeine, had been an addictive and treasured feature of my snack packs. "I've got one left," she said. "It's for you." She tossed it to me and handed me my hot water, and I mixed it and sat there in the dark, thinking about where I had been and where I would be tomorrow.

At this point, we knew who was going to be in Port St. Charles to meet us. I had wanted to bring my children to Barbados but had found the logistics difficult—the kids had school and work schedules, and nobody had a clue as to when we might arrive. Plus Barbados is a premium tourist island, and flights and hotels can be expensive, particularly on indefinite stays with uncertain arrival and departure times. As it turned out, my friends Margie Bettiol and Doug Flegel, who had many times welcomed me to their wilderness home when I had writing to do and needed the isolation, had flown down from Thunder Bay. And Trish would be there. She and Steve's wife, Janet, along with Nigel's girlfriend, Kim, were already in Barbados—later that night they would phone the boat from where they were partying at a seaside nightclub.

So I was excited—was far too restless to sleep. I was also feeling a trickle of self-satisfaction. I had survived, had done what many had told me I could not do, what I myself had occasionally doubted I could do. The feeling, I admit, was not very convincing, particularly in the shadow of my now desperate desire that these awful stresses be over.

If I was feeling a deeper ambivalence, it was about the completion of an endeavor that while it had nearly killed me had also, paradoxically, become a part of me, that I had become addicted to, and that some profoundly sane (or profoundly disturbed) aspect of me was reluctant to see end. If it had taken gumption to get on the rower more than eighteen months ago and eventually to face the sea, it would take every bit as much to get up out of my rowing seat some thirty-six hours hence and disembark for good from *Big Blue*.

We rowed hard on the 10-to-12, and at midnight, when I rose from my seat and turned to the bow, I experienced a deep, childlike satisfaction. There, in the distance, rising off the horizon, was a great green arc of illumination, the glow above the city of Bridgetown—a light that, for me at that moment, was as lyrical and mystic as the stars.

Ten times on the next watch (and then the next) I turned and stared at it, until finally dawn erased it, and we were left peering into the haze above the horizon, looking for our first glimpse of land.

During the night, a flying fish had hit Ernst in the teeth, giving him a slightly swollen lip. For all of us, it was the final evidence, the cartoon confirmation, of the degree to which David's fishing efforts were irresolvably jinxed. "What does it saying about his skill," pleaded Ernst, "that for seven weeks they iknore his line and are now trying to jump directly into our mouths?"

For breakfast, I ate a handful of stale peanuts, then crawled into my bunk. But couldn't sleep—so pulled my shorts on and went back out on deck. As I stepped from the cabin on to the bridge, Steve was standing there, explaining to Dylan that on the way into Port St. Charles he intended to be right where he liked to be, which was to say "leading from behind, ready in the background" should his guidance or direction be required, as some of us imagined it might be. Even so, it struck me as a curious thing for him to say, especially since he had so recently and resolutely declared himself outside of the boat's direction and command.

Ironically, Angela had told me the previous day that *she* intended to be "large and in charge" as we came into port— "not like Tarfaya," she added, obviously still haunted by her unexplained, perhaps inexplicable absence when we most needed somebody "large and in charge."

At around nine o'clock I took out my notebook and attempted to condense a paragraph or two on the meaning of where we were and of our long weeks at sea. But the more I fussed with it, the more frustrated I felt at trying to reduce something that was essentially irreducible to a few manageable sentences. In some part, it seemed, I had lost my enthusiasm for attempting to unravel the complexities around me—was more aware than ever that the over-examined life is not worth living either. Which is not to say there were no decipherable lessons, but only that their meaning was not as neat or germane as it had seemed in the projections of several months back, when I had not rowed a stroke.

If one of those projections more than others had maintained a presence in my consciousness, it was the significance of living boldly, of embracing a degree of risk, as we add years. I had by no means turned back the clock during our weeks at sea. If anything, it had turned me back. But for a few weeks I had at least stared it in the face. And in that I took a small measure of pride. If I had proven anything about what was possible for those who refuse to accept the Verdict— to "go gentle into that good night," as Dylan Thomas famously put it—I had proven it only to myself. I had gone, I had not croaked, I had returned. And for the rest of my life I would carry with me perhaps not the messages in any speakable sense so much as the immensity, the imponderables, of an experience that I would never have had if I had accepted conventional wisdom and avoided the risks inherent in such a journey. And in the deepest recesses of my awareness, it was enough.

Perhaps the only other thing I could say about the lessons at that point was that in a way they had been *un*lessons. It is one of my longstanding themes, and I think a reliable one, that inner progress is at times less about accumulating than about letting go and clearing out assumptions. The voyage had given me a chance to see myself free of most of what was comfortable and assumed about my life. I am talking about everything from safety and privacy and a measure of circadian order to social standing and professional credibility. For nearly two months, I had lived on the margins of chaos—had observed myself vulnerable and for who I am. And who I am not. And had observed those around me in the same compelling state. And had treasured the view—as well as the confirmation of what is needed in a life and what is not. For me (if I may risk an indulgence) those needs include a connection to the planet, the more intense and varied the better (a need not just endorsed but redefined by the expedition); and a sense of community to balance off my need for independence; and a purpose, or several of them, particularly of the sort that are born and nurtured in the depths of the imagination; and enough risk to keep the juices flowing; and the freedom to think and act; and a boatload of patience; and another of forgiveness, both incoming and outgoing; and a range of defenses, most especially those that preserve me from myself.

What I don't need at this point in my life—more accurately, what I don't want (heartily confirmed by my weeks at sea)—is orthodoxy, conformity, contrived goals. I do not need "management," although many would disagree. I am, perhaps needless to say, a less-than-sterling candidate for a row across the ocean.

AT ABOUT 11 A.M., as I rowed behind Ernst on the port hull, Sylvain, who had lingered on the tramp after his watch, announced at stentorian volume that he could see land, could see Barbados. Dylan appeared with the video camera and ordered him to see it again—for the first time, so to speak. He was to see it with the cry "Land ho!" which Sylvain, who is no actor, delivered with approximately the zip he might have applied to declaring that a skunk had appeared in his backyard.

As it had thrilled me the previous night to see the lights, it thrilled me now to see the mountains—although at first I could *not* see them, for the simple reason that I was looking for something subtler, for some sort of spider-line that I imagined would rise a speck at a time from beyond the curvature of the sea. Instead, they emerged whole out of the sun-silvered mists, a long north–south band of greeny cliffs, more impressive and alluring than anything I had anticipated.

As the day passed, they got bigger, looked more like actual countryside, and I could not keep from glancing at them, or staring, several times drifting into a contemplation of the travelers who had seen them from the ships of other centuries. It was a sight that at this distance had not changed, at least not much, in ten thousand years. I am perhaps misguided to suppose that my own crossing of the Atlantic, with its lumps and lesions, its waves and weather and anxieties, gave me a better understanding of what the early sailors and their subalterns (if not their slaves) had faced. Many of them never saw land again. Or arrived sick or with a leg amputated, or beaten up for insubordination, or mutilated by pirates.

At this point, my own deteriorating carcass was more fragile and depleted than I have perhaps let on. I was down thirty-five pounds from my skeletal norm (was in other words at burial weight). I had broken not one tooth but three, and in the absence of my normal infusion of 222s was experiencing such intense pain in my left knee and hip that in order to step from the tramp up to the bridge, a difference in height of perhaps eighteen inches, I had to hoist myself with my arms, unable any longer to count on the muscles in my legs. The wound on my shin was a brown and swampy stain, no longer a scab but not exactly skin either. I have debated even mentioning that on the previous night my exhaustion was such that during the pre-dawn watch I fell asleep on the rowing seat, waking only as my face crashed into the gunnel, which ripped several inches of skin off the orbital bone at my left temple. Sylvain joked scornfully (at least I assume he was joking) that I had inflicted the wound myself so that I would "look tougher" when we arrived in Port St. Charles. While I have not spent a lot of time over the years attempting to look tough, I will admit that at 135 pounds, limping and with broken teeth, I would have welcomed a little toughening in my appearance. There are photos of me during those last days—ribs showing, skull prominent—that I refuse to circulate, having heard enough people joke that, compared to most corpses they had seen, I looked great.

Big Blue, too, was ready for the infirmary. Apart from the cabin cracks, the metal-and-cord fasteners that held the tramps in place had begun to disintegrate. Eight or ten of perhaps 150 of them had given way entirely. The wind-powered generators had quit, and several of the sliding seats had broken down. The holds were full of garbage.

I could go on. However, as an antidote to this rather despairing litany, I might mention that not long after we returned from sea, I noticed on a popular boating website that our beloved if eccentric rowboat was said to resemble some elaborate, whimsical Lego construction. In elucidating our peculiarities, the site compared *Big Blue* to the more conventional rowboat *Hallin Marine.*

What caught my attention about this smirky comparison was not so much the fact of it as a pair of accompanying video links, one showing *Hallin*'s durable and remorseless crew, the other offered as evidence of the "interesting" and eccentric nature of *Big Blue*'s crew—to wit, a six-minute film made by the director Kelly Saxberg, featuring my personal and implausible self in training to row the ocean. Imagine my joy in discovering that I was no longer merely a misfit on his way to the library but had become a poster boy—a poster geezer—for all that is unlikely and idiosyncratic about an unlikely sport that seduces normalish human beings into rowing the Atlantic or Pacific!

I hasten to add that *Hallin*'s crossing of the Atlantic happened in a world-record thirty-one days, twenty-three hours—a record broken exactly a day later by *Sara G,* another three-seater, which crossed in thirty-one days, thirteen hours.

It hardly needs emphasizing that our own somewhat inflated ambition to set a record ended well over two weeks behind the world mark. Our time, according to the Ocean Rowing Society website, was forty-seven days, eighteen hours, from Tarfaya—more than fifty-two days from Agadir. If there were regrets among the crew, they were at this point overshadowed by a welter of realizations and acceptances—of the fact, for example, that the boat, with its all-but-crushing tonnage of provisions and equipment, was far heavier than anticipated and didn't surf as we'd hoped; and of the vagaries of the Atlantic winds and weather.

Quite beyond the fact that our toothbrushes had handles and our watch changes were a trifle sluggish, there was also the rather embarrassing recognition that we were unable to rebuild our flawed boat in mid-ocean, or calm the waves, or redirect the wind as Christ had done at Galilee. Or for that matter that we were unable to row more than twelve hours a day on limited sleep and nourishment. In other words that we were mere human beings against a rather resolute opponent in the Atlantic Ocean.

Nor were we able to transform on the fly the often grisly little minstrel show that was ourselves. I for one would not have wanted to. As I have implied many times or said outright—and despite our occasional antipathies— I loved these people, I cared about them, I believed in them. And at least a few of them believed in me. They were funny, they were tender, they were fierce. Some, at times, would have torn one another's throats out, torn *my* throat out—but in the aftermath would have stitched it back in and begged for forgiveness. Much has been said (indeed much of it by me) about our failures. Yet to this day, I would like to meet the crew who, under any captain on earth, could have brought *Big Blue* across the Atlantic, amidst the conditions we faced, more than half a day quicker than we did.

WHEN DARKNESS settled on the last full day of our journey, we were still nearly twenty miles out. The lights along the coast came on hazy at first, as if seen through silk, more a glow than separate points of light. But as we got closer, individual lights began to emerge. Before long, we could see street lights on the slopes and bluish industrial lights along shore, could see bright white headlights and red taillights going up and down the hills. I was rowing behind Dylan, and the two of us gassed away about what exactly we were witnessing. When he put his iPod in, I began thinking about my children, wishing they were in Barbados, as Sylvain's were. Part of me envied his good fortune.

Between watches I lay on my bunk, relaxing fitfully but unable to sleep. While for the first time in weeks it was easy to get up out of bed, the rowing remained a challenge to the end, a battle against unexpected cross-currents.

We rounded the north point in the wee hours, and as the sun rose were moving tenaciously down the back side of the island, a land mass of about 300 square miles, twenty miles from top to bottom. Close up, the shores were a tangled version of paradise—high, verdant banks, atop which slave owners from another century had developed sugar cane plantations and built pastel-colored mansions.

At 9:55, when I came out of the cabin to row, I got a surprise that at any point during the past fifty-two days I would have welcomed but did not welcome now: basically an order from Angela that I should go back to bed and wait. The current was so strong against us that she wanted what she called her "300-watt rowers" in the seats. However, I could not bring myself to go back inside—was far too restless. Plus, I wanted to be present and ready when the call came. In short, I wanted to be rowing when we arrived in port—not for the sake of those waiting but for my own sake. In effect, I wanted the most out of these last couple of hours aboard.

For now, David was in my seat, stroking hard, as he had not done in weeks because of his damaged knees. But he was tiring, having more or less relinquished his fitness during a month of inactivity. Just six feet down, we could see the ocean floor passing at a snail's pace as the tidal current flushed up the coast into our prow: starfish, sea urchins, bits of coral from the reefs farther out. At one point, a good-sized stingray rose in an explosion of sand and swam lazily into deeper water.

Somehow Tom, who is an exquisite oarsman but whom

Angela did not consider a 300-watt man, had insinuated himself into the mix of rowers, and Angela asked him now if he would give up his seat to Liam. When he lingered, Liam leapt out of the shadow of the cabin and began screaming at him, frantically and profanely, to *move* damn it, to get up, to get out. The fuss had barely resolved itself when Angela, who was standing on the bridge, began scanning the shoreline, talking about going ashore right here and now. I could barely believe what I was hearing. Her thinking seemed to be that the rowers were tiring, that if we began losing ground we might gradually be carried away to the north or west. She may also have been thinking about Liam and Ernst—"Ernest," as she called him—whose flights were scheduled for early in the afternoon. My only thought was what a terrible heresy it would be to go ashore just three or four miles from Port St. Charles, to forego recognition for our voyage when, despite the current, we were moving steadily south at pretty close to a knot and a half.

"See if you can find a place to land," Angela said, handing me the binoculars from the controls shelf, explaining that for some reason she couldn't focus them.

I trained them along the shore and after a few seconds said, "There *is* no place; it's all rip-rap—it'll tear the boat apart."

It was a lie, but before anybody could question it we came onto a shoal, and David hollered at Angela to move the boat into deeper water. And that was that. The idea of a premature landing passed.

David was by this time rowing with one hand, a sure sign that he was exhausted; I had done it a thousand times. I bounced down the tramp and said, "Why don't I give you a break?" And within seconds was in the stirrups, aware that the only way to stay there was to pull with the persistence of a mule. I was soon plowing so hard through the power phase of my stroke that my bruised and bony ass at times flew right off the seat.

In front of me, Ryan and Nigel were trading places at five-minute intervals, pulling like Percherons, leaping in and out of the trench with such athleticism that they did not miss a stroke in the exchange.

A sailing yacht had fallen in alongside us, under power, keeping pace, as a woman snapped photos and waved an enthusiastic welcome from its deck. So out of touch was I with reality, it did not occur to me that she would have any idea about the identity of the strange-looking rowboat and crew that had come into local waters. But of course she knew—had sailed out of the very yacht club at Port St. Charles where we would soon be putting ashore.

I found it ironic, and rather touching, that the only two members of our crew who were holding flags, the Australian and Canadian respectively, were Margaret and Steve, who had positioned themselves so their colors could be seen ashore. A few minutes later Tom had the flag of Toronto Island up and flying. The U.S. flag was aloft above the bridge.

When we were perhaps a quarter mile out, somebody noted that there were *people,* a lot of them, spread out along the stone jetty that protected the harbor. From somewhere on the jetty, a flare went up. But the cabin was in my sight line and I could not see what was happening. "Are they our people?" I asked Nigel, who was standing on the tramp. But he did not hear me in the developing hubbub. "Nigel," I said again, more loudly, "are they our people?" I wanted to know.

"Yes," he said, giving me his attention, "they're our people."

At that moment a small Zodiac outboard came racing out from behind the jetty and circled us twice, corralling us like a border collie. It was the harbor master, come to lead us into port. But even as we drew within shouting distance, I could not, despite the welcome, bring myself to look at those who had gathered. Because of the positioning of the cabin, I was hidden from them as we made our approach—and was no more ready for the landing when it came than if we had crashed into the dock at a hundred miles an hour.

For a few seconds I sat in my seat, still hidden from view as the others got up and moved onto the bridge and the gangway. Needing a moment or two of privacy, I ducked into the cabin, where my kit and clothing were packed on the bunk beside Sylvain's. From the small yellow bag in which I carried my treasures I took my good sunglasses and exchanged them for the wrecks I had been wearing. From my dry bag, I pulled a white long-sleeved T-shirt that bore the insignia of the Montauk Tackle Company, one of our Long Island sponsors. I sniffed its armpits, the better to return to civilization, and put it on. And sniffed and repositioned my peaked hat. I had not seen my reflection since the barbershop in Agadir, and on a whim picked up a tiny frameless make-up mirror that I believe belonged to Louise Graff. People eventually told me that I had looked "fragile," had looked "haunted" as I stepped from the boat. One woman told me she had been "shocked" by my appearance. But from what I could see in the glass I was no more emaciated or "shocking" than any other old man who had had his teeth knocked out, his eye blackened, and had lost a fifth of his body mass in relatively short order. Oh, and had not slept for more than ninety minutes at a stretch in fifty-two days.

Outside, a celebration was going on. Beer was beginning to flow. Food was on the grill. Measured against the elation of arrival was the forfeiture of our lives at sea. And of our freedom: not absolute freedom, which would be meaningless, but freedom from getting and spending, from the never-ending imperatives of life on land. Sir Richard Burton felt that in traveling we search for what is missing in ourselves. I am inclined to think we go in search of what affirms us, of what we already are and know. For some, our days at sea were a journey into the lessons of exactitude. For me they appealed largely to the imagination—to the imponderables at the core of what it is to be a human being. They had also, I now knew, been a much simpler kind of journey, the kind that ended with its second-oldest citizen, which is to say myself, peering into a tiny magic casement caked in salt, seeing a skeleton in Ray-Ban sunglasses, a creature he did not recognize, and beginning quietly, perhaps crazily, to laugh.

It was in this capricious mood—haunted, fragile, perhaps damned, but wearing a genuine and satisfied smile—that I emerged from the cabin, climbed gingerly over the port hull, and stepped ashore.

EPILOGUE

O N ARRIVAL IN Barbados, Ernst Fiby and Liam Flynn celebrated briefly with the crew, then raced to the airport in Bridgetown and caught afternoon flights to Vienna and London. Since then, Ernst has worked for the Vienna-based shipping company with which he communicated onboard, and has built a small business of his own, investigating shipping losses. At some point in 2013, he will again embark on a transatlantic row—with Captain Roy Finlay. Liam returned to Norwich in time for his medical exams and at last word was doing internships in oncology and cardiothoracics in Scotland. Meanwhile, he is training for the Marathon des Sables, an annual six-day, 251-kilometer footrace across the southern Sahara—considered the world's toughest running event.

Shortly after her return, Liz Koenig moved from Long Island to Connecticut, and later that year into New York City, where she works as a social media manager for an eBay-owned company called True Action. She is simultaneously taking an MBA in social media at Southern New Hampshire University.

Aleksa Klimas-Mikalauskas remains with North Babylon's first-response team, and with the volunteer fire department in Deer Park, NY. During November 2012, she worked for ten days, nonstop, helping victims of Hurricane Sandy, which hit the eastern seaboard hardest within minutes of her family's home on Long Island.

Zach Scher spent the months following his return at his mother's home in Panama, where his primary aim was to refine his capability as a surfer. Since then, he has lived in Guelph, working as a stonemason, building straw-bale houses, and learning hang-gliding. During the summer of 2013, he returned to northern Ontario as a fire-fighting crew chief and has since entered the engineering program at Dalhousie University in Halifax.

Dylan White flew to Guatemala upon his return and spent a number of weeks with his girlfriend, Zoe Barrett. Since then he has worked as an itinerant field ecologist based in Guelph, where he also teaches music. He continues his career as a stand-up bass player and composer, and tours regularly in southern Ontario with his jazz band, the Upside Trio.

During the summer of 2011, Tom Butscher rowed the length of Lake Ontario, solo, and during 2012 the length of Lake Erie. In July 2013, he will row from St. Joseph Island, at the north end of Lake Huron, to Sarnia at the south end, more than 400 miles. He wrote recently in an email, "Sometimes in blustery weather I close my eyes and I am back aboard *Big Blue*, rolling with the waves, hearing the sounds of the Atlantic. I see and treasure every face of our remarkable crew." As ever, Tom lives on Toronto Island with Luisa and makes his living as a carpeting installer in Toronto hotels.

For several months in mid-2011, Nigel Roedde trained as a bicycle mechanic in Guelph, Ontario. During the spring of 2012, he and his girlfriend, Kim McKone, pedalled from Vancouver to San Diego, stopping briefly in Long Beach to surf with Angela Madsen. Nigel divides his energies and time between bicycle road racing, working with disadvantaged athletes, and making a living as a bike mechanic at Mountain Equipment Co-op in Burlington, Ontario.

In late January 2012, Margaret Bowling skippered a crew of three rowers on an attempted crossing of the 200-mile-wide Bass Strait, between Australia and Tasmania. Partway across, their boat capsized in a storm, injuring one of the rowers and necessitating a dramatic rescue and a tow into port. Margaret is currently working in line production at an animation studio in Buenos Aires, where she lives with a group of Meher Baba yoga followers.

By her own estimation, Louise Graff has been "sticking close to shore" since returning to Charleston, where she and her partner, Noreen Powers, have a home on the city's famous salt marshes. Louise paddles dragonboats and occasionally gets out on her rowing skiff. She has what she calls "selectively fond memories" of her days aboard *Big Blue*, and refers to the expedition as "the pinnacle of freedom and also of captivity."

In November 2011, while cycling downhill at speed, Ryan Worth was thrown from his mountain bike, suffering near-fatal injuries to his back, ribs, and sternum. Within a week of removing his full-torso brace four months later, he led a climbing expedition through the White Mountains of New Hampshire, carrying an eighty-pound pack. Otherwise, he has spent the months since his return rowing, kayaking, and climbing—as well as completing a degree in environmental science at the University of Tennessee, Knoxville, where he is currently doing an MA in sports psychology. In June 2014, he will join three friends in rowing the Pacific from southern California to Hawaii.

During the spring of 2011, Angela Madsen began a year of intense training for the Paralympic Games in London. There, in September 2012, she won a bronze medal for the U.S. in the shot put. In February 2013, she married her partner, Deb Moeller, on Shelter Island. The ceremony took place in the same guesthouse where the pair had stayed during training maneuvers for *Big Blue*'s crossing of the Atlantic. As of this writing, Angela is about to embark alone, in a boat named *Positive Outcomes*, on a 3,000-mile row from southern California to Hawaii—an endeavor dedicated to veterans of the U.S. military.

Sylvain Croteau remains a fixture in the emergency ward at Gatineau Hospital. But he has also started a software company called SEKMED (Software for the Evolution of Knowledge in Medicine). The program will allow physicians across the globe to share awareness and information related to medical diagnoses and treatment. In June 2012, Sylvain fulfilled a long-standing ambition to row the St. Lawrence River from Montreal to Quebec City, a distance of 150 miles, in less than twenty-four hours—and did so with half an hour to spare. Later that summer, he and his wife, Suzanne, won the Canadian Sculling Marathon for the second time.

Steve Roedde made it back to St. Joseph Island just in time to harvest the sap from his maple bush and to "sugar off," as they say in the syrup business. Since then, he has traveled, farmed, and rowed—and in early 2012 shed twenty-five pounds in six weeks so that he could compete as a lightweight in the C.R.A.S.H-BS, the world indoor rowing championships—which is to say, rowing-*machine* championships—in Boston. There, five pounds below the weight at which he arrived in Barbados, he became world champion in the men's "veteran" category (aged fifty-five to fifty-nine), a feat he repeated, with an improved time, in February 2013.

After a brief vacation in Barbados with his dad, David Davlianidze returned to his Shelter Island boat shop, where for the past eighteen months he has been working overtime to repay his substantial debts from the expedition. During the summer of 2011, his fiancée, Lali, emigrated permanently from Tbilisi to join him. Together they have a baby son named Dachi.

I myself have spent much of the past year and a half thinking and writing about our lives aboard *Big Blue*, as well as recovering from the effects of the rowing, which seem permanently to have altered my spine and range of motion. More than a year ago I was denounced by Angela for declaring that I intended to tell our story "as it happened," which she took as a betrayal. Even the title offended her. Others believed, as I did, that the betrayal (to both crew and reader) would be in *not* attempting to tell it as it happened. So I told away, unfiltered, restricted only by the limits of my awareness and perspective. And by my subjective interpretation of events.

One of the few stories I did not tell in the book is about the crew member who, when we saw Barbados from perhaps thirty miles out, groaned, "Thank God. It's over. We're home!"

But when I saw that crew member six months later and asked how he'd adjusted to being back, he said, "I haven't. Too much of me is still out there."

A part of me, too, is still out there. And I suspect will be out there for a long time yet. Meanwhile, one of the questions I get asked is: Would you go again? And the answer is simple: For now, I don't have to. But I'll consider it when I get back.

Big Blue, bless her heart, is still in Barbados, afloat in the shallows near Port St. Charles. David's intention, well noted in these pages, was to bring her home to Shelter Island. But during late 2011 she was hit hard by vandals, who stole everything they could remove from her cabin and hulls. Since then, sun and salt have destroyed much of what remained. In mid-2012 David gave the deteriorating vessel to her Barbadian caretaker, noting that while it broke his heart to abandon his beloved boat, he had decided it was "time to move on." At last word, her new owner had scraped and painted her, added a string of patio lanterns, and was operating her as a floating bar.

If you happen upon her while in Barbados, you are encouraged to go aboard and raise a glass to her days on the Atlantic, and to those who brought her across.

CW

May 2013

ACKNOWLEDGMENTS

THE MAKING OF a book is invariably a complex and lengthy endeavor. But, for me, this one set new records in all stages, beginning with sixteen months of intense physical training, a long and demanding journey by sea, followed by all the customary implausibilities of getting the story down—in notes, then drafts, and finally a finished manuscript. As the months passed, so many people became part of the process, providing generous and good-humored support, that it would be difficult for me to cite in detail the nature and variety of their many valued contributions. Suffice it to say that to all of them I am far more grateful than the mere listing of their names might suggest. I am talking about John Sifton, Carol McLaughlin, Chris Casuccio, Betty Carpick, Jake MacDonald, Sue Langer, Kelly Saxberg, Damien Gilbert, Tom Hazenberg, Jim Crooks, Peter White, Mary and Bryan Frost, Mary Louise and Peter Crooks, Caitlin Crooks, Bob Edwards and Carol Bruni, Kevin Cleghorn, Jim Stevens, Joan Baril, Richard Alguire, Kevin and Adele Parkinson, John Parkinson (1924–2010), Sue

Bishop, Karen Keeley, Stewart Kallio, Joan Skelton, Stan Kurisko, Janet McLeod, Steve Roedde, Heather Blois, Jan and Ron Saddington, Mary and George Morrison, Paddy Bailie, Sally Colquhoun and Dan Newton, Kal Nikkila (1934–2010), Erica Burton, Celina Reitberger, Alf Petrone (1925–2009), Doug Morrill, Sue and Mike Bryan, Liz Stewart, Dorothy and Pete Colby, Gerry and Rosemary Waldron, Kate and Clint Harvey, Keith Travis, Lori and Aldo Ruberto, Deborah and Paul DeBakker, Mabel and Jamie Crooks, Larry Dustin, Cappy and Jim Colquhoun, Peter Leclair, Ann and John Hargadon, Lainie Burton, James Arthur, John Warner, Elleda Warner (1919–2011), Patrick Newman, Laura Robinson and John Cameron, Joe Fiorito, Mary Roach, Deb Kinsella, Dale Syme, Rhonda Beck, and Al Zikovitz.

I am also much indebted to my literary friends at the Stories in the North writers' festival and Bookends Book Club. And to my business and corporate backers, all of them friends: Gargoyles Grille & Ale, Gerry Waldron Consulting Ecologists, bfusion design, Young Living, and Cottage Life Media.

I would be remiss if I did not make special mention of a number of people who, at crucial times, gave me invaluable moral or literary support—among them Dan Diamond, who read the manuscript when I most needed a reader and advisor and gave heartening encouragement; Philip Syme, who listened closely, appraised generously, and went paddleboarding with me when I needed a break; Margie Bettiol and Doug Flegel, who housed and fed me and always listened with great patience and care; Frank Pollari, whose spare room and late-night conversation were invariably a welcome respite; and my sisters, Susan and Ann, who have been in my corner a long time.

Many thanks as well to James Little at *explore* magazine, who published my earliest writings about the journey, and J.B. MacKinnon for his assertive editing of those early efforts; and David Hosking for the training advice; and Anne Maurissen, a one-time crew member who was injured before departure but remained a supportive and sadly missed part of the expedition.

I am equally indebted to Rob Sanders of Greystone Books, who saw merit in the project long before it began and signed me up to tell the tale—and stuck with me. And to my agent, Jackie Kaiser at Westwood Creative Artists, who has always been one of the truest believers in my writing. Sincere thanks are also due my editor, Lucy Kenward, an astute and fearless observer of the writer's art, who made numerous insightful suggestions for improvement as the book took shape (and was patient with my occasional reluctance to do what needed doing). And to Peter Norman, a most exacting and erudite copyeditor, whose sensibilities as a poet and novelist were a ready resource as I polished the manuscript. And to Nancy Flight for marshaling the project at headquarters, and Zoe Grams for promoting the book with such enthusiasm, diplomacy, and skill.

And, once more, without embellishment, to my fellow rowers. I am profoundly grateful to them.

Finally, I wish to thank my friend Trish Wilson for her support throughout the months of training and writing—and my children, Matt, Georgia, and Eden, who, as always, are my foremost reason for doing and being, and to whom, at the deepest level, all of my efforts are devoted.

My love and warm wishes to you all.